Pursuing the Endless Frontier

Pursuing the Endless Frontier
Essays on MIT and the Role of Research Universities

Essays by Charles M. Vest

The MIT Press
Cambridge, Massachusetts
London, England

First MIT Press paperback edition, 2011
©2005 Massachusetts Institute of Technology

MIT Press books may be purchased at special quantity discounts for
business or sales promotional use. For information, please e-mail
special_sales@mitpress.mit.edu or write to Special Sales Department,
The MIT Press, 55 Hayward Street, Cambridge, MA 02142.

This book was set in Sabon by The MIT Press.

Printed and bound in the United States of America.

Library of Congress Cataloging-in-Publication Data

Vest, Charles M.
  Pursuing the endless frontier : essays on MIT and the role of
research universities / Charles M. Vest.
      p. cm.
  ISBN 978-0-262-22072-9 (hc. : alk. paper)—978-0-262-51678-5
(pb. : alk. paper)
    1. Massachusetts Institute of Technology. I. Title.
T171.M4493 2004
387.744'4—dc21   2004049862

10 9 8 7 6 5 4

Contents

This book is dedicated to my wife, Rebecca McCue Vest. Becky has been my constant companion and selfless source of support throughout the journey that is partially chronicled in this volume.

It is further dedicated to the memory of Constantine Simonides, Jim Culliton, and Margaret MacVicar.

Foreword

Norman R. Augustine

Not long ago I was writing an article that compared the demands of management in government, business, and academia. When I would mention my interest in management in academia to friends who are presidents of universities, the not uncommon response, invariably delivered with a wry smile, was, "Did you find any?"

Well, for those who may harbor any degree of doubt, I can report that management is indeed alive and well at the Massachusetts Institute of Technology, in the person of one Charles M. Vest. More important, I can report that *leadership* is also alive and well at MIT. The distinction, it has been said, is that management merely concerns doing things right, whereas leadership involves doing the *right* things right. My study, incidentally, concluded that management and leadership in a university environment are by far the most difficult of the categories I addressed.

Chuck Vest has led MIT for nearly fourteen years—years of enormous challenge for that institution as well as for the academic enterprise as a whole. Intriguingly, however, the collection of his annual messages that forms the foundation of this book seems to skim over major internal challenges that were well met to focus on broader policy issues confronting academia, science and technology, and indeed the nation and the world at large, making the difficult look easy and the impossible appear manageable.

While there were financial issues to confront, personnel matters to engage, and even an occasional crisis, one could never confuse leading MIT with running a business. In fact, most business-persons would probably question the difficulty I assigned to academic leadership, asking, "How hard can it be to lead an organization whose would-be customers are almost literally beating down the door?" In fact, MIT turns away more than eight out of ten of its potential customers. Given such a powerful position in the marketplace, one can only imagine how the average business-person might price his or her product; MIT charges tuition that covers only about half the cost of educating a student. How does MIT "stay in business"? This book addresses this and other conundrums of operating a world-class university, together with some of the more global issues that surround it.

While this is indeed the story of a great institution, it is even more the story of science and technology and educational policy in America as we enter the twenty-first century. There are few individuals, if any, better suited to address these matters in a knowledgeable and balanced fashion than Chuck Vest.

Vest has always been considered a statesman by his colleagues, one who is willing to look beyond his immediate responsibilities and interests, and beyond the unique priorities of his own field of expertise, science and technology, to see the big picture. He has won the respect of his peers in academia and those in industry, as well as the people who set public policy in our nation's capital. He is invariably among the first to be called to testify at Congressional hearings when a particularly difficult and contentious issue involving science, engineering, or education is confronted. He has been selected to serve as a member of the President's Council of Advisors on Science and Technology for presidents from both political parties. So attuned is he to the public-policy scene that MIT even maintains its own Washington office.

But while highly respected as a statesman, Vest is also revered for his courage. Examples are legion. Consider just three:

MIT has long embraced the view that financial aid to undergraduates should be granted solely on the basis of financial need, a view shared not only by MIT but also by each of the Ivy League schools as well as certain other, mostly private, institutions of higher learning. But in 1991 the U.S. Department of Justice disagreed with this point of view, for reasons that will be cited later, and the attorney general of the United States filed a complaint of collusion against MIT and the Ivy League schools—collusion in the form of conducting meetings to ensure that financial aid was indeed distributed equitably based purely on economic need. A confrontation with the Department of Justice on a high-profile issue is not a particularly attractive undertaking, and the eight Ivy League schools concluded that their interests would best be served by entering into a consent agreement with the government. Not so Chuck Vest and MIT. Under his unwavering leadership, on behalf of a cause that he and his institution's governance board considered just, a prolonged battle was waged with the federal government. The result was a clear victory for MIT in the federal courts, where a decisive ruling was issued in the Institute's favor.

A second example concerns the long-enduring tradition at MIT whereby freshmen could pledge fraternities and live in fraternity houses, and that they had to make the decision to do so within their first few days on campus. The custom had become an important element in the economic underpinning of the fraternities that populate the Institute—and a tradition held dear by many alumni. Vest had questioned whether this system best served the educational and social experience of the students, but there was a great deal of push-back from students and alumni alike. But when a freshman tragically died as a result of an incident at a fraternity house, Vest decreed that freshmen would no longer be allowed to live in fraternities but must all reside in dormitories—on campus. He then took the necessary steps to build additional housing in order to create a stronger sense of community and a more holistic and academically oriented introduction to MIT and to assist the fraternities in meeting the new financial challenges they confronted. Even in the face of intense questioning of his decision, there was no compromising the actions he deemed necessary to ensure the well-being of MIT's students and maintain the reputation of the Institute.

A third example of this remarkable leader's courage relates to MIT's decision to make the primary course material for most of the 2,000 courses taught at MIT freely available, via the Internet, to all who might desire it, whenever they might want it, wherever they were located in the world—be it Beijing, Mombasa, or New Haven. This was MIT's contribution to furthering educational excellence on a global scale. How many businesspersons—or even academics—would simply *give away* what comprised a significant part of their competitive advantage? Such was Vest's confidence in MIT's faculty and its academic strength that the benefits to humanity of making these materials broadly available seemed to far outweigh any potential diminution of the Institute's stature in the educational hierarchy. In fact, it might well embellish that stature.

In addition to such not infrequent examples of courageous actions that reside in the pages that follow, readers will witness another of Chuck Vest's qualities—that of "telling it like it is." No equivocating. No sugarcoating.

• Commenting on a report concerning the status of women faculty in science at MIT, Vest chose the following words: "(The study) portrayed a long-term pattern of bias or discrimination against senior women in the school."

• On the politically volatile subject of nuclear power, he notes simply, "It is difficult, if not impossible, to construct a scenario that does not involve substantial use of thermonuclear fusion reactors."

• And, regarding the causes of the ills that beset our nation's public school systems, he excuses no one, citing "parental indifference, students with low expectations, outdated and decaying infrastructure, political infighting, misplaced ideology, meaningless bureaucracies, and insufficient financial support."

Underpinning the statesmanship and personal courage for which Vest is broadly recognized are a strong moral compass; a commitment to ethical comportment; and a dedication to establishing a responsible "tone at the top." A not-uncommon reaction among young engineering students when it comes to ethics is that "engineers don't confront ethical issues": Engineers, they reason, deal with the laws of nature, and those laws are absolute. Indeed, Mother Nature is a wonderfully fair—albeit unforgiving—judge of one's work. But when Vest discusses the responsibilities of an academic institution to its students when they leave the classroom, the first thing he mentions is the matter of moral and ethical decision-making. He goes on to say that "Colleges and universities teach by their actions as well as their curricula." This conviction is evident throughout the book.

The focus of this collection of what could be called "State of the Union" addresses is on pervasive public policy issues rather than "local" issues, sometimes even making the task of leading an entity such as MIT appear almost incidental—perhaps even easy. Nothing could be further from the truth, even for an individual of Vest's enormous energy and ability. For starters, the institution he leads encompasses 10,000 students, over half of whom are pursuing graduate degrees. Such is the ability of these students that nearly 60 percent of the undergraduates scored at least one "perfect" (800) on the standardized admissions tests. The faculty is world-renowned, spiced with Nobel Laureates and winners of numerous other major recognitions. One study conducted a few years ago indicated that MIT graduates had founded literally thousands of new companies and had provided jobs for over a million individuals. The scope of research conducted at MIT spans from exploring the nature of the Dark Matter that is said to permeate the universe, to probing human cells in search of the causes of cancer. Much of the research focus today is on the "three O's," *info, bio,* and *nano*—info-technology, biotechnology, and nanotechnology. In addition to MIT's well-established position in the fields of science and technology, the Sloan School of Management has earned a solid reputation in the business world, and the Institute manifests a small but excellent School of Humanities, Arts and Social Sciences.

Then there is the matter of sustaining all this excellence—of managing an endowment of $6 billion, a sum that would be the envy of most other schools in the world. A fundraising campaign launched in the late 1990s began with a goal to raise $1.5 billion; under Vest's leadership this goal was handily surpassed. Nearly one-fourth of the buildings on MIT's campus have been constructed during his tenure. In his spare time, he is a devoted husband, father, and grandfather. One marvels that one person can manage to do all these things, do all these things well, and still have time to contribute to the formulation of national policy in so many arenas. (One possible explanation of this enigma is that he is not required to spend time doling out tickets to alumni for football bowl games.)

Among the factors that make this collection of papers particularly valuable is the increasingly significant role that science and technology play in our daily lives. Developments in these fields provide a particularly important part of the answers to such challenges as protecting the environment, providing energy, ensuring the security of the homeland, expanding the economy, providing food and water, and curing disease. At the same time, there are, unfortunately, unintended consequences associated with many, even most, scientific and technological advancements, ranging from the highway deaths and environmental damage associated with the advent of the automobile to the threat to our national safety posed by nuclear weaponry.

There is an increasing awareness that simply because science and technology can achieve something, it does not necessarily follow that they should do so. Witness the absence of nuclear power-plant construction in the United States, America's refusal to build a supersonic transport, controls placed on stem-cell research, the cancellation of the Superconducting Supercollider, and the on-again, off-again program to land humans on Mars.

In the face of the technological explosion we are witnessing—over half of the growth in the gross domestic product during the past few decades has been attributed to advances in science and technology—the number of engineers being produced in the United States has actually decreased, with many of the nation's most talented young people opting to pursue careers in business, law, and other fields.

The character of science and technology has itself changed markedly. We find ourselves in an era increasingly dominated by "Big Science"—involving projects that range from sequencing the human genome to conducting experiments in high-energy physics. Further, this collaborative nature of science and technology has not displayed any great respect for geographical borders; indeed, science has become an international enterprise, with individual projects involving collaborators in many parts of the world, all linked together in cyberspace.

Profound changes have also occurred in the funding of science and technology. Perhaps foremost among these is that national defense no longer propels the leading edge of basic research in America, that responsibility now having shifted in large part to our nation's academic institutions. In 1965, federally supported research efforts approached two-thirds of MIT's total campus budget; today they amount to less than one-third. Further, U.S. industry, responding to pressures for quarterly earnings growth and the harsh penalties of the marketplace for failing to meet these short-term objectives, has increasingly turned away from the conduct of fundamental research. The response to shareholders who ask "What have you done for me today?" has included shutting down or reducing the scope of corporate research laboratories, such as the famous Bell Labs, and focusing on pursuits with financial outcomes that were nearer-term and more predictable. It is in this environment that Vest has become a leading spokesperson for research—with particular emphasis on the still largely neglected "hard sciences" and engineering.

At the other end of the spectrum, U.S. industry was rudely awakened in the 1970s and 1980s to the fact that it had been ignoring manufacturing and quality assurance as fundamental disciplines. MIT thus embraced a growing and important role as an exponent of modern manufacturing techniques and product-quality disciplines.

A systems engineering entity was established in recognition of the fact that many of the problems encountered in modern engineering projects were no longer with individual components but rather related to the manner in which components were combined to form complete systems. This integrative facet of engineering has long proved troublesome in the academic sphere, given the subject's "orthogonality" to the classical organizational structure and culture of engineering departments—which are generally structured along the lines of traditional engineering disciplines: civil, mechanical, chemical, electrical, and so forth. It also became increasingly evident that engineering curricula would have to focus more on team projects, on multidisciplinary pursuits, on manufacturing and quality control, and on design engineering, as well as on such long neglected but fundamental skills as verbal and written communications. The "systems engineer" of tomorrow would need to be exposed not only to the underlying foundations of physics, chemistry, and mathematics and to the engineering disciplines themselves, but also to the liberal arts, economics, public policy, and management. And all this would have to be done within the context of the rapidly globalizing world of technology, in which factories move to Mexico and the Pacific Rim and knowledge functions shift to India and China.

Today, if one has an X-ray in a U.S. hospital there is a not inconsiderable likelihood it will be read by a physician in Bangalore. Vest writes, "MIT is of and for America. Today, however, in order to serve America well, we must participate in the broader (world) community." Indeed, Americans have a stake in the education of the doctor who interprets that X-ray, as well as in the research results emanating from emerging world-class laboratories around the globe.

Vest concludes that our success in adapting science and technology to the betterment of humankind will require the cooperative efforts of academia, industry, and government, a truism that, unfortunately, is more readily stated than realized. The inherent differences among these institutions are profound. Industry, for example, marches to a "time constant" that increasingly approaches one business quarter, that is, three months—and prefers to hold its scientific and technological advancements very closely until they can be introduced into the marketplace ahead of those of competitors. In fact, there is a growing trend in U.S. companies to not even register for patents in view of concerns that such efforts merely place a spotlight on the firm's most sensitive initiatives. In contrast, university research tends to be longer-term, loosely keyed to the number of years it takes to achieve a PhD, and is premised on the notion that new knowledge should promptly be shared with the world—a tenet that is underscored by the imperative to "publish or perish."

Various studies have indicated that there is not a large number of institutions—of any kind—that survived throughout the past several hundred years; predominant among those that did are universities. It has also been noted that universities are among the least changed organizations to have endured over that time. The exception seems to lie in the province of science and technology, where the content of material that is taught—if not the pedagogy—has changed markedly.

Charles Darwin's observation about biological organisms seems to apply to human organisms as well: "It is not the most intelligent of the species which survives, nor is it the strongest," he wrote, "rather it is the one that is most adaptable to change." But change does not come easily in most cultures, and that is particularly true in academia—even with strong leadership. Perhaps this is for a good reason. As a provost of MIT once told me, "You can't imagine how hard it is to overcome one hundred years of excellence and success!"

It is in these contexts that Vest addresses a broad spectrum of public-policy issues. His approach to resolving an issue, at least as I have observed it, is first to listen carefully to the views of others. It is this ability to keep an open mind while steadily narrowing the uncertainty surrounding the issue at hand that has made him so very effective in building bridges among disagreeing—and sometimes even disagreeable—parties. Consider but a few of the perplexing topics that are addressed in this volume:

• How will it be possible for America to maintain what are generally recognized as the best universities in the world while harboring one of the world's worst public K–12 educational systems? (In this regard, it was my privilege to serve on the Hart-Rudman Commission on National Security, where it was concluded that the second-greatest threat to America in the twenty-first century would be the failure properly to manage science, technology, and education; the first being the danger—which was soon to become a tragic reality—of massive terrorist acts.)

• To whom should universities grant "scholarship" assistance (read, "financial aid")? Should it, like most other benefits in America, be allocated on the basis of merit—that is, the "best" student gets the scholarship? Or should scholarships be devoted to qualified students with the least ability to pay? Certainly in the business world the concept of favoring customers who can afford to pay their bills is not a foreign notion, nor in much of the academic world is the idea that good quarterbacks should be given greater financial assistance than mediocre quarterbacks. But does it serve the greater overall good to give financial aid to those who do not need it and ignore those in need? The manner in which student financial aid is distributed is of particularly great consequence in the field of engineering, since this has often been the specialty of choice for students who represent the first generation in their family to attend college (as was the circumstance in my own case).

• Should admissions preference be given to women and minorities? Women now constitute over 40 percent of the MIT undergraduate body, with under-represented minorities comprising a lesser but growing proportion—clear progress, but with a great deal remaining to be accomplished. Or, in a self-proclaimed meritocracy, should admissions simply be granted to those deemed most highly qualified to pursue a higher education, as indicated by their test scores and prior grades? Interestingly, in deciding this issue the Supreme Court chose words very similar to those expressed by Vest a number of years earlier, "I believe that the time will come when affirmative action programs will no longer be necessary, but for now, we still have a compelling need for proactive efforts."

• Has faculty tenure outlived its usefulness, simply promoting job security? Or is tenure still an essential shield against those who would seek to limit freedom of academic inquiry? Or is the central point that the process of granting tenure also comprises an important means of filtering candidates for professorships?

• Are there avenues of research that simply should not be pursued? Is it appropriate to deny federal research support to such areas as stem-cell research and in-vitro fertilization? Who is to decide what areas should be banned? What is the net benefit of doing so, if other nations simply continue their own pursuits of such topics?

• Should federal support be provided to those researchers deemed by their peers to be best qualified to pursue a given research undertaking? Or should federal funds be distributed to universities more nearly in geographical proportion to those who are paying the bills (that is, the taxpayers)? Should research grants be used to promote social goals—or should their provision be confined to the optimal pursuit of knowledge?

• When a university provides faculty members salaries and laboratories, who should own the teaching materials they develop, the rights to the books they write, and the companies they establish to apply their research results? How much time should a faculty member be allowed to devote to such external pursuits?

• How should a faculty member balance his or her obligations to students as a teacher as opposed to the pursuit of knowledge as a researcher?

• Universities generate information that can be valuable in helping protect our nation's citizenry against terrorists and other foreign threats. Some argue that portions of this information need
to be protected from open dissemination, that is, "classified." Is
it appropriate for universities to conduct classified research? If
so, under what conditions should that work be undertaken,
given the long heritage of our nation's academic institutions with
respect to openness and transparency? If the answer is that classified work should *not* be conducted, what does this imply with
regard to any obligation a university might have to serve the
nation?

• If foreign students are admitted to a U.S. university, should
they be considered to be full members of the university community—or should they be relegated to some lesser status? Should
there be limits on the courses in which foreign students are permitted to enroll? Should foreign students from all nations be
treated alike? Should they be permitted access to hazardous biological materials? Should academic institutions provide the U.S.
government information as to whether individuals holding student visas actually show up for school? Should institutions provide the government information on what courses such students
are taking? Or which library books they are borrowing?

• While the cost of higher education in recent decades has grown
at a rate moderately in excess of the Consumer Price Index, it
has done so for a sufficiently long period of time that even "moderate" increases, when compounded, can pose large problems to
families with college-age children. To help alleviate this growing
financial burden, should universities enter into relationships with
corporations, say in support of joint research or providing
endowed faculty chairs? If so, to what extent might universities
find themselves influenced by those who are helping pay the
bills? Should faculty members be permitted to consult for

corporations that are financing research in the university's laboratories? If cooperative research arrangements are permissible with one set of companies, what is the fairness of this activity to those companies that are not included? How much time should be permitted for such outside activities? To whom should these relationships be disclosed?

• About half of the engineering and computer science graduate students in American universities are foreign citizens. Should there be some limit placed on the number of such students in our universities to make more room for American citizens? Or would doing so merely deny our country a proven source of talented contributors? In the past, after graduation, nearly half of all foreign students remained in the United States (which raises a question regarding the propriety of wealthy nations "skimming" talent from poorer countries), but in more recent years that proportion has declined markedly as more and more students return home to work for enterprises that compete with American firms for jobs and for profits. On the other hand, foreign-born individuals have been among the brightest stars as faculty at our universities, playing leading roles as creators of knowledge, as recognized by the concentration of Nobel Prizes among this group. About one-third of all the science and engineering PhDs in American industry were born in other countries, and nearly half of those in engineering and computer science were foreign-born.

• Should taxpayer funds be used to support research projects at U.S. universities if the results are to be published openly and thus made available to foreign competitors as well as to U.S. companies? In this regard, what *is* a U.S. company? Is it one with headquarters in the United States and factories abroad? Or is it a company whose owners live abroad but have purchased their shares on the New York Stock Exchange? Or perhaps it is the subsidiary of a "foreign" company that maintains factories and research laboratories in the United States. Or is it a company whose facilities are all in America but whose customers are mostly abroad?

• What will be the impact of distance-learning on the American residential research university? If students anywhere in the world can share in the courseware of America's finest universities, watch on television the lectures of the world's foremost professors, and enjoy access to the Library of Congress stored in a device the size of a sugar cube, what is the value of paying tuition to be present on a university campus? How great *is* the value of living with other students, including those from other lands, of informal discussions with faculty; of sitting down to dinner to discuss the issues of the day, face-to-face with people who are actually shaping those issues; of helping one another in the learning process?

All of these questions—and more—are addressed in the pages that follow, with implications that extend far beyond any single university, the fields of science and technology, or even any individual nation. Those who read these pages cannot help but find their thinking stimulated and their understanding enhanced. Such was certainly my experience.

Norman R. Augustine is the retired chairman and CEO of the Lockheed Martin Corporation. He has served as undersecretary of the Army, chairman of the American Red Cross, and a lecturer with the rank of professor at Princeton University. He is a former chairman of the National Academy of Engineering, a former trustee of MIT and Princeton University, and a current trustee of the Johns Hopkins University.

Acknowledgments

Above all, I acknowledge with gratitude and respect MIT vice president Kathryn A. Willmore, who worked with me in crafting every chapter in this book. More important, she has contributed immensely to the institutional environment and ethos that I have attempted to portray in many of these essays. I also want to acknowledge the MIT presidential search committee whose members in 1990 created the opportunity for me to serve in this role, and who suggested that I communicate my personal views on major issues during my presidency. The essays in this volume were written in response to their suggestion.

Jack Crowley tutored me in the ways of the federal government. He also read drafts of most of these essays and made many helpful suggestions, as did Larry Bacow and Kirk Kolenbrander in recent years. Laura Mersky, assistant to the president, guided the flow of my activities in a manner that enabled the writing of this book and the myriad of experiences and activities that underlie it. Ellen Faran, Michael Sims, and Lois Malone of the MIT Press deftly guided the transformation of a collection of essays into a book.

Chapter 6, "What We Don't Know" reflects substantive contributions from several MIT faculty leaders, including Alan Brody, Claude Canizares, Tom Eagar, Richard Hynes, Tom

Jordon, Paul Joskow, Mujid Kazimi, Philip Khoury, Steve Lippard, Nicholas Negroponte, Paul Penfield, Phil Sharp, Nam Suh, Samuel Ting, and Glen Urban.

Finally, I acknowledge my most senior associates in the central administration: Bob Brown, Joel Moses, and Mark Wrighton, who each served as provost during my presidency; Larry Bacow and Phil Clay, who each served as chancellor; and Bill Dickson and John Curry, who served as senior vice president and executive vice president, respectively. Each of these colleagues contributed immeasurably to my thinking, and to the accomplishments of MIT during the period 1990–2004.

1

MIT: Shaping the Future
Inaugural Address, 10 May 1991

I was elected president of MIT in June 1990 and formally took office the following October 15. The inaugural ceremonies would not take place until May 1991, when the New England weather would permit us to convene in the great venue of Killian Court; I spent those months interviewing the MIT faculty and others, learning their views of what was needed for the Institute to go forward. The inaugural address was in some measure a distillation and shaping of their insights. It also contained several components that I felt were especially important for MIT, as an icon and leader of American science and technology, to address— the shrinking and rapid interconnection of our planet largely because of information technology, the increasingly apparent need to steward our environment on a global scale, the sorry state of much of public secondary education, and the continuing quest to bring people of color into the nation's scientific and engineering workforce and leadership.

It seemed especially incumbent on MIT to take an active and visible role in rebuilding trust and investment in science and technology among the American public and the federal government, because at that time highly publicized claims of scientific misconduct had negatively affected the views of the public and of Congressional policymakers. Indeed, ameliorating this would turn out to be a constant personal quest during my tenure.

Finally, I chose as a theme "MIT: Shaping the Future," to connote a university strongly dedicated to driving change in the world beyond its campus boundary, as well as purposefully directing its own institutional evolution.

This is, indeed, a splendid moment—as we gather to celebrate a great institution, to renew our commitment to a set of ideals, to mark a passage, and to set a course for the future. Yet for me and for my family, it is also an intensely personal experience, and one that we are honored to share. A journey that began in a warm family in a small town in West Virginia has led to center stage in Killian Court—where my own path and that of the Institute have come together in this symbolic moment. It is a profound privilege to walk with four great and gracious men—Jay Stratton, Howard Johnson, Jerry Wiesner, and Paul Gray. Your trust and guidance give me great comfort and courage for the task ahead.

* * *

On the banks of the Charles River an institution has arisen that is recognized throughout the world for its unique contributions to our life and times. Established one hundred thirty years ago this spring, MIT did not become yet another comprehensive university. Nor did it become simply an "engineering school" or a "polytechnic institute."

Rather, it became a wellspring of scientific and technological knowledge and practice and a place where musical creativity thrives. Its inventive and entrepreneurial faculty generated a great economic engine, and they have created revolutionary insights into the structure of language and the nature of learning. They have led the quest to decipher the molecular foundations of life, and they have influenced the political and economic policies of nations. MIT's engineers and scientists made critical contributions to our nation's security when that was largely a military matter, and its graduates have given architectural manifestation to humankind's highest cultural and artistic insights.

MIT has been home to distinguished scholars from around the world, men and women who have stretched the human mind and spirit. Above all, it has provided an intense and effective education to generations of the brightest young men and women that this nation and the world have brought forth.

Now MIT prepares for the passing of the twentieth century and the advent of the twenty-first. We seek form and substance appropriate for these times, even as we seek to shape the future of our nation and world.

But we enter more than a new temporal era. We stand at the dawn of a new global age. Our lives are interwoven across national boundaries in unprecedented ways—connected through our earth's environment, whose stewardship we all share; through our economic and production systems; through instantly shared information; through universally shared dreams. These dreams include the vision of a world in which the security of nations is defined by economic and social dexterity rather than by military might. And they include the vision of a nation that has regained its sense of social justice and is truly the land of opportunity for all.

MIT has played a remarkable role—at critical moments—in shaping our nation and our world. We have done so through individual creative genius and through grand institutional ventures. Like America itself, we have responded in a heroic and innovative manner to sudden challenges, such as the onset of World War II or the launching of Sputnik. Today we are challenged once again on a grand scale, but this time by slow, corrosive forces rather than by sudden, galvanizing events: by the erosion of our global environment rather than by explosions at Pearl Harbor; by declines in scientific literacy and industrial competitiveness rather than by the launching of a satellite.

This morning I would like to share with you my view of the challenges that confront us and to offer a growing vision of the opportunities they present for the future of MIT.

A New Global Age

There is a remarkable image etched in the mind and psyche of our generation. We were the first to view a shimmering, seemingly peaceful planet Earth from the depths of space. Still, here below, we know that we inhabit a raucous global village. We are connected, across time and space, as never before in human history. Many of these connections have been made possible by the advances in science and technology. We must learn to deal with this interdependence in new ways, creating new forms of organization and incorporating new points of view.

Let me give three examples.

First, the earth's environment, a fragile envelope that bears witness to the degrading effects of human activity. It is no longer possible, if it ever was, for individuals or nations to think that the way in which they treat their land, air, and water has no bearing on their neighbors. Nor is it possible for us to work on each aspect of this damaged environment as a separate problem. Ironically, many of the scientific and technological advances that so enhance human comfort and well-being—advances in transportation, energy, and agriculture—concurrently pose threats to our biosphere. This presents a challenge and an opportunity for us here at MIT. I believe that we must marshal our interests and capabilities to understand these issues and to develop solutions. Such an endeavor will require a new generation of scientific computation for atmospheric modeling, new instrumentation for monitoring environmental conditions, new modes of analysis, and new technologies to correct or avoid problems.

Beyond this, we need to come together in new ways—from different fields, different organizations, and different countries—to understand not only the physical but the cultural, economic, and political forces that affect the health of the natural world. The stage has been set at MIT by the establishment of the Center for Global Change Science and by the new Council on the Global Environment. Only with this kind of integrated approach—drawing on faculty from disparate fields—can we hope to meet the profound challenge of making and keeping our planet livable.

Another challenge—and set of opportunities—in our increasingly inter-dependent world lies in the realm of electronic communication. Instantaneous communication, both verbal and visual, has reduced our planet to the electronic global village once envisioned by McLuhan. Knowledge has become a capital asset, at least as important as physical resources. Bits of information flowing through copper wires, optical fibers, or satellite links have become a new currency: the currency of the information marketplace. Increasingly, the commerce of this new marketplace will be conducted along fiber optic information superhighways that will connect computers, telephones, high-definition video systems, and hybrid technologies yet to be developed.

This information infrastructure already exists in rudimentary form. MIT has the opportunity to play a pivotal role in bringing increased capabilities and coherence to this system and in defining the currency of the new information marketplace. In doing so, we must not only increase the power and ease of computing and communications but we must do so in ways that enhance our intellectual and social capabilities, that help us make wiser decisions, and that enable us to bridge cultural and political barriers. Here, too, we must invent new ways of combining our talents across disciplinary and institutional boundaries in order to give form, substance, and humanity to the dawning information age. To this end, I am pleased to announce the establishment of the MIT Information Infrastructure Initiative—a project that will bring together eight different organizations within MIT with the goal of working with industrial partners to develop a very-high-frequency, entirely optical network and to establish within our campus a working model of the information marketplace.

My third example derives from the increasing political and economic connections throughout the world. These connections pose the question of whether the MIT of the future will be a national or an international institution. What does it mean for MIT to be a citizen of a world where common problems or interests are often more powerful than geographic distances, yet where national differences exist?

The issue is complex. MIT is a national institution, but America is no longer isolated. MIT was born as a manifestation of Yankee ingenuity and know-how, it has served as a driving force for the creation and improvement of American industry, it is funded to a very significant extent by the American taxpayer, and above all it is centered on the education of many of the brightest and most talented young people of the United States. MIT is of and for America.

Today, however, in order to serve America well, we must participate in the broader global community. Basic science has always prided itself in being the prototype for true international cooperation, but today this viewpoint and system are being strained—strained because of the increasing economic value of university-generated knowledge and technological concepts.

There are those who look at this country's position on the economic balance scales and call for greater protection of our ideas, especially those having to do with science and technology. Some look at this country's troubles in the world marketplace and are quick to blame our overseas competitors. Others cast the issue into the framework of Pogo Possum's famous saying: "We have met the enemy, and he is us." And still others quickly respond along the lines of Robert Reich, who asks, "Who is us?"—that is, in this day and age, what defines an American corporation?

Clearly, we must be concerned with this nation's economic well-being. We must not, however, endanger the very essence of our institution by retreating into simplistic forms of techno-nationalism. To draw boundaries around our institution, to close off the free exchange of education and ideas, would be antithetical to the concept of a great university. The list of nations that, at difficult historical moments, closed their universities to the outside world is not one we would be proud to join.

This does not mean that we could not, on occasion, establish special programs directed at the solution of national problems. However, any such programs must also fit one fundamental rule: All students, once admitted to MIT, must be able to participate fully in our educational and research programs, without regard to their citizenship.

In my view, a much more important concern of MIT should be the establishment of programs to ensure that our students are educated in such a way as to prepare them to lead full, responsible lives as world citizens. It is time we made the matter of international context and opportunity an integral part of an MIT education.

The Changing Face of America

Just as we develop new connections among nations, so too must we seek new connections within our own. The face of America is changing significantly and rapidly. Our society is increasingly pluralistic, yet our connections across racial, ethnic, and sometimes even gender boundaries are frayed. Securing America's promise for all remains a crucial goal. The nation's potential will not be fully realized until all racial and ethnic groups have full opportunity to realize their own potential and, in doing so, to contribute fully to the health and vigor of our society.

MIT has traditionally educated engineers, scientists, and others to develop technologies, lead businesses, and serve as professors, researchers, and scholars. To continue this leadership in the era ahead, we must better reflect the changing face of America in our students, faculty, and staff.

We can clearly see such changes in our undergraduate population—thanks to the leadership, commitment, and concerted effort of many here with us today. Among our graduate students and our faculty, however, we see far less evidence of this change as yet. We must double and redouble our efforts to attract the brightest and best from all races, both women and men, not only to our undergraduate program, but to our graduate school and to our faculty. There are many social and historical forces militating against success in this endeavor. It will require renewed commitment on the part of each of us to identify and recruit these scholars and, once they are here, to do our part to see that they attain their full potential.

As one step, we will begin implementing during the coming weeks a program proposed by the Equal Opportunity Committee to recruit more women to our faculty. And we will reaffirm and reinvigorate our policies and programs for bringing more underrepresented minority members to our faculty. As we succeed—and in order to succeed—with these and other efforts, we must work to ensure that MIT is a place that respects and celebrates the diversity of our community. Just as we celebrate learning about the physical universe or the political and economic worlds or the creative arts, so must we celebrate learning about, and from, each other. Such change is rewarding, but it is seldom easy. During the years ahead we must refuse to let the centrifugal forces of intolerance and injustice pull us apart. We must be held together by respect for the individual and by a commitment to the values we hold in common.

Education: To Move a Nation

Just as we as individuals are part of an interwoven social fabric, so too is MIT part of an interdependent educational system—one that begins before kindergarten and extends through postdoctoral studies. Within this system, America's colleges and universities stand as national treasures. But the strength of these institutions, and thus of our society, is imperiled—imperiled by the state of our primary and secondary schools and imperiled by the declining interest and ability among our young people to pursue rigorous advanced studies, particularly in science and engineering. These trends must be reversed.

It is my firm belief that national educational strength is the essential prerequisite for economic and social prosperity. Education can move a nation; the future belongs to those who understand it. At all levels, active, informed participation in our economy and our democracy now requires an ability to understand basic scientific and technical concepts. And yet, American popular culture pushes us in the opposite direction. We need no less than a change in the culture of this country, a revolution in attitude about the importance of education and, in particular, of scientific and mathematical literacy.

Until we as a nation wake up to the fact that we must increase our investment in the growth of human capital—that is, people and ideas—our educational system will spiral downward, pulling our economy and our way of life with it. This is a danger of the first magnitude and we must all work to address it.

Thirty years ago, MIT played a key role in launching a nation-wide wave of education reform in the sciences. The time has come again for us to place our expertise and stature in the service of a major national effort to rebuild the strength of science and mathematics in American schools. I believe that MIT not only can but must draw on its special strengths to help renew effective, accessible education for the young people of this country.

An MIT Education for the Future

The education that we most directly influence, however, is the education of our own students. Among them are people whose passion is to engineer a better world; among them are people with a particular, concentrated brilliance; among them are profoundly creative people who tread new and different pathways. We are gifted with some of the very brightest young people of our nation and of the world. It is through these students that MIT will have its greatest influence on the world of the future.

In recent years, our faculty has been involved in a long-term review of the undergraduate program. The intensity of this review is testimony to the fact that education, and particularly undergraduate education, is at the very core of MIT. No one has been more engaged with these matters over the years than our engineering faculty—indeed, the engineering curriculum in this country was largely developed by MIT faculty in the 1950s and 1960s. They spearheaded the infusion of basic science into engineering education and practice.

The results were astounding: We produced engineers who created a revolution in computing and communication, developed vehicles to explore outer space, and started not only companies but entire industries based on high technology. While this curriculum has been continually refreshed, its fundamental approach and content have remained essentially unchanged for thirty years. The world in which engineering is practiced, on the other hand, has changed dramatically and rapidly.

Take, for example, the decline in the United States' ability to compete in the world marketplace for manufactured goods. The reasons for this decline are complex, but a major issue has certainly been the attitude of industry and of universities toward the design and manufacture of consumer products. We need to infuse our engineering students with an increased respect for and enjoyment of effective, efficient, and socially responsive design and production. Today, we must prepare engineers who have the self-discipline, analytical skills, and problem-solving abilities so highly valued in MIT graduates, but who are also prepared for the challenge of production and leadership in the world marketplace of the next century.

This is but one of the challenges to engineering education. But it is indicative of the concerns that face our faculty as they design a curriculum that will serve our students well into the twenty-first century. They will do so in the setting of this research university: a setting in which the unique blending of graduate education, undergraduate education, and research creates unparalleled opportunities for learning and for discovery—a setting that keeps both our education and our research forward-looking and robust.

All do not agree with this view. Many believe that our mission has become distorted and that education has been lost in our desire and responsibility to excel in research. This is clearly a central issue for MIT—one that must be openly discussed in all corners of the Institute. This fall, as an event of the Inaugural year, we will hold a major colloquium on the topic of teaching and learning within the research university. I intend this to be a no-holds-barred debate that will illuminate our efforts to shape the future of education at MIT.

Educational success at MIT depends, above all else, on the commitment and inventiveness of our faculty. Excellence in undergraduate teaching must be rewarded and encouraged. To this end, we are establishing an endowed program to recognize faculty members who have profoundly influenced our students through their sustained and significant contributions to teaching and curriculum development. A select number of faculty will be appointed as Faculty Fellows, each for a ten-year period, and will receive an annual scholar's allowance throughout their appointment. The first Fellows will be appointed this year, and we expect their ranks to build to at least sixty during this decade.

The strength of an MIT education is its depth and intensity. Our graduates value above all else their self-discipline, their analytical thinking skills, and their confidence to take on great challenges. Today, science and technology, culture and policy, industry and government, production and communication, are interwoven as never before. The nation needs broadly educated young men and women to be leaders of the next generation. An understanding of science and technology is surely part of what such leaders must possess. Similarly, those who practice science and technology need an ever-greater understanding of the world in which they will work and must be able to contribute wisely to policies affecting the development and uses of technology.

What does this mean for education at MIT? Surely it means a careful balance among the humanities, arts, and social sciences on the one hand and mathematics and the physical and life sciences on the other. And it means a continuing look at our departmental programs to ensure that—in content and approach—they give our students the best possible foundation for intellectual growth and professional achievement.

Our campus should be a place where humanistic and artistic scholarship and creation can flower in unique and important new ways. I further believe that we at MIT have an unusual opportunity for the humanities and engineering to enrich each other. While the continuum from the humanities to the natural sciences has long been recognized, the continuum from the humanities to engineering is less well explored. In general, such exploration has been hindered by a utilitarian view of the humanities and social sciences on the part of many engineering educators, and by a lack of appreciation of the intellectual content of modern engineering by many humanists. An MIT education should enlarge an individual's choices—and so should include a common experience in science and mathematics; a serious exploration of the humanities, arts, and social sciences; and a continuing conversation among these fields.

I believe that the creative tension generated by these varying interests and cultures can serve us well as we continue to review and renew our undergraduate programs. We have a common currency of excellence and creativity—regardless of field—that will enable us to develop new modes of inquiry and teaching that make the most of the unique intellectual community that is MIT. We have a special set of talents and focus that give MIT its distinctive character. By building on these special strengths, MIT will contribute in rich and often unique ways to the times and the nation's needs.

We should not expect to be all things to all people. One of the strengths of the American educational system is the great variety of public and private colleges and universities. This condition allows for, and indeed demands, experimentation, variation, cooperation, and competition. The resulting synergy is the yeast that keeps our system strong.

Rebuilding Trust in Science and Technology

For four decades, the American research universities have served this nation exceedingly well. From virtually any perspective, they have paid enormous dividends in return for the public's trust and investment, dividends in the form of educated leaders in academia, business, and government; of advances in medical care and nutrition; of national security; of new and revitalized industries; of increased understanding of our physical, social, and natural worlds. But today, the American public is calling into question the value of our research universities and no longer tends to view science and technology as the foundation of progress. The public's attention is caught not only by the debate over the costs and quality of undergraduate education but also by the debate over the costs and conduct of research.

The doubt of the moment, however, must not be allowed to weaken the basic concept of the American university system, one that is universally recognized as being the best in the world. This system is founded on a social contract with the American public and enhanced by partnerships with government and industry. We cannot keep our flexibility, our vigor, our quality—as a nation or as an academic community—by taking this partnership for granted. We need to rebuild trust in this nation's research universities and its scientific enterprise. We must ensure that the foundation of scientific and scholarly research is secure. What is this foundation? Jacob Bronowski stated it with deceptive simplicity when he wrote, "The end of science is to discover what is true about the world."

In seeking scientific truth, ideas and hypotheses are debated, tested, proved, disproved, revised, built upon, or rejected. This activity is carried out by researchers in different laboratories, in different universities, indeed in different countries. This is what makes science, indeed most scholarship, simultaneously an individual and a communal activity. And it is why we have usually been able to rely on this system to detect and correct error. Like all human endeavors, science is not, and cannot be, totally free from error or even occasional abuse. And so it rests upon us— as scientists and scholars—to do a better job of strengthening, continually renewing, and transmitting our system of values.

Great teachers impart and stimulate the passion, excitement, and beauty of intellectual endeavor. But it is equally important that we impart and stimulate the meaning of, the necessity of, and the passion for the pursuit of truth with integrity and ethical rigor. But whatever we say, ethical lessons will be taught primarily by the ways in which we undertake our own scholarly activities.

These lessons will also by conveyed by the ways in which our institutions handle problems if they do arise. How we deal with alleged misconduct will also affect the strength of society's confidence in and regard for our universities and colleges and for the enterprise of science. We have heard great outcries—for and against—the policing of science. Our response as an academic community must not be one of knee-jerk defensiveness against our critics. Rather, we must engage seriously with our thoughtful critics as well as with our colleagues as we develop ways to continuously foster academic integrity and deal forthrightly and fairly with problems when they arise. If we are not able to do so, we can be sure that others will be only too glad to do it for us.

Public confidence in our universities must be fully restored. Our social compact must be reestablished. But in the discourse required to do so, we must avoid the trap of justifying all that we do on utilitarian grounds. Clearly, we have been great contributors to the nation's economy, and this must continue to be a cardinal element of MIT's mission. But we must take care not to over-emphasize these contributions as the justification for investing in universities. If we overuse such arguments, we might unwittingly endanger our traditions of intellectual excellence, innovation, integrity, openness, worldwide service, deep scholarship, and independent criticism. Ultimately, our contributions to social progress and well-being rest on our ability to steer our own course, with imagination and intellectual daring.

MIT: Shaping the Future

What then is my vision of MIT a decade hence?

MIT will be a preeminent wellspring of scientific knowledge and technological innovation. MIT will foster the pursuits of individual scholars, whose work so often leads to truly fundamental discoveries. We will be known for our ability to establish new and effective methods for analyzing complex and pervasive issues facing the nation and the world. In an invigorated partnership with industry, the government, and other educational institutions, we will contribute profoundly to their solution. MIT will be known for educating engineers who combine the spirit of innovation and invention with a passion for the highest quality and efficiency in design and production.

MIT will better reflect in our students, faculty, and staff the changing face of America. We will find ways to instill the excitement and romance of science and mathematics in new generations of young people. MIT will spearhead efforts to rekindle our nation's belief in the importance of scientific research and education. We will have found renewed commitment to the deepest values of the academy. MIT will stand for integrity in all that it does. MIT will serve our nation well, but also will be of and for the greater world community.

Above all, the Massachusetts Institute of Technology will be a place to which the brightest young men and women will come for their educations. They will be able to attend MIT regardless of their financial circumstances. They will be taught and counseled by dedicated teachers who themselves define the leading edge of human knowledge and invention. Their education will be robust: deep in scientific content, yet providing the flexibility and learning skills to serve them well in ever changing and expanding circumstances. They will be attuned to the complexities of their world, a world that they will help to change. Through that wonderful blend of undergraduate education, graduate education, research, and creative activity that is MIT, our students will be enriched and they, in turn, will enrich the Institute.

Mens et manus: With mind and hand we set forth. Our promise will be secured by the collective energies and wisdom of those who are drawn to this great magnet for intellect and creativity. Together, we will give shape to the future—the future of MIT, our nation, and our world.

2

From the First Year: MIT in National and International Context 1990–1991

During my first year in office, American higher education, especially in our research universities, was sailing in unusually troubled seas. A "whistleblower" at Stanford University brought about highly publicized hearings, chaired by John Dingell, the powerful Chairman of the House Commerce Subcommittee on Oversight and Investigation, on alleged misuses of public funds through inappropriate overhead charges to federally sponsored research grants and contracts at universities. This, coupled with high-profile accusations of scientific misconduct, tore at the fabric of the longstanding and productive partnership between our universities and the federal government.

This same year, MIT alone went to court to fight the U.S. Department of Justice's suit against nine universities, accusing them of violating the Sherman Antitrust Act by sharing certain financial information about their applicants in order to maintain the discipline of awarding undergraduate financial aid to students on the basis of their financial need, rather than on perceived "merit." Another tempest arose, largely in Congress, because MIT maintained research relationships with other countries, especially Japan, that were perceived by some as counter to our national economic interests. These were difficult times that called for institutions like MIT to stand tall on behalf of fundamental principles, to carefully consider their role in a rapidly changing world, to wisely steward public investments in our research and education, and to thoughtfully answer our critics.

Observations on the First Year

My first year as president has been marked particularly by the need for MIT to respond to a host of challenging external forces.

At a time when I wanted to concentrate on setting a long-range agenda for the future of the Institute and primarily on involving the community in strategic planning, MIT has faced a flood of external actions and issues that have demanded unremitting attention. Some of these issues—such as the matter of intellectual integrity in the conduct of research—touch all universities. Other external actions were more narrowly focused on a few universities—such as the Justice Department allegations regarding "price-fixing" on financial aid.

Many of these outside forces are troubling; some could be seriously damaging. But while I regret the sheer time and effort that dealing day-to-day with these matters has required, the fact is that they are by no means unrelated to the long-range planning on which we need to concentrate. Indeed, they have served as a lens to bring into focus many of the issues that we must address in defining and shaping our future. They speak to us of a changing nation and world. And many represent an erosion of the partnership of the federal government with our research universities.

Changing Public Attitudes

Yet the matter is deeper than the erosion of the sense of partnership between the government and the universities. In our democratic system, the actions of Congress and the executive branch ultimately reflect the views and will of the people. Thus, we must look more closely at public perceptions and attitudes toward our research universities. MIT historically established the paradigm for these universities and retains its preeminence today; hence these are critical matters for us.

I surmise that the origins of changing public attitudes toward our research universities are twofold. First, there is a growing wave of populism and an associated widespread distrust of expertise, excellence, and privilege, whether real or perceived. Second, there have been direct assaults, largely on ideological grounds, against our universities. These began in earnest when William Bennett used his pulpit as Secretary of Education to attack American higher education. The flames he ignited were fanned by others, including the picture of the presumed decline of higher education painted by Allan Bloom in *The Closing of the American Mind*, and the intemperate portrait of the American professoriate by Charles Sykes in *Profscam*.

Criticisms of universities have resonated with the public, which had taken account of rapidly rising tuitions and come to believe that, almost antithetically, the quality of teaching and the commitment to undergraduate education, had degenerated. It is a resonance that we must worry about. It calls for serious self-examination.

Catalytic Federal Actions

Against this backdrop came this past year three catalytic federal actions—the investigations at Stanford of alleged abuses of the system for reimbursement of indirect costs of sponsored research; the further investigation of the matters surrounding fraud charges associated with the *Cell* paper by Weaver, Baltimore, and others; and the continuing investigation by the Justice Department of alleged conspiracy and price-fixing among universities.

While these activities captured the headlines, still other actions were proceeding with less public attention. They included the decline of peer review of academic research and facilities proposals and the corresponding increase in political earmarking; investigations about conflicts of interest on the part of faculty with strong ties to industry; debates about technology transfer from U.S. universities to foreign countries, particularly Japan; criticisms about the numbers of foreign students studying engineering and science in American universities; and a continuing decline in the effective level of federal financial support of students.

Diagnosis and Prognosis

What does all of this mean? To what extent are these forces aimed at MIT specifically? What is the prognosis? What can we do? There are no definitive answers to these questions, but I would like to share some thoughts about them.

First, what does it mean? It means, basically, that our universities are not immune to the strains present in our society, and that tight budgetary times and shifting, or indeed uncertain, federal priorities are likely to have profound implications for us. It means further that we must strive energetically to understand the forces at work and their causes, and then develop ways of dealing with them. Thoughtless defensiveness is neither an appropriate nor a helpful response. We must listen to and talk with our critics as well as serve as critics. We must correct those areas in need of correction. We must adjust to new realities, recognizing the opportunities and responsibilities as well as the difficulties we face.

When I arrived in Cambridge last fall, MIT had been buffeted by several adverse interactions with various agencies of the federal government in rapid succession. Many believed that there was a strong anti-MIT attitude abroad, but I have not found it so. For over twelve months now, I have made monthly trips to Washington, each with a saturated schedule of visits to senators, representatives, agency heads, and other policymakers. I come away with the impression that MIT is still highly respected and viewed as an important national resource. However, I do not believe that we are viewed as being as far apart from the crowd as we have been in the past. There are also small pockets of resentment of our quality and a belief that, while many other institutions need help, MIT can take care of itself. And there is, most regrettably, a serious lack of recognition of what is required to maintain the wide range of excellence at an institution like MIT and of how very different that is from what is required to build one or two spires of excellence at other kinds of institutions.

What is the prognosis? These are treacherous times. We need to take a leadership role in restoring public confidence in our research universities and in engendering a better understanding of their past contributions and of their importance to a vibrant future. These tasks should follow from our own self-assessment and dedication to leadership in a changing world. Above all, the United States must re-establish a strong and fundamental belief in education and in the importance of scientific and techno-logical research. In his recent book *The Next Century*, David Halberstam speaks of the Japanese educational system. Regardless of one's views of the nature of that system, he states, the Japanese believe that if the young people are educated well, all else can be achieved. It is this attitude—that the development of our human capital, of people and their ideas, is prerequisite to all else that we want to accomplish—that we must regain in the United States. If we succeed in doing so, a bright future for the country, and an exciting mission for MIT, will be assured.

Changing Federal Relations

Let me now turn to some of the specific elements in the nature of MIT's relationship to the federal government that require careful analysis and action. We begin that task from a history and background of strength. Previous MIT administrations have been very well represented in the highest councils of the executive branch. Moreover, MIT faculty remain very well connected to the agencies of the federal government. They are sought out for service on key planning panels and understand the missions of the agencies very well. Nonetheless, I believe that the Institute today needs new responses to the apparent growing shift of responsibility for science and education policy into the more chaotic domain of Congress. In addition to devoting a major portion of my own time to federal issues, I concluded early on that it would be wise to have a continuous presence in Washington. Accordingly, we have opened an MIT Washington Office, directed by Dr. John C. Crowley, former vice president of the American Association of Universities. This office will enable us to observe and interact more continuously with federal policy initiatives and the related authorization and appropriation processes that affect us and our colleagues. We intend to work largely through coalition-building and close collaboration with our sister institutions. The Washington Office will also serve as a gateway to MIT, assisting in bringing MIT faculty expertise to both principals and staff members in Congress and in the executive branch. Good scientific and technological advice is needed as never before in the government, and our faculty can contribute much.

Indirect Costs of University Research

The subject of indirect costs of university research, long considered something of an arcane topic, became headline news in 1991 as a result of allegations of erroneous and inappropriate charges to the federal government by Stanford University. The subsequent government investigations riveted both congressional and public attention on indirect costs of research and on the accounting/auditing procedures used to reimburse universities for those costs. These investigations and the manner in which they were conducted and reported by the press have tended to erode public confidence in our universities and have unleashed forces in Congress and elsewhere that have the potential to do great damage to the nation's system of higher education and research.

These investigations have also raised authentic issues, however, and the response of the university community must be to correct any legitimate problems. In particular, further tightening, clarification, and greater standardization of accounting procedures are needed to prevent erroneous charges to indirect-cost pools. What is not needed is a rush to judgment that will produce an ill-considered quick fix that will harm the long-term health of our universities and our national system of research. I am particularly concerned that the responsibility for indirect cost matters should remain centered in the executive Office of Management and Budget (OMB). The specter of the details of indirect-cost accounting becoming part of the annual appropriations process in the Congress is daunting.

A particularly troubling aspect of the present indirect-cost debate is the lack of recognition of, or commitment to, the concept that federal research support to universities serves the dual purpose of accomplishing research and educating graduate students, who comprise the next generations of researchers. In some of the debate, funding of university research has been viewed as simple government procurement—an approach that draws no distinction between supporting university research, with its intimate involvement of graduate students, and purchasing goods and services from an ordinary supplier. This approach also appears to be promoted by some funding agencies in support of policies that effectively encourage the employment of postdoctoral researchers rather than graduate students. In an era when projections show looming shortfalls in the numbers of PhD scientists and engineers in the United States, such an approach is unwise, and we have worked hard to counter it wherever we have found it.

We are especially concerned about recommendations by some to disallow the payment of graduate research assistants' tuitions as employee benefits. The disallowance of this practice would drive an immediate two-thirds increase at MIT in the annual cost of supporting a graduate-student research assistant on an individual faculty grant or research contract. A lack of supportiveness of the graduate student component of research is also displayed in various proposals for handling the partial support of library costs and the recommendation by some in Congress that the student-services component of indirect costs be eliminated.

Fundamental to the process of restoring confidence in this system of cost accounting is the tenet that policies and practices should be based on principles. Therefore, I believe it is particularly important now, while we are reviewing these accounting guidelines, that we not lose sight of the fundamental principles of OMB Circular A-21, which has governed for many years the financial relationships between government and universities receiving federal funds in research. In brief, these principles are that university faculty, graduate students, and staff will perform research at low cost, and that simultaneously they will maintain and advance the scientific, technological, and intellectual infrastructure of America by educating the next generation of researchers. In return, the U.S. government will recognize the diversity among American universities and the dual role of graduate students in research and education, and will bear its full and fair share of costs. These philosophical and economic principles have proved extraordinarily sound and have helped make our university research system the world leader. Any restructuring of Circular A-21 must be solidly based on considered analysis, careful redefinition, and the preservation of the principles that have served so well.

Academic Integrity

Universities exist to pass on knowledge to succeeding generations and to generate new knowledge, analyses, and insights. We, in addition, have an overarching responsibility—to imbue in our students and ourselves a dedication to intellectual honesty as well as an understanding of the methodologies of objective analysis and the respect for reasoned discourse that lead to the establishment of scientific and scholarly truth.

Recently, a few highly publicized cases of alleged scientific misconduct have captured the public's attention. While the press and others seek to sensationalize these events, we must do more than attempt to persuade the public that if such misconduct has occurred it is a rare event—as in fact it is. In every case of alleged misconduct, we must look to the substance behind allegations, and we must continually review and refresh our commitment to basic academic values.

What are these values? What is the foundation of scientific and scholarly research that we hold fundamental? The foundation is truth, and certain intimately related concomitant values, which Jacob Bronowski identified so well in his book of essays, *A Sense of the Future*. As discussed by Bronowski, these include, importantly, independence and originality; a belief in the value of dissent; and an adherence to freedom of thought and speech. Central to these values is the importance of respecting another's point of view. Points of view and hypotheses are there to be debated, tested, proved, disproved, revised, built upon, or rejected. This is what makes science—indeed most scholarship— both an individual and a highly communal activity. And it is why we say science is a self-correcting enterprise that strongly counters any forces that might tempt one to cut corners or act with less than full honesty.

Nonetheless, there are forces that push the modern university researcher in other directions. Among them are the following:

• First, the *rapid expansion and communication of knowledge*. Nearly instantaneous promulgation of research results by various modern means contributes to a sometimes frenetic pace that can run counter to the careful review and reworking of research that might reduce ultimate error.

• Second, the *nature of incremental advances in some fields*. In some fields undergoing rapid development, it is often the case that relatively modest advances may have great, albeit fleeting, significance. This, too, can produce a rush to disperse results that can reduce care, review, and reflection, thereby increasing the probability of error.

• Third, the *culture of instantaneous news and fame*. Scientists and scholars do have egos. They are often highly competitive, a characteristic that generally works to the advantage of science. However, when this trait is combined with the American public's unquenchable thirst for sensation and for daily dosages of revolutionary advances, extraneous temptations and inappropriate forces are created.

• Finally, the opportunity for *monetary gain*. Universities have become great engines of the modern economy, and we have increasingly worked together with profit-based industries in arrangements that have contributed significantly to the common good. Yet some of these ties between university scientists and the corporate world, with their enhanced opportunities for personal financial gain, may not always be free from the possibility of troubling conflict of interest.

The basic challenge before us is to do a better job of passing on and strengthening our system of values. How can this be accomplished? The easy suggestion is to establish formal courses and perhaps require them of all students. But this is not necessarily practical or effective. We can also, as I have asked MIT to do, establish broader mentoring of new colleagues—faculty and students—and create occasional forums designed to help develop an environment in which the importance of intellectual integrity and scholarly values is widely understood and prized. Ultimately, however, it is in our individual and institutional actions that our values are manifested. Whatever we say, we teach by example. And the lesson will be conveyed best, therefore, by the ways in which we undertake our own scholarly activities and by the ways in which we deal with problems if they do arise.

We have heard great outcries for and against the policing of science. Our response, as an academic community, must not be one of knee-jerk defensiveness, but rather one of developing an effective method of self-governance regarding integrity in research. If we are not able to do so, we can be sure that others will be only too glad to do it for us. And what we don't need is more bureaucracy and increased overhead expenses for programs to enforce scientific integrity. To strengthen our self-governance at MIT, the provost and I asked a group of distinguished faculty, chaired by Professor Sheila E. Widnall, to review our responsibilities and articulate our values in the conduct of academic research; to look at our own policies and procedures in light of those values; to compare these policies and procedures with federal and professional standards and guidelines governing research and suggest revisions where appropriate; and, finally, to propose creative ways of introducing mentoring and educational programs regarding both the conduct of research and the provision of broad career guidance throughout the entire academic community. This committee has produced an interim report that will provide the framework for Institute-wide discussion during the fall and a set of specific recommendations thereafter.

Student Financial Aid and the Justice Department
A rather strange episode in our relations with the federal government continues to play itself out in a suit against MIT by the Department of Justice. Since 1989, a number of universities and colleges have been the subjects of an investigation by the Department of Justice seeking evidence that they have conspired

to violate the Sherman Antitrust Act. Hoards of government attorneys have, at great expense to the American taxpayer and to those who pay tuition and make charitable donations to these schools, combed through the records of this "industry" to spot evidence of "collusion" in restraint of trade that would suppress free-market forces acting upon faculty salaries, tuition charges, or financial aid to students. In May the U.S. Attorney General brought a formal complaint against the eight Ivy League universities and MIT for colluding in the Overlap Group—meetings held by those institutions to assure that their student financial aid to applicants in common be awarded only on the basis of financial need.

The eight Ivy League universities settled the complaint out of court by agreeing not to engage in this practice for the next ten years. MIT, after careful deliberation, decided not to sign this consent decree and therefore is being sued by the Department of Justice. We took this position for three reasons. We do not believe that we have violated the Sherman Act; we believe that there are distinguishing differences between us and the other eight universities in this matter; and we believe that our approach to need-based financial aid, and the manner in which its implementation was assisted by the Overlap Group, serves an important social function and is the best use of the limited financial-aid funds available to us. We do not believe it is in the nation's interest for universities to compete financially for students.

The Department of Justice apparently believes that financial aid would better be based on merit. It concludes that if the highly competitive schools named in its action had not jointly agreed to provide aid based on need, that some students would have received greater financial assistance, and therefore a lower effective price for their educations, and that this would be appropriate. MIT, on the other hand, has long believed that, while students should be admitted to the Institute on the basis of intellectual merit, they should be awarded financial aid based solely on their and their families' ability to pay. Ironically and remarkably, this long-standing MIT student-aid policy is exactly the approach that was later mandated by Congress for the use of federal financial-aid funds to undergraduates.

MIT has defended and will defend its beliefs in this suit in a considered manner, seeking thoughtful and expert advice, and remaining cognizant of all the costs and ramifications of its actions.

The Changing Face of America: Implications for MIT

Besides these federal actions, there are a number of other external issues that impinge strongly upon us. Foremost among them and of deep concern is the issue of race in America. Universities are both susceptible to aspects of this issue and, in my view, responsible for working vigorously toward the solution of certain components of it. Moreover, regardless of differing views regarding the social responsibilities of higher education, the fact remains that the racial and ethnic structure of the American populace and workforce is changing rapidly in well known and absolutely predictable ways. Students who are to be optimally educated for the world they will enter must learn from the experience of living with and learning with and from students and faculty representing the diversity of people who now comprise the country's population. Furthermore, as we look at the various projected shortfalls of engineers, scientists, and PhD-level scholars in numerous fields, it becomes apparent that attracting and educating people from segments of our population who have traditionally not been well represented in academe is in the national interest.

MIT has played a leadership role by significantly increasing the numbers of underrepresented minority students in our undergraduate programs. Underrepresented minority students make up 16 percent of the class of 1995. Enrollments in our graduate programs and representation on our faculty of under-represented minority scholars, however, have not kept pace. It is imperative that we improve this situation appreciably. At the faculty level, the provost has recently announced a reinvigorated, funded program designed to assist departments financially in increasing the number of underrepresented minorities on the MIT faculty. We also are accelerating the conduct of programs aimed at making the opportunities for graduate study at MIT clearly known to underrepresented-minority undergraduate students around the country.

MIT has also played a leadership role in the education of women in engineering and the sciences. Women make up 35 percent of the new entering class. Substantial progress has been made during the last two decades also in attracting women to our graduate programs and to our faculty, but more remains to be done. Here, too, the provost will provide certain assistance for hiring women, especially at tenured levels in departments where they constitute less than a third of the faculty.

But attracting a more diverse faculty and student body to MIT is only part of the challenge before us. The entire environment for living and working in our universities needs concerted attention as the society of which we are a part changes. Single parents, dual-career couples, and an aging population have become the norm. Although the university cannot be expected to solve all of the problems that accrue from these changes, they require that we give proper attention to the development of a campus that is open, rewarding, and enjoyable. Accordingly, following the recommendation of a recent faculty and staff committee, a Council on Family and Work will be appointed to advise and assist the administration in establishing at MIT the most satisfying environment possible.

MIT: A National and International University

Yet another set of challenges has to do with the increasing inter-dependence of peoples and enterprises throughout the world. Our world is interconnected as never before—through our physical environment, through communications networks, through our production and economic systems, through politics, and through expanding common knowledge bases. Similarly, our research universities have become increasingly international, an inevitable change that has led some legislators and others to question the nature of the international connections of research universities in general, and of MIT in particular.

The basic questions are obvious. Is it appropriate that so many international students are studying science, engineering, and business in American universities? Nationally, for example, approximately 50 percent of the graduate students in engineering and physical science are foreign citizens, while at MIT one-third of our graduate students come from other countries. Is it appropriate for universities to receive support in the form of donations or research funding from foreign countries and companies? And the most difficult and emotionally charged question—given that our universities receive so much federal research support—do foreign companies "skim the cream" by carrying off critical technological knowledge, commercializing it, and then out-competing U.S. firms?

During much of this past year an Institute-wide committee chaired by Professor Eugene B. Skolnikoff considered these and other issues involving our international connections and proposed a number of policies for MIT. We have disseminated this report widely among colleagues in government and industry, and it has received, generally, very favorable comment.

The basic principle set forth in the report is that MIT is first and foremost an American institution. We have served, and will serve, the United States well. We best serve our nation, however, by being a preeminent institution of higher education and research emphasizing science and engineering. We can maintain this preeminence only if we maintain strong intellectual, professional, and personal ties throughout the world.

Science has always prided itself in its internationalism— judging people and ideas on their merit alone. This principle served us well earlier in this century, when large numbers of American scholars studied in Europe, bringing back leading-edge knowledge and establishing fine academic departments and laboratories here. American universities also greatly value the numerous faculty who have immigrated to this country and have become great academic and scientific leaders. I believe that we are now entering an era when the flow of scholars and knowledge across many national boundaries will be the prerequisite for first-rate science and technology and for first-rate universities. We must act accordingly.

The issue is admittedly complicated to an extent because of the diminished distinctions between basic and applied research in many fields, the shortened times from laboratory to commercialization, and the more intimate relationship between universities and industry. However, I believe that it would be a serious strategic error for the country to attempt to establish impermeable boundaries around our universities. Rather, we must work to gain more assurance that communications with visitors to our laboratories are two-way, that knowledge and expertise flow in as well as out.

Having said this, in my view the fraction of international students in U.S. graduate science and engineering programs is too high. It should be a goal of our secondary and undergraduate schools to educate and inspire U.S. students to move into such demanding and important programs of study rather than standing aside while more intellectually energetic and disciplined students from other nations take up the challenges. Furthermore, we must educate our U.S.-citizen students appropriately and encourage them to gain experience overseas, that is, we must prepare them for leadership in the kind of world in which they will live and work. (MIT's Japan Program is an example of leadership in this area.)

Education at MIT

All aspects of undergraduate education continue to be very actively discussed at the Institute, as they are in public forums, where university faculty are frequently criticized for allegedly caring more about graduate education and research than undergraduate teaching. With such criticism in mind, I recently asked one of our graduating seniors how he had found the quality of teaching at MIT. He answered that it was excellent in the lower level subjects, but spread over a wide range in the more advanced subjects. Expanding on this, he explained that the faculty expended enormous effort and creativity in doing a truly first-rate job in the large freshman and sophomore introductory classes, but that a student was expected to learn more independently—more like a junior colleague, if you will—in many of the more advanced subjects. This senior's response demonstrates yet another aspect of MIT's uniqueness. At most research universities the usual complaint is that the faculty seem uninterested in the large introductory courses, and only as one progresses into the advanced classes does their interest become more deeply engaged.

While American students themselves appear to be satisfied in many dimensions, they seem also to have the sense that somehow things should be better still. Undergraduates often believe that they have too many teaching assistants as instructors, not enough direct faculty contact, and insufficient academic and career counseling. And such criticism is aimed most often at research universities, the thesis being that undergraduate teaching is not valued there and that faculty often neglect their teaching responsibilities because of the emphasis on research.

What then is the situation regarding undergraduate teaching at our research universities, and at MIT in particular? In contrast to what some educators are arguing today, I believe that the American research university has created a matrix within which the best possible education for the twenty-first century can take place. Its novel blending of undergraduate education, graduate education, and research is what truly makes these universities the best in the world. At MIT, moreover, there is a permeating belief that our undergraduate curriculum and education constitute our institutional core and are the key to our national and world leadership. Still, vigilance is required to maintain teaching excellence and to renew and revitalize the curriculum. I believe that our record in this respect is exemplary.

In a major curriculum development this past year, the faculty voted to establish a subject in modern biology as a new general Institute requirement for undergraduates, effective with the class entering in 1993. We believe that we are the first university to recognize, by requiring it of all students, the growing general importance of modern biology and the uniqueness of its methodologies. This will enhance still further the quality and relevance of an MIT education.

I am pleased to report also something of a quiet revolution in student counseling and personal contact between students and faculty. As we enter 1991–92, so many faculty have decided to offer freshman advisor seminars that over two-thirds of our new students are having the experience, at the very beginning of their MIT education, of meeting weekly in small groups with Institute faculty for study, discourse, and counseling.

To encourage further attention to teaching, we have just established a program of Faculty Fellows. These endowed awards will recognize faculty for outstanding contributions to our under-graduate educational programs. They are intended to have asso-ciated with them a level of prestige equivalent to endowed professorships, and will provide a discretionary scholar's allowance for a period of ten years. The provost will solicit nom-inations from the community and will appoint approximately six fellows per year. Thus over a decade, on the order of sixty outstanding teachers will be acknowledged in this manner.

A Personal Note

I have narrowed the scope of my first presidential report to focus on a few trends and problem areas that are of particular signifi-cance nationally and at MIT in 1991. There is so much more that could fully and pleasurably have been addressed. Since accepting the privilege of serving this great institution, I have found MIT to be intellectually vibrant, replete with creativity and entrepreneur-ship, well managed, and a great asset to this nation and world.

On a personal note, Becky and I wish to express our deep appreciation for the manner in which we have been accepted and welcomed by the MIT community. To have that friendship, warmth, and collegiality coexist so wonderfully with the excel-lence and professionalism of our faculty, staff, and students has made our transition to our new home and institution as much of a pleasure as it has been an honor.

MIT's commitment to education, its uniqueness in mission and education, and its effective service beyond the confines of its campus have served the nation and world well for many decades. Our central challenge is clear—to continue and enhance MIT's excellence through these uncertain and changing times and into the next century.

3

Excellence in an Era of Change and Constraint
1991–1992

"A slow sort of country!" said the Queen.
"Now here, you see, it takes all the running you can do, to keep in the same place. If you want to get somewhere else, you must run at least twice as fast as that!"
—Lewis Carroll, *Through the Looking Glass*

This was a time of both boundless opportunity and financial constraint for MIT and our sister institutions. Molecular biology; biotechnology; neuroscience; the Internet and communications technologies; management in a global context; sustainable development; better design; and the need to further vitalize the liberal, visual, and performing arts all presented marvelous opportunities and responsibilities to MIT. Yet the combination of bad economic and business climates, with continuing downward pressures on federal research investments, limited the resources available to pursue these opportunities and responsibilities. A structural deficit had developed at the Institute, and a pending change in federal reimbursement policies shook the foundation of support for our graduate-student research and teaching assistants. In this environment, universities had to adopt better management practices and learn from the experiences of businesses through quality management and process reengineering. We did so haltingly, and sometimes painfully, but in the belief that industry, government, and individuals would not strengthen their investment in universities unless we were seen to act responsibly. At MIT we also began to develop additional sources of revenue through new research and educational initiatives of interest to the private sector. Even as we worked to adjust to a world becoming less inclined to support us, we did not lose sight of the fact that excellence costs money and that we must be nimble and inventive, but only while staying true to our basic purposes and values.

America's research universities are faced with a central challenge—to retain and enhance excellence in a time of fiscal constraint and societal uncertainty. We are experiencing a deep sense of frustration because never in our history has the field of intellectual challenge and opportunity or the need for our services to the nation and the world been so great; yet never in recent decades have we experienced such fiscal constraint or sensed such a fall from grace with the public and the government. We are not in crisis, but we are in a precarious state, one that may be more difficult to grasp and respond to than crisis.

But respond we must, because this is a time in which we at MIT and our colleagues around the country should solidify and expand our roles as leaders in this increasingly complex world. We must define new disciplinary futures and invent new intellectual pathways to understanding the physical, biological, economic, and artistic universes. It is a time in which we must do our part in shaping the future.

The challenges before us are great. We must:

• continue to lead the revolution in molecular biology and advance the promise of biotechnology;

• come to understand the workings of the human brain and the nature of intelligence;

• bring the highest quality of mind to assessing and ameliorating humankind's effects on the earth's environment;

• secure the advances of computers, communications technology, and the information marketplace for the social good;

• better understand organizations and businesses and how to make them more effective in building vital and sustainable economies;

- combine the aesthetic and the technical in the design of the physical environment and in the creation of more livable cities; and
- renew—through our unique intellectual and creative environment—the liberal, visual, and performing arts that in such large measure define what it is to be human.

Leadership and Management

University presidents, provosts, deans, department heads, laboratory directors, and other academic administrators rightfully understand their tasks to be to lead and serve, rather than to manage in a narrow sense. Universities are not, and must never become, simply businesses. Our essence and our human purpose run far deeper than that. Nonetheless, leadership for the 1990s requires an understanding of rapidly shifting conditions, opportunities, and resources. The human resources of America's research universities are truly extraordinary, but our fiscal resources are dwindling in real value. I believe that the times require of us uncommon attention to financial and organizational planning and, indeed, management. This attention must come not only from administrators, but also from faculty and staff throughout the academic community. We must all act concertedly and with wisdom and dispatch if we are to serve our societal purposes.

Forces Driving Finances

The budgets of American universities have been affected for the last several years by opposing forces. On one side we are faced with declining rates of revenue increases and a general decline in the climate for support of higher education. Dominant factors include the concern of students and their families about college costs, a leveling trend in federal resources for education and university research, and a loss of national will to address the broad spectrum of the country's educational needs.

On the other hand, we are faced with increasing costs, expectations, and obligations. The cost of what we already do is rising, and there is an escalation in what we expect of ourselves and what society expects of us.

One of the fastest-growing components of most campus operating budgets has been student financial aid. The combination of rising tuition, rapidly declining federal scholarships and grants, and, more recently, the effects of the national recession on family incomes, has rapidly accelerated the need for financial aid. Federal grants to students have declined in real value by a factor of two since 1980. As recently as 1975, 70 percent of federal student aid was in the form of scholarships and 25 percent was in the form of loans. Following the trend of so many other things in our society, by 1991 only 31 percent of federal student aid was in the form of grants, while 66 percent was in the form of loans.

At MIT, 45 percent of MIT's student aid came from the federal government in 1975, compared with 31 percent in 1991. In 1975, the federal government provided 19 percent of scholarship grants at MIT, while the Institute provided 67 percent. By 1991, the federal portion had dropped to 11 percent, while MIT provided 81 percent. The reduction in the level of federal support and the shift from grants to loans have significant financial consequences that have been borne by the Institute.

Research universities are subjected to strong market forces associated with hiring new faculty members of the highest quality. Salary competition is pervasive, and the costs that universities are expected to bear in order to start the research career of a new faculty member in many branches of science and engineering are measured in hundreds of thousands of dollars. In many fields, the bidding for faculty members has included the promise of greatly reduced teaching loads—a trend that we must resist.

Establishment of a healthy and vigorous research environment is often very expensive. Major costs include modern equipment and instrumentation and the associated technical support staff.

During the past decade, the revolution in information technology has brought with it an indispensable but very costly budget line that hardly existed theretofore. Microcomputers and workstations, campus network infrastructures, and the corresponding staff to manage and maintain information systems have become pervasive and essential features of university campuses. The demand for increasing capacity, speed, and sophistication has accelerated rapidly. This revolution has greatly expanded the breadth and complexity of educational and research topics with which we can deal. Yet these advances are costly. It is already common for 2 or 3 percent of a campus operating budget to be associated with information technology.

Libraries, even in their most traditional form, have been sources of particular cost escalation. The cost of acquisition, storage, and preservation of scholarly books and journals has grown rapidly during the last decade or two, and most libraries have also had to carry the capital investment in automation of many of their records and functions. As we have moved into new optical and electronic forms of information storage, libraries have tended to add to, rather than replace, traditional printed materials. Every campus library has been engaged in cutting back on the numbers of its journal subscriptions and book acquisitions. During the last two decades journal subscription rates have often risen by many tens of percents in a year.

Not surprisingly, there is a rather large litany of regulatory and legal matters as well as social mandates that have caused costs to grow very rapidly on campuses. Issues of campus safety, access for the disabled, substance-abuse monitoring, financial-aid eligibility of students, conflict-of-interest matters, investigations of research misconduct, environmental regulation, the compliance reporting associated with affirmative action, matters of sexual harassment, and a variety of personnel issues in an increasingly litigious society, are but a few of the many and substantial costs that are of relatively recent origin.

New intellectual trends, especially the growing importance of organizing to conduct highly interdisciplinary research and education, tend to bring new organizational overhead with them. The formation of new laboratories, centers, and institutes is sometimes encouraged by research sponsors and is often believed to be necessary, in order to conduct many interdisciplinary activities. These new organizations often require new space, as well as additional staff and services.

The past two decades have brought an expanded societal role for many of our colleges and universities. We all share a responsibility to be more reflective of the rapidly changing racial and ethnic makeup of our nation, and a need to make all career paths fully accessible to minorities and women. In addition, institutions have increasingly assumed, or had thrust upon them, various roles in the economic development of their states or regions. The daunting problems facing primary and secondary education have led many universities to undertake a variety of active roles in the improvement of K–12 systems and curricula.

Finally, there are many new services that we have either taken on, or very much wish we could better assist with, as socially responsible employers. These services reflect the changing nature and economic characteristics of the families and careers of our faculty and staff. Matters such as health care, childbearing, childcare, housing, and retirement, not to mention care of the elderly, all impose new or rapidly growing costs or potential costs upon our institutions.

New tasks, new roles, and new responsibilities—but no corresponding new revenues—have become a familiar situation in academe.

A National Perspective

Academia today exemplifies the adage that misery loves company. Last year, nearly 85 percent of the nation's colleges and universities reported that securing adequate financial support was one of their three most serious challenges. During 1990–1991, 45 percent of our colleges and universities announced mid-year budget cuts. This was not a one-time anomaly; 57 percent implemented mid-year cuts during 1991–1992. The budgets of public universities, because they are subject to the variations and changing priorities of state legislatures and administrations, tend to fluctuate more rapidly and over a wider range than those of private institutions. But the basic financial trends of both types of institutions are depressingly similar, and the private institutions have fewer options available to them for the long-range amelioration of their financial problems.

To put higher education's revenues into some historical perspective, we must examine both how the levels and sources of revenue have changed and also how the use of those revenues has varied. The total operating budgets of all public and private doctoral-granting universities grew in constant dollars by 109 percent, from $31 billion to $65 billion, during the last 20 years. More than doubling operating budgets in 15 years hardly seems like austerity, so why are we sensing such constraint? The answer seems to be twofold: We are taking on more tasks and we are teaching more students. Enrollments have grown (99 percent in public institutions and 50 percent in private institutions) during the last twenty years, continuing to grow monotonically even during the years in which the number of 18-

to-24-year-olds in the United States declined by more than 20 percent.

The operating revenue of private doctoral-granting institutions has grown from roughly $12 billion to around $23 billion in constant dollars during the last twenty years. The most dramatic change in the source of these funds is that the federal government supplied nearly 30 percent twenty years ago, but only about 18 percent today. The fraction of operating revenue (26 percent) derived from tuition and fees has increased slightly during this period, while that arising from endowment has remained constant at about 9 percent. During this period, the fraction of operating revenues derived from auxiliary activities, including hospitals and federally funded research and development centers, has increased substantially, from 29 percent to 40 percent. The trends for public universities are similar, but, of course, they have a high dependence on state support (approximately 40 percent across all such schools, but with wide variations among them).

Tuition across the country, especially that of private universities, has rather consistently followed the ups and downs of variations in the consumer price index (CPI), but for fifteen years the annual increases have been greater than the CPI. This is because the cost of the majority of goods and services needed by universities—such as scholarships and fellowships, books and journals, faculty and staff salaries—tends to rise more quickly than the CPI. Hence, while general inflation has been a primary driver of tuition, the specific costs borne by tuition have grown even more rapidly. It should be noted that while the tuition of the major private universities grew by nearly 300 percent from 1976 to 1991, its real growth, that is, growth adjusted for inflation, was 55 percent. Interestingly, the contribution of tuition to the operating budgets of these universities grew by only about 3 percent during the past fifteen years.

MIT'S Budget

How is MIT's budget faring in the current climate? The simple answer is that we are in a stronger position than many of our sister institutions, but that the forces on our budget have reached a critical point, one that requires concerted, Institute-wide action if we are to remain excellent and rebuild some flexibility to do the things that we believe to be important.

Our situation differs somewhat from that of most research universities. Because of our focus on science and engineering, and the consequent dependence on federal funding, we are particularly sensitive to government policy and budgetary changes. On the positive side, our historically strong relations with the private sector are important and growing assets.

To examine our current situation, note that we have only three primary sources of revenue—tuition, federal and industrial research funds, and private support, including gifts and investment income.

Tuition rates are set annually at the Institute's discretion, but obviously must reflect the realities of the nation's economy, the corresponding need to supply financial aid, and our desire to remain accessible to bright students regardless of their families' financial situation. While tuition will continue to grow somewhat, MIT has begun to slow its rate of growth; this year's increase was 6.5 percent, the second-lowest increase in 20 years.

Federal research support is earned by the efforts, innovation, and high intellectual quality of MIT's faculty, but it also depends on the congruence of our goals with those of the federal government and is subject to the shifting nature of the federal/university partnership. Research support at MIT has nearly leveled out during the last two years.

Private support is received in the form of gifts, grants, and bequests from alumni, alumnae, and friends of the Institute and from foundations and corporations. The development of private support requires considerable concerted effort and stewardship, and ultimately is a function of our institutional quality. Donations to MIT have increased very substantially during the five years of the Campaign for the Future, and our endowment has grown from $1.2 billion to $1.6 billion in market value over that period, while total invested funds have increased in market value from $1.4 billion to $1.95 billion.

The state of the budget is crystallized when we set tuition levels and, of course, when we balance costs and revenues. Flattening research income, despite the increase in private support, has left us in a position in which there is nearly a direct relationship between annual tuition increases and the magnitude of faculty and staff salary increases. This is not a healthy circumstance. I believe that we must constrain the rate at which tuition grows, but also that we must retain our ability to pay the salaries and wages required to retain and appropriately reward faculty and staff of the highest quality. This dilemma must be resolved.

MIT's endowment grows through the receipt of gifts and the investment of its funds. During the period of the Campaign for the Future, we have done well by both measures. For example, we have been able to create 58 new full-professorial chairs and 33 career-development professorships. Each year we spend a portion of the interest earned by the endowment equaling between 4.5 and 5.0 percent of its principal. Of course, on the average, the endowment earns more than this, but by policy we plow the difference back into the principal of the endowment so that it will grow at least at the rate of inflation. In this way, we maintain the purchasing power of the endowment over time so that, for example, professorial chairs and student fellowships retain their value in perpetuity.

There are two key measures to consider when we attempt to balance our operating budget—the *deficit* and the *operating gap*. The operating gap is the difference between our expenditures and directed revenues such as tuition, research funds, fees for service, and most endowment income. This gap must be filled by discretionary resources in the form of annual unrestricted gifts, grants, and bequests. If the addition of these discretionary resources still does not bring our available resources to the level of our expenditures, we are left with a deficit. For the past 15 years, the operating gap has averaged around $5.7 million, but for the last three years this gap has ranged between $9 million and $13 million. The deficits between 1976 and 1988 were very modest, averaging nearly zero, with small surpluses in a few years. In 1989 and 1990, deficits grew to around $4.5 million. In 1991 we were able to bring it down to $300,000, but only because there was an unexpectedly large amount of unrestricted gifts and bequests received that year to fill the operating gap. In 1992 our deficit grew to $6.3 million.

The result of recent budgetary pressures, therefore, has been that our annual deficit has been running at about $5 million and is projected to increase further. This is troubling. Despite the fact that this is less than 1 percent of the campus operating budget, it is clear to all who have observed the federal deficit that, if unchecked, its effect will grow over time and leave an unfair penalty for the Institute in the downstream years. In my view, however, it is the development of a decidedly substantial, structural operating gap of at least $10 million that is of the most serious concern. The use of much of our annual, unrestricted gift income to fill the operating gap represents a loss of flexibility to fund new initiatives, to seed innovative educational and research projects, and to ameliorate our growing financial aid burdens. It also does not bode well for the appropriate compensation of faculty and staff if this situation is left unchecked.

Growth

A recent examination of the growth of faculty, students, and staff at MIT over the last 15 years indicated that in many ways our trends are similar to those of other major research universities around the country, although in one important measure, faculty size, we are somewhat distinct. We have maintained an essentially constant faculty headcount during this period while many other institutions expanded. Currently, we have 966 assistant, associate, and full professors, 73 percent of whom are tenured. The discipline of maintaining this constant faculty size, I believe, has lessened the depth of financial pressures at MIT relative to that at some universities, but it has not eliminated them.

MIT's undergraduate enrollment has stayed essentially stable at 4,300, while our graduate enrollment has grown by almost 1,000—to 5,200—during this period.

As at virtually every other research institution, there has been an increase in staff during this fifteen-year period, especially during the first few years. Administrative, support, and service staff have increased roughly 7 percent, from 3,699 in 1976 to 3,976 in 1991. Why? This growth was the result of such factors as an increase in services required by faculty for their research and educational activities: a 70-percent growth in the headcount of other academic staff;[1] the increasing bureaucratic overhead required to conduct sponsored research programs and to comply with the upward spiral of federal regulation; the establishment of a pervasive computing environment; the establishment of a major organization for fund raising; and the development of a comprehensive medical department. Simply put, we have grown in complexity in response to enhanced internal needs and expectations and to externally imposed requirements. Unfortunately, many of these new tasks have not brought with them new revenues.

It is fair to say that by far the bulk of growth of administrative, support, and service staff has been driven by academic needs. Indeed, the size of the staff on the administrative side of the house (i.e., those reporting to the vice presidents) is at virtually the same level (2,200) as in 1976, having grown slightly and then been reduced in the early 1980s. The administrative, support, and service staff in the academic sectors (schools, departments, and laboratories), however, has grown by 16 percent—from 1,481 to 1,721—during this period, reflecting the increasing need and demand for academic support services. Similarly, research staff increased in headcount by 47 percent—from 650 to 953. Each of these additions has been a conscious, local decision, ultimately agreed to through the deans or directors and the provost.

Revenue Enhancement

There are only two ways to bring a budget into balance—increase revenues or cut costs. In my view, both are called for at the present time. In examining both options we must always remember the obvious—our mission is not a financial one; it is one of teaching, research, and service. Our revenues are only the means to an end, and the structure of our budget should be a direct reflection of our substantive goals and aspirations.

I am confident that the excellence of our faculty and students and the quality and innovative nature of faculty activities will ensure that our federal research support will remain strong. But there are two caveats. First, by small step upon small step, federal agencies are backing away from paying the full costs of the programs that they sponsor, including research and fellowships. Second, the directions of federal research policy are in flux as a natural consequence of the end of the Cold War era and because of the advent of new concerns associated with issues such as the environment, health care, and industrial competitiveness. America's research universities must respond to these changing conditions, but more important, they have a responsibility to help shape policies and programs in the national interest.

There are many object lessons and reasons for optimism in recent MIT initiatives. Let me cite two—the Leaders for Manufacturing Program and the MIT Japan Program. Leaders for Manufacturing is an innovative master's-level program designed and implemented in close working partnership with several U.S. manufacturing firms to educate a new breed of managers and engineers equipped with a broad, integrated understanding of manufacturing and management science, technology, and organization in a contemporary, international context. The MIT Japan Program provides a number of MIT undergraduates with in-depth Japanese-language training, combined with education in Japanese culture, history, and business practice, and places them, upon graduation, as interns in Japanese industrial and research organizations. These students then return to the United States with a detailed working knowledge and understanding of Japanese practices and techniques, as well as with the general benefits of international acquaintances and cultural experiences. Both of these programs respond to a clear national need; both are conducted in a world-class manner; and both have created very substantial new revenue streams for operations and student support, because the importance and effectiveness of the investment have been made clear to corporations and to the government. It also should be noted that both are primarily educational activities.

We should move forward with confidence that programs conceived with excellence, educational innovation, and long-term economic and social relevance will still find appropriate partners and sponsors. These partners and sponsors should come increasingly from the private sector, but it would be unrealistic to imagine that this will to a major extent replace federal funding. It remains a necessary function of the federal government to support the advanced education and research on which the future so directly depends.

We and our colleagues must continue to press for federal support of the full costs of programs and to press for merit as the prime determinant of grants, contracts, and facility funding. Academic earmarking has reached the extraordinary level of nearly a billion dollars in the new federal budget—more than was contained in the total of budgets during the previous decade. Although we must recognize legitimate concerns such as geographic distribution, it is not in the interest of the country to cut off the tops of its mountains in order to fill in the valleys. Surely the wisest policy for the country cannot be random selection for awards, based on the location of schools in particular congressional districts and funded with monies removed from the already stressed resources of programs and agencies. The great public and private institutions must be maintained. They are magnets for the best thinkers and researchers, and their facilities and graduate schools are the peaks of excellence to which students from schools and colleges all over the country aspire and matriculate. The set of these institutions is dynamic, with new universities moving into its ranks the old-fashioned way—by hard work and good ideas.

Having said this, the clear prognosis remains that the rate of growth of federal funds is being attenuated and the number of universities capable of productively conducting high-quality research and education is expanding. Substantial growth in overall research funding is therefore unlikely in the near term.

The outlook for private support is something of a mixed message. Through the very successful Campaign for the Future, we have significantly increased MIT's level of private support. Our alumni and alumnae, as well as our staff and faculty, have worked very hard and effectively to make this happen. We must meet the challenge of continuing the momentum generated by the campaign. Resource development will need to become more deeply ingrained in the MIT culture. Continuing to increase the level of private support will be a strong challenge, but one that I have confidence we can meet.

The other side of private support, of course, is that the real value of our endowment depends on the performance of the market and the quality of our investment strategies. Our track record is good, but it also appears to most observers that returns will not be as great in the coming years as those that were possible during the last decade. Thus, major expansion of private support is somewhat problematic.

Learning Institutions

We cannot assume that the resources of universities in general, and of MIT in particular, will grow significantly in the years immediately ahead. Thus, the only way to ensure that we maintain excellence and have the flexibility to strike out in exciting new intellectual directions, to be a high-quality employer of faculty and staff, and, above all, to meet our responsibilities to our students and the nation, is to do less, do different things, or gain efficiency. In my opinion, we must do all three. Indeed, there is no choice. We must be as open to new ways of thinking about how we operate and how we teach as we are to new lines of research and scholarly inquiry.

Universities must thoughtfully and continuously review and prune their programs and organizations in addition to creating new ones as times and intellectual frontiers change. Similarly, we must continuously review and renew the services that we provide to our faculty and students. Only in this way can we ensure the excellence of what we are and what we do.

I am fond of quoting Frederick Terman, an MIT alumnus who became engineering dean and provost at Stanford. When once asked whether he wanted his university to be a teaching institution or a research institution, he replied that it should be a learning institution. Today, universities must also be learning organizations in the sense developed by Peter Senge of the Sloan School of Management: organizations that come to understand and react wisely to the opportunities and constraints they face. We must study the work of our own management scholars and we must learn from the substantial transformations of industries and other organizations around the world during the last decade or two.

The MIT Ad Hoc Faculty-Administration Committee on Indirect Costs and Graduate Student Tuition, for example, has proposed an MIT Quality Initiative to adopt the principles and lessons of Total Quality Management (TQM) within the Institute. I would use the term "adapt" rather than "adopt," because we are a university, not a manufacturing or commercial service organization. However, the results of quality initiatives in a variety of settings have been so substantial that we cannot afford not to commit ourselves to serious exploration, experimentation, and implementation of these concepts and techniques.

In fact, there are three major areas in which such activities are already underway. First, the entire Information Systems group has for several months been studying and planning full-scale implementation of a TQM program to improve their service to the Institute community and to gain efficiencies in their operations. Second, campus departments that provide human services, ranging from Admissions to the MIT Press, and from Personnel and Public Relations to the Medical Department, have been meeting and working with external and internal experts to develop an approach to quality management that is appropriate for the MIT culture and that merges with their Building on

Differences program—a program designed to enhance produc-tivity and the quality of professional life in an organization of highly diverse individuals. Third, a faculty initiative resulted in a major grant from the IBM Corporation that made possible a week-long seminar in their facilities that was attended by 50 fac-ulty members and 25 staff and administrators from MIT in early September. The opportunity for this cross-section of the Institute community to study and plan together how to enhance the excel-lence of all that we do as an institution was extraordinary. We shall build upon the momentum developed by this group.

It is my belief that we must increasingly consider and operate MIT as an integrated organization. Our faculty, students, and staff must act more as a seamless community. Despite the fact that we must always be an environment in which individual achievement and disciplinary excellence are fostered, we must pay increasing attention to integrated activity and teamwork. In research and education, new approaches to teamwork and inter-disciplinary problem-solving are flowing naturally from the complexity of many of the most interesting areas of modern research and scholarship. Similarly, institutional complexity and constraint require that we approach our administrative support activities with greater communality of purpose and explicit cross-linkage.

We must in these and many other ways seek to improve the quality and efficiency of our support services. But these efforts must also touch the heart of what we do—teaching and research. Are we teaching the right courses in the right way? Do we main-tain archaic approaches to classrooms and laboratories? Are we making the appropriate use of the very information technologies that we develop here? Is the information flow among faculty, stu-dents, and administrators designed to enlighten or to generate entropy? Can we gain greater efficiency in the more mundane of our duties in order to free time and resources for the really

important aspects of academia? Do we have too many committees? Do we have the proper balance of formal and informal contact with our students? Are research proposals prepared in such
a way that faculty can concentrate on their essence and quality
rather than the bureaucratic details? Do we communicate effectively with the public, the government, the business world, and
our alumni and alumnae? Are there redundancies in our operations? Do we consciously determine where we should cut back
in order to make new programs possible? Do we maintain the
proper balance of teamwork and individual activity? Do we
allow responsibility to be exercised and decisions made at
the levels where knowledge and understanding are greatest? Do
we strike the congruence between the goals and needs of the
Institute as a whole with those of individuals within it? Do we
plan for and invest our intellectual and financial resources in
the future, or squander them on issues of the moment? Do we
learn and improve as an organization as well as individually?

Ensuring the Future

Our times are times of change and uncertainty—and promise. In
four decades, we have moved from an era in which the United
States produced over half of the world's gross product to one in
which we produce just over 20 percent. It is a world in which
challenges of energy, environment, and human survivability are
becoming paramount. It is a world in which idealism and
concern for our fellow men and women have become rare
commodities.

And yet, it is a world in which our understanding of the basic
nature of life and of the physical universe is expanding expo-
nentially. It is a world in which the integration of knowledge
across seemingly disparate disciplines is producing startling new
insights and intellectual directions. It is a world in which the

range of temporal and physical scales with which engineers and scientists can operate has become vast beyond belief. It is a world in which the blending and cross-currents among men and women of different races and cultures can give rise to new synergies for the advancement of civilization.

It is a world in which we at MIT can and must dream of new futures. And as we do, we must cherish those values that have made us great. We must demand excellence. We must celebrate both the solitary, iconoclastic scholar and the multidisciplinary group. We must value both abstract thought and practical application. We must treasure both the diversity of our community and the communality of our deeply rooted values. We must, in sum, hold to a vision of MIT that draws on the best we have and the best we are, and that gives to the world the full measure of our talent and imagination.

These are the things that are at stake as the economic and societal underpinnings of the American research university, and of MIT in particular, shift and change. These changes must be met with a clear-headed view of financial realities. We must be both prudent and farsighted, and we must act carefully but decisively to shape our finances, our activities, and our organization in order to retain and enhance the excellence that is so critical to a vibrant future for ourselves and for our fellow men and women.

Note

1. "Other academic staff" includes instructors, technical instructors, lecturers and senior lecturers, adjunct faculty, visiting faculty, postdoctoral fellows and associates, senior research scientists, visiting scientists, coaches, and medical staff.

4

Embracing Complexity, Moving toward Coherence
1992–1993

Still follow sense, of ev'ry art the soul,
Parts answering parts shall slide into a whole.
—Alexander Pope, *Epistles to Several Persons*

The theme of response to change was very heavy on my mind, especially the continuing tension between fragmentation and integration in both the intellectual and social fabrics of universities. Were we properly serving society? Were we organized appropriately? How could our values serve to bring greater coherence at a time when we increasingly identified ourselves, and our fields of study, through fine partitioning, even as we were surrounded by evidence that integration and systems approaches were becoming increasingly important? In no aspect of MIT was change more dramatic than in the makeup of our student body: It had moved in a few decades from being mostly white male engineers to become a highly diverse group of young men and women whose backgrounds, objectives, and world views were remarkably varied. This diversity brought challenges and stresses, but also expanding horizons, excitement, and valuable discourse. MIT engaged in deep thinking and reorganization of much of its engineering curriculum, as it recognized a need to address issues of design, product development, and manufacturing in an era of global organization and production. We were moving away from near-total emphasis on engineering science, and closer to our industrial roots. Thinking about and adjusting to the scale, complexity, and rapid time-frame of much of contemporary engineering and business created new subjects and programs, many of them joint between the School of Engineering and the Sloan School of Management, which enhanced our resolve to solve grand problems.

These are times of change that call for a rethinking of how American higher education can best serve the nation and the world. As our universities and colleges evolve to meet the new intellectual and social challenges before us, we must find ways to deal with the fragmentation, both intellectual and social, that has accompanied change. It is time to seek a new balance within our intellectual and organizational constructs. Our fundamental values will help us stay on course, but we need a vision that embraces the complexities of our times while helping us to move toward greater coherence around common goals.

The American dream has become more complex, and the people who dream it are more diverse, but our higher educational system remains the most important vehicle for reaching that dream.

At one level, the American dream and the goals of higher education remain congruent and unchanged. Simply put, they are to provide the opportunity and the means for each person to meet his or her needs and aspirations and to contribute to the well being of our society—with understanding, skill, responsibility, and, one would hope, compassion.

These goals are fostered by a set of fundamental values that are held in common by essentially all institutions of higher learning. We believe in the importance of education, of rationality and objectivity, and of discovering and transmitting knowledge. We respect varying views, value the role of our institutions as critics of society, and believe in an elitism that is based solely on talent and accomplishment rather than wealth or social status. As a corollary to this last point, we believe that in a democratic society, our institutions of higher education must be both excellent and accessible—for the sake of the individual and for the sake of society.

These values give continuity of purpose to our colleges and universities. At the same time, they ensure that we will encounter continual change in the students we educate, in the faculty who teach them, and in the expectations of both. So, too, we will continually generate change in what we teach, in how we teach, and in the fields we invent and discover.

Change

Sometimes intellectual, social, and organizational changes are precipitated by sudden, dramatic events or insights followed by a long period of diffusion and adjustment throughout an institution. More often, they come slowly and painfully, as a result of adjusting to the tensions that arise from conflicting forces, goals, and realities.

American campuses, like society as a whole, change at an awkward pace. On a historical time scale, they change very quickly. On the time-scale of a faculty member's career, they change slowly enough to be missed in day-to-day perception, but rapidly enough to create confusion of goals over time. On the time-scale of an undergraduate's education, they seem to change not at all.

The student body of MIT has changed remarkably since the time of the Institute's founding, when a group of 15 young men gathered in Boston at the end of the Civil War to study the practical arts and sciences that would serve the needs of a rapidly industrializing society. Today, MIT's students are a remarkably heterogeneous group of nearly 10,000 men and women who come to our Cambridge campus from all over the world to study in fields ranging from molecular biology to music composition, from computer science to economics. One-third of the graduate students now come from other countries, as do 9 percent of the undergraduates. The undergraduates, one-third of whom are women, are a particularly diverse group. Of those who are U.S. citizens or permanent residents, 56 percent come from the majority white population, approximately 28 percent are Asian-

Americans, 9 percent are Hispanic-Americans, 6 percent are African-Americans, and 1 percent are Native Americans.

By contrast, when I began my teaching career in the mid-1960s, engineering was widely regarded as a man's world and it was rare to have more than one or two women in an engineering class. Most of my students were born in this country, and most were white. For the most part, students, especially in science and engineering, shared rather common personal goals, aspirations, and world views. At that time, federal funding was creating rapidly growing research programs, mostly at a handful of leading institutions. The structure of DNA had only recently been discovered, computing was done by batch-processing of programs entered on punched cards, and the engineering science revolution was propagating from MIT to the rest of the country.

A faculty member looking back over three decades sees social and intellectual changes that have been significant, even dramatic, but consider how things must look to a graduating senior reviewing his or her four years at MIT. Since the class of 1993 entered in 1989, the General Institute Requirements have changed by only one subject, molecular biology. The organizational structure remains pretty much the same, although the deans of every school are new and two departments have changed their names to reflect new emphases. The campus looks about the same, with the very notable exception of the Biology Building rising on Ames Street.

To put it simplistically, students think nothing changes. Many faculty and administrators view the world through eyes that grew accustomed to the academic light twenty, thirty, or forty years ago. And William Barton Rogers would be hard put to discern any connection between today's MIT and the Institute he founded.

Intellectually, we have sometimes advanced in sudden bursts, as when an entirely new approach to technological development and applied research was created in the World War II Radiation Laboratory, or when Noam Chomsky reconceptualized linguistics, or when Edward Lorenz developed the basic ideas of chaos theory. More often, we have slowly and collectively evolved ideas, approaches, and academic disciplines by a combination of incremental insights, external forces, and growing infrastructure.

Organizationally, we adjust to changing circumstances. Traditionally, the pattern has been the following: Research leads to the establishment of laboratories and the creation of graduate subjects; graduate subjects are combined to form graduate programs; and as the intellectual mass develops and as demand for graduates and applications accumulates, departments are formed. Faculty entrepreneurism, both intellectual and in terms of developing funding for research and education, have been and remain essential elements of change. The administration and support services of the Institute have developed to meet growing faculty and student needs and to deal with the ever-increasing administrative requirements of government funding and regulation. Thus, we now have major institutional organizations to provide our scholars with information technology resources, to attract financial support from individuals, foundations, and corporations, and to provide housing, food, advising, and medical services to our students.

Socially, we also adjust to evolving circumstances, but often only with difficulty. MIT is a collection of extraordinary individuals who, time and again, have redefined intellectual fields and have risen to the challenges presented by the larger society. And now these challenges include incorporating more rapid cultural and demographic change into our life as an academic community. In the past four years, the number of underrepresented-minority students has increased by 9 percent, while the number of minority students overall (that is, including Asian-American students) has increased by 26 percent. At the faculty level, the number of women in the professorial ranks, while still small, has increased by 15 percent (from 95 to 109). The number of underrepresented-minority faculty has increased by 15 percent as well, but remains distressingly low, at 31.

Many of the changes that we face today—some with relish, and some with anxiety—seem to me to have in common tensions between fragmentation and coalescence. Furthermore, they cannot be classified neatly as intellectual, organizational, or social, but involve all three aspects simultaneously. As I contemplate these changes, I have come to believe that there is a growing imperative to deemphasize fragmentation and to reemphasize coalescence. We must seek greater commonality of vision in the many dimensions of our life at MIT.

The Multicultural Campus

As noted, the gender, race, and ethnic composition of MIT is far different than it was three decades ago and is characterized by remarkable heterogeneity, especially among the students. Even though MIT is a more focused institution than most, we find that the values and aspirations among our students are increasingly diverse as well. This heterogeneity, depending on the context, is viewed as providing a great resource and opportunity, as demanding new institutional services and responsibilities, or as establishing new tensions on campus. Each of these views is correct. None can be escaped.

As faculty and administrators across the country grapple with these new realities, they are caught in a vise of political opinion—the "politically correct" arguments of the left and of the right. From the left, political correctness condemns us if we do not fragment every academic subject indefinitely along gender, racial, ethnic, and other lines. It seems to strive to make us so self-conscious about differences, terminology, and "isms" that open, objective intellectual and social discourse becomes both difficult and unproductive. On the other hand, the politically correct on the right cry "quota" and "standards" at the first sighting of a minority student on a prestigious campus; find it inappropriate when our studies of history, politics, and literature become more inclusive and view the world through many eyes and experiences; and see the decline of American civilization if a group of black students eats together in the cafeteria.

Now, it is true that the growing diversity of our campuses is accompanied by a tendency toward fragmentation in many academic communities. There are a variety of reasons for this. Some delineation along racial, ethnic, and other lines is appropriate. It certainly is true that studies of human affairs require examination from the perspectives of the various peoples who have led or participated in them. Then, too, individuals gain a sense of identity, a sense of history, and a sense of purpose that derive in part from exploring and affirming their personal heritage. That is why it is appropriate for there to be ethnic interest groups, women's groups, and other culturally based activities on our campuses.

But there are lines that can be crossed from the productive to the counterproductive. This occurs when we move into too much self-centeredness, and when we fall victim, for example, to what Cornel West calls "racial reasoning," which creates a closing-ranks mentality stemming from fixation on racial authenticity.[1] At some point, a community ceases to be inclusive if its constituent groups all define themselves in exclusivist terms, regardless of whether they comprise a majority or minority, or whether they have come recently to the table or have been there since the inception.

The tensions introduced by diversity into the academic community are very real. So are the opportunities and responsibilities that it makes possible. We need to find ways for our differences of experience, culture, and perspective to enrich, rather than divide, our community. As Alfred North Whitehead said in his 1925 lectures on Science and the Modern World, "Other nations of different habits are not enemies: they are god-sends."[2] This is true whether we speak of societies, professions, or single institutions. The electrical engineer and the mechanical engineer are able to build systems together that neither can build alone. Men and women together create a balanced discourse and world view. Black and white, brown and yellow, red and tan create a campus and a nation far more meaningful and creative than any alone.

Speaking to this issue, Paul Penfield, the head of the Department of Electrical Engineering and Computer Science, concluded in a recent thoughtful essay that "a diverse faculty can carry out the mission of our department better than a nondiverse one." This mission, he said, includes attracting the best students, providing them the best environment for learning, and helping them to develop the necessary personal and professional skills for a fulfilling life. These goals are well served by at least three benefits of faculty diversity—providing role models, enriching the intellectual environment, and improving counseling and mentoring.[3]

Penfield's key point is that a diverse faculty can better accomplish our central mission—the tasks that we collectively consider to be our core activities. The very term "university" denotes a gathering together for common purpose, with learning as the unifying force. We are all here at MIT for the same fundamental purpose: to pursue our intellectual interests and to improve ourselves and our society through teaching, study, and research. We must be more determined to use this common focus to overcome the centrifugal forces of separatism. Through community and civility we enhance our ability to grow as individuals. This is particularly important in times of change.

Writing of such times, Martin Luther King warned that "our very survival depends on our ability to stay awake, to adjust to new ideas, to remain vigilant and to face the challenge of change. . . . Together we must learn to live as brothers or together we will be forced to perish as fools."[4]

A Dynamic Intellectual Map

Fragmentation has accompanied the changing racial and social profiles of our university communities, but fragmentation is part of our intellectual history as well. Over the past century, the exponential expansion of knowledge—coupled with the increasing complexity of society—has resulted in fields of knowledge becoming increasingly specialized and distinct from one another.

Most twentieth-century science has been reductionist in nature. Despite the goals of discovering the great unifying principles, much of what scientists do is to refine and narrow; to burrow deeper and deeper into structure; to move from systemic description to component to cell to gene to molecule. Over time, this narrowing—together with the consequent explosion of factual knowledge—led to division and specialization. This fragmentation was codified ultimately as scientific disciplines, subdisciplines, and specialties. We became increasingly technical and less concerned with the larger issues that give rise to scientific curiosity to begin with.

The same was true—perhaps more so—of technologists. After World War II, engineers, especially in academia, began to specialize. Even systems engineering itself became more of a specialty than a unifying concept.

For a time, the humanities and social sciences followed much the same path—in part because the knowledge base was expanding, although not so dramatically and not for the same reasons. Expansion and diversification in the humanities and social sciences came about with the inclusion of knowledge about aspects of society and human experience that had heretofore been largely neglected in academia. I refer here to non-Western cultures and civilizations, to groups that have not been economically and socially powerful, and to popular culture, for example. This, coupled with the pattern of increasing specialization in other disciplines and the lure of the powerful quantitative techniques of the sciences, tended to break down the humanities and social sciences into increasing numbers of specialties as well.

In all of these fields, specialization was a natural response. It was one way of dealing with the information explosion. But in many ways, it led to an intellectual tower of Babel.

But now there is a shifting of the tide, as scholars and researchers pay more attention to how disciplines can inform one another. Within the humanities and social sciences, for example, scholars are applying the methodologies of anthropology to social and cultural history. And in the sciences, the line between biology and chemistry is increasingly difficult to draw.

The forces calling for greater communication among fields do not stop at the boundaries of science and engineering on the one hand, or of the social sciences and humanities on the other. A greater synthesis is becoming paramount in response to many of the challenges that we face.

Perhaps the ultimate example is global environmental change. The problem of humankind's effects on the earth's atmosphere cannot be understood by physical scientists without data collected by sophisticated engineering instruments, and the meaning of the data and its projection into the future cannot be contemplated without the use of prodigious calculations carried out on state-of-the-art computers created by engineers and computer scientists. More to the point, all of this scientific knowledge is useless unless we understand the human, emotional, cultural, and political responses to potential changes in the earth's climate and ecosystems. And still more to the point, if scientists discover ways in which escalating or irreversible damage to the earth is caused by human behavior, the historians and economists, political scientists and psychologists, writers and artists must be called upon to suggest ways in which that behavior can be changed.

This is but one example of how changing questions and challenges are making us increasingly aware of the interconnectedness of both things and ideas that make up our research and that must be reflected in our teaching. Interdisciplinary research and study are hardly new. Indeed, it has been a catchphrase on campuses for about three decades, and at MIT for even longer. A variety of approaches to academic organization have been attempted to foster such work. Centers and institutes have been formed for this purpose, and administrators have been assigned the task of promoting interdisciplinary work. Many of these efforts failed. As far as I know, none of the experiments of dissolving traditional academic departments and rearranging them along cross-disciplinary lines has been successful. Yet there is a decided recent upturn in truly interdisciplinary work. Why?

The reason is obvious: Many of the really interesting and intellectually challenging issues of the day simply transcend disciplinary boundaries. Scholars need their colleagues' expertise. The sheer complexity of these problems demands it. Form is again following function. Ralph Gomory once indicated that as senior vice president for science and technology at IBM, he had tried many different ways to get researchers to work well together across disciplinary boundaries. Organization charts were redrawn, and offices and laboratories were regrouped and rearranged. Nothing really worked well. Finally, the truth that should have been apparent all along emerged. Researchers worked well across disciplines if they were engaged in solving a problem that interested and excited them and that required each others' expertise. The same is even more true in academia.

This trend of people and ideas from intellectually disparate disciplines coalescing to gain new insights and solve new problems will continue. It will be very dynamic—not a matter of creating a few new centers or institutes but a shifting and changing scene that will require institutions like MIT to be very nimble. We must be able to reorganize and rearrange our efforts without having to continually build and dismantle bureaucratic structures—or physical ones, for that matter. The idea of virtual centers is one powerful way to accomplish this, and in the last two years, four virtual centers have been established at the Institute.

Advances in information technology will soon enable us to take a quantum leap in the way we deal with issues that emerge from the continual reorganization of knowledge. Work will increasingly be done in "collaboratories," that is, through computer-mediated collaboration that transcends geographical and temporal distances. As the national and international information infrastructure expands in scale, sophistication, and ease of access, the traditional meaning of creating, archiving, disseminating, and accessing information will be lost. We will readily sift through national and international data bases to garner, combine, and shape information from an unimaginably wide variety of sources.

Thus the complexity of important problems and areas of research and study is expanding rapidly, as is our knowledge base. Progress will depend on our ability to effectively combine knowledge and expertise of many different sorts. Specialists and in-depth, disciplinary explorations will still be needed, but the critical factor will be our ability to work together as teams and to collectively focus our disparate knowledge and expertise on problems and issues of importance.

Integrative Education in Engineering

Our curriculum, and even our way of teaching, derives from our research and scholarly activities. Thus, we will see this trend of integration and greater interdisciplinary activity expressed in our educational programs as well. Nowhere at MIT is this more evident than in the School of Engineering.

Engineering education in the United States generally follows a format originating in the 1950s and 1960s. This was the period of the engineering science revolution. Stimulated by the foresight of leaders in engineering education, especially at MIT and Stanford, faculties developed curricula that brought scientific tools and approaches to bear on engineering problems. This was driven by the need to address the challenging issues presented by space flight, the development of computing, the sophisticated defense needs during the Cold War, and the rapidly evolving electronics industry. All benefited enormously from this approach and still do. During this period there also was a rapid development of research and graduate education in American universities. Engineering faculty members increasingly built their activities and approach to research and education on the model of the physical sciences. Inevitably, engineering subjects and activities became increasingly specialized.

The results of the engineering science revolution were, and are, remarkable in terms of the increased sophistication of engineering analysis and the depth of knowledge possessed by engineering graduates. This revolution was so powerful that the basic structure of engineering curricula in this country has been unchanged for over three decades. Of course, curricula have been revised and improved, especially through the influence of computing, but the basic structure has been rather static.

The context within which engineering is practiced, however, has changed dramatically during the last decade or two. The

Cold War has come to an end, bringing with it a rapid redirection of federal, industrial, and public priorities toward civilian concerns. And because of shifting geopolitics, changing economic structures, and rapid communications, many of our central concerns are of a much less isolated and national nature, and are marked more and more by interconnectedness and global perspectives.

In this changing world, many American industries have lost their positions of dominance and have moved, sometimes grudgingly and sometimes enthusiastically, from national to international perspectives and operations in order to remain competitive. There are other changes as well. Large corporations have dispersed their functions internally and externally in new ways. More technical work is outsourced, both domestically and internationally. Emphasis has been placed on reducing product development times; improving the quality of manufactured products; integrating design, development, and process functions; and developing new management styles and methodologies. Engineering graduates are increasingly ill-adapted to this new environment, because they lack sufficient flexibility, systems perspective, understanding of manufacturing processes, teamwork, communication skills, and experience, as well as appreciation of the broader context.

It must be said that the lack of skills needed for immediate deployment as practicing engineers has been the theme of various national reports for many decades. Yet the immediacy of this view today, in my opinion, is much greater and more accurate than in the past. The scale, complexity, and rapid time frame of much contemporary engineering is different—and will continue to increase.

Our students need more exposure to the integrative aspects of engineering design and practice—to the analysis and management of large-scale, complex systems. They need more experience with, or at least appreciation of, the integration of mechanical, electronic, computational, and perhaps optical systems. They also need an increased understanding of the larger economic, social, political, and technical system within which scientific principles and engineering analysis and synthesis operate in order to create technological change. And these must be presented as what they indeed are: difficult intellectual challenges.

So here is the paradox. We have developed an educational approach that provides students with an unsurpassed grasp of the fundamentals of individual engineering and science disciplines, which are organized as fragmented disciplines and sub-disciplines. But our graduates increasingly need integrative experiences and subjects. How do we shift the balance? What is the optimum?

It is generally agreed among advisors from industry, as well as our own faculty, that a strong working knowledge of fundamentals is the most important goal of an undergraduate engineering education. This strength must be retained, as must the encouragement of flexible thinking and innovation. We cannot run the risk that ten or twenty years from now our engineers will be adept at reducing product development cycles and at manufacturing high-quality products through continuous improvement, but will have lost their edge in creativity so that the new ideas that are driving a knowledge-intensive world are generated elsewhere.

Still, we must build greater cooperative strengths in our students by increased attention to teamwork and collective enterprises. The MIT tradition of "design-build-operate" experiences obtained by many students through the 2.70 design contest and the Undergraduate Research Opportunities Program are good examples. The ideas embodied in these and other programs, such as Concourse, the Experimental Study Group, the Integrated Studies Program, the freshman advisor seminars, and the new team approach to introductory chemistry subjects, can provide lessons that we can incorporate more broadly into the education of our students. If our faculty become committed to the idea of change in the undergraduate curriculum, their creativity and directed energy will ensure success.

Dramatic curricular change, however, most naturally flows from graduate programs. The Leaders for Manufacturing Program, which is jointly organized by the School of Engineering and the Sloan School of Management, in partnership with a number of U.S. manufacturing firms, has already demonstrated a new paradigm in the education of engineer/managers. The goal of the program is to discover and translate into teaching and practice the principles that will produce world-class manufacturing and manufacturing leaders. Working together, faculty and their industrial partners have brought disparate disciplinary expertise and perspectives to the development of a curriculum of study and research organized around the themes of Foundations, Integration, and Leadership. By involving many faculty and by opening LFM subjects to other students, the program is having an ever-increasing influence on education at MIT and elsewhere.

The next few years afford us an opportunity to play an even more dramatic and effective role in promoting a more integrative approach to the education of engineers. MIT faculty, in the context of a major five-year planning exercise, are debating the merits of a number of proposals—including the establishment of a cross-school department concerned with linking technology, management, and policy. Several departments are looking at the possibility of restructuring their curricula with an eye toward finding or creating common sequences of courses that could serve multiple departments, thereby emphasizing the commonality of objectives, knowledge, and techniques across disciplines.

In addition, the dean of engineering, Joel Moses, has proposed the establishment of a second professional degree to be offered through a radical new master's program in systems engineering/systems architecture. This is an idea whose time has come. The program, which would span engineering and the Sloan School of Management, would address the needs of first-rate engineers who have been in practice for five to ten years and who demonstrate the talent to become systems engineers and architects in their fields and/or to move toward positions such as vice president of engineering. The program would be based on a combination of campus and industry experiences that would develop and teach approaches to the engineering of large-scale complex systems, including those having considerable public policy implications. Just as with the Leaders for Manufacturing Program, the philosophy, insights, and approaches developed in such a program would soon influence the entire engineering curriculum.

The move toward greater emphasis on common fundamentals and a more holistic approach to engineering education is apparent at the national level as well. A number of engineering deans and university presidents who are engineers have joined with colleagues from industry to work together with the Accreditation Board on Engineering and Technology (ABET) to establish a far more flexible approach to accreditation—one that measures outcomes against principles instead of counting credits for discrete elements in the curriculum. This cooperative effort recognizes that engineering schools need the flexibility to develop curricula appropriate to the times.

And these times call for a more integrative experience for engineering students. By returning closer to the roots of engineering practice, armed with the knowledge and sophisticated approaches of engineering science, but with an eye on the nimbleness and flexibility required by a future of rapid change, we can best prepare our students to lead through engineering.

A Closing Word

The intellectual and social map of MIT, and the world in which MIT operates, is marked by increasing diversification. These changes are the cause of discomfort and tension. They are also the source of renewal and growth.

We should welcome these changes and the opportunities they bring. And we should rise to the challenge they present: to recognize the importance of our varied talents and backgrounds while renewing a sense of common vision and purpose. We need to value, celebrate, and build on our differences, but also to rediscover and renew our mutual commitment to the shared values of academia. We must have community. We must have mutual respect. We must have common purpose.

It is a time to come together, to rediscover unifying forces, and to integrate our energies to solve grand problems.

Notes

1. Cornel West, *Race Matters* (Boston: Beacon Press, 1993), chapter 2.

2. Alfred North Whitehead, "Requisites for Social Progress," in *Science and the Modern World* (New York: Macmillan, 1925), p. 185.

3. Paul Penfield, Jr., Memorandum on Faculty Diversity, February 26, 1993, sent to the Faculty of the Department of Electrical Engineering and Computer Science and other colleagues at MIT.

4. Martin Luther King, Jr., *Where Do We Go from Here: Chaos or Community?* (Boston: Beacon Press, 1967), p. 171.

5

Higher Education and the Challenges of a New Era
1993–1994

A state without the means of some change is without the means of its conservation.
—Edmund Burke, *Reflections on the Revolution in France*

In this period the relationships among industry, government, and research universities were changing rapidly, presenting opportunities and challenges, and requiring fresh thinking. As the cold war faded into history, military security as a dominant motivation for federal support of university-based research and advanced education faded with it. The challenge of the highly competitive global marketplace drove fundamental transformation of the R&D function in U.S.-based corporations. Industry generally ceased to do research with moderate or long time-frames and absorbed R&D directly into its product-development process to accelerate product cycle times and improve manufacturing quality and efficiency. Various federal policymakers and appropriators sought to focus more university research on near-term application and commercialization; policy debates raged about the relative merits of "applied research" versus "basic research."

This turmoil gave universities a rare opportunity to respond to changing national needs and to sort out and clarify the relative roles of industry, government, and universities in funding and performing research and development. We needed to form a broad consensus that it is a necessary function of government to support the conduct of research of a fundamental nature and/or a long time-horizon to potential application, and to seek recommitment to the U.S. system in which universities are the primary performers of such research. The elegant system in which federal research dollars do double duty—supporting the research and creating the next generation of researchers and scientific and engineering leaders—

needed to be reaffirmed. Modern industry, fast-paced, innovation-driven, and globally connected, presented fascinating new intellectual challenges to engineering and management researchers. Industry and universities needed to find new ways of working in partnership, ways that would add value to each, enhancing education and filling the developing national void in research that has medium time-horizons. While doing so, universities needed to reaffirm and adhere to basic academic values, and to establish sound and effective policies for avoiding conflicts of interest.

American higher education must address the challenges of a new era. This requires not only introspection regarding our mission and the changing environment in which we serve society, but also rethinking our relationship and interaction with both industry and the federal government. Global economic competition and accelerating social and technological change have altered much of what is needed in our educational and research programs. Changing national priorities and attitudes, including an increasingly pervasive cynicism, are remaking the landscape of federal science and technology policy, with strong ramifications for our universities.

We must enthusiastically address the challenges of this new era, yet it is essential that fundamental values of the academy not become victims of short-term or localized thinking, despite the necessity for evolution and change within the system of higher education. Likewise, commitment to academic values must not imply rigidity and resistance to change.

Consideration of both the larger issues and specific instances of opportunity and challenge illuminate the new pathways we must pursue.

A Changing Environment for Education and Research

The end of the cold war, the stunning advances in information technology, global economic competition, and the changing demography of America are rapidly creating new expectations, responsibilities, and opportunities for institutions of higher education, especially research universities. The military needs of the cold war era and the culture of superpower competition created a public and political climate of support for advanced education and research. Defense became the dominant driver of high technology and provided an underlying rationale for the support of much basic science as well. The benefits of this support extended far beyond our security, narrowly defined, to build new industries and national capabilities through an enhanced knowledge base and a more highly educated citizenry. This now has changed abruptly. The cold peace that we have won has eroded this supportive climate, and left the compass of national policy spinning, rather than locked onto new directions that would unite, inspire, and advance us.

In a generation, computers have grown from curious devices to a ubiquitous technology of unprecedented power and influence. Information technology now links us across time and space in a manner that is revolutionizing human organizations. How knowledge is acquired and operated upon, and how work is accomplished in the future, are likely to be so influenced by information technology as to be unrecognizable in today's context.

We already live in a global society. Most notably, our corporations buy, sell, produce, employ, and compete in countries all over the world. They interact continuously across national, cultural, and linguistic borders. Even so, most American citizens continue to lead rather isolated lives, particularly during their childhood years. Second languages are not acquired, and the experience of living in other countries, or even visiting them on more than a superficial plane, is rare. International leisure travel is beyond the financial grasp of most children as they grow up. Yet these young men and women will have to work in a highly global environment when they reach adulthood.

The face of America is changing, and changing rapidly. Our minority populations will continue their rapid growth in the next generation. We are experiencing immigration from the east and south on a scale comparable to the waves of Europeans coming to our shores early in the century. The range and extent of professional activity and leadership accessible to women continues to expand.

From these changing realities and contexts, a new agenda for universities must emerge—one that will emphasize their contributions to civilian issues: improving health and welfare; creating industries and societies that are sustainable in terms of energy and environment; increasing quality and productivity in both manufacturing and service industries; understanding the origin, development, and reduction of violence; establishing and replenishing our physical and information infrastructures; and preparing students to live, work, and exercise leadership in an increasingly international context.

The Mission of Higher Education

The central mission of universities is to educate students. Drawing on the German model, America added to this mission the generation of new knowledge. In the period since the Second World War, we continued this evolution to create the uniquely American research university. At their best, these institutions are communities of learning that respect the intrinsic value of new knowledge and understanding, and at the same time emphasize the importance of interacting with and influencing the world beyond campus boundaries. The nature and raisons d'être of these communities are generally well understood and held in common by their members.

The external perception of universities' mission, however, is increasingly unclear. For many decades both the public and government held a fairly common understanding that the underlying role of education in America at all levels was to prepare citizens to operate a democracy. This essentially Jeffersonian view has served the nation well, bringing a commitment to education for all citizens, and a healthy mingling of practical education with humanistic, artistic, and scholarly endeavors. It provided the fertile soil that supported the growth of the post–Civil War land-grant universities and the post–World War II research universities. There now is a great sense of turbulence and uncertainty that suggests that some new educational form will emerge in this immediate post–cold war era. At the least, the social contract among the taxpaying public, and the private, government, and academic sectors will be rewritten.

Universities and the Federal Government

Nearly 50 years ago a confident America, seeking to build a strong future for its citizens, established an approach to advancing science, technology, and education that is unique in the world. The government, noting the critical role that university faculty and researchers had played in World War II, turned to the universities to conduct the basic research that would undergird our national goals.

For half a century, federal agencies have funded research and graduate education programs that have been uncommonly successful. Federally supported university research has generated essential components of our technology base, produced new generations of scientists and engineers, and driven the economy in important ways.

Federal spending at research universities was viewed as an essential investment in the future. The economic payback on this investment is hard to determine, but the economic analysis of University of Pennsylvania economist Edwin Mansfield suggests that in recent decades, the annual rate of return on investment in academic research is on the order of 25–30 percent. The Congressional Budget Office reviewed this analysis and concurred with this estimate of the remarkable rate of economic payback to the country on its investment in academic research. Nonetheless, the public and Congress now increasingly question the value, priority, and relevance of this investment. The sense of partnership between government and universities has decayed dramatically.

Establishing a renewed partnership and common vision requires that we look forward, not backward, and face the challenges of a new era. It requires that we strike a good balance between immediate national needs and the long-term good of the country. It also requires that we recognize the increasing scale, cost, and complexity of research. But above all, it requires that we establish a sense of common purpose.

A key mechanism for setting the tone of the evolving relationship and nature of federal support of higher education is the establishment of national research policy. Once the relatively clear domain of the executive branch, such policy is increasingly set in Congress through the appropriation process. This makes the job of establishing purpose and commitment much more difficult.

America knows better than any other nation *how* to do research, but we have lost our common understanding of *why* to do research.

Our national R&D pendulum swings fast and wide. We commit the nation to advance fundamental physics by constructing the Superconducting Supercollider, spend $2 billion, and then decide not to do it after all. We declare that industrial policy or even technology policy is verboten, then within a couple of years we commit to a national clean-car initiative organized by the Department of Commerce. National laboratories, mostly dedicated to weapons production and accustomed to noncompetitive, steady funding, suddenly aim to become adept at assisting industry. And in industry itself, central research laboratories with a strong commitment to basic research have for the most part been transformed into organizations with entirely different missions.

These swings are manifestations of the vagaries of our political system, but they also are indicative of an unstable search for policy in a time of fundamental change. Synergy and common understanding among the universities, the federal government, and industry have been lost. They must be regained.

Balancing the Short and Long Views

A major issue for the future of research universities will be the emerging federal view of the proper balance between clearly applicable research and the fundamental pursuit of the unknown. Ignoring fundamental research is just another way of living for the short term at the expense of future generations. How to develop this balance and how to continually renew and draw fully on the talents and expertise of our faculties is the essence of a set of questions that must be addressed by those who establish policy in America for science, technology, and research. In the final analysis, establishing congruence between the driving passions of researchers and societal goals is the central issue of science and technology policy.

The last several years have seen considerable angst and strain among universities, the federal government, and industry regarding the nation's research and development profile, policies, and in particular the role of academia. We have begun to think about research in new and often unfamiliar terms. Some would turn rapidly to highly applied research, redirect the activities of scientists and engineers, and increasingly foreordain the specific directions of scientific research and technological investigation.

After all, the argument goes—with considerable validity—
Congress and the American taxpayer expect a strong return on
their investment, preferably in the form of measurable improvements in our economy, and especially in high-wage employment.

Such arguments and actions greatly worry those who understand the dynamics of science, its unpredictability, and its dependence on curiosity and sudden insight as well as on hard work
and a supportive environment. In order to prosper, and to provide maximum long-term benefit to society, science needs flexibility, continuous support, and passion.

These conditions are endangered by the current state of
federal/academic relations. The past few years have seen a continuing attempt on the part of both Congress and the Administration to shift substantial portions of the cost of conducting
university research away from the federal sponsors of that
research. Rather than reimbursing universities for the full cost
of the research conducted on our campuses, the government has
expected the universities to shoulder more of those costs. This
means using our tuition, gift, and endowment revenues to cover
unreimbursed costs of federally sponsored research. At MIT,
such changes already account for a recurring annual shortfall of
$10 million in federal reimbursement of actual and legitimate
costs of research. There is a continual stream of further actions
to arbitrarily cap reimbursement or otherwise undermine the
support of our nation's research.

For example, this year the House of Representatives passed
an appropriations bill that would have instantaneously
decreased Department of Defense support of research at universities to 40 percent of its current level. The potential damage of
this was imponderable. This is the primary source of federal
support of engineering graduate education and research in the
United States. It supports over 75 percent of all electrical engineering research on our campuses, and it accounts for approxi-

mately 50 percent of research in other critical fields such as mechanical engineering, computer science, materials science, and engineering. Only at the eleventh hour during a Senate-House conference was this cut modified, but we still were left with a destructive 14-percent cut—a $200 million reduction in funding for DOD-sponsored research on the nation's campuses.

Such instances have caused the university community to work with great intensity to promote understanding of the issues by members of Congress and their staffs. We have enlisted the help of leaders of American industry to explain the disastrous consequences to our economy and competitiveness. In the process of fighting each of these difficult, defensive, political battles, the universities have had to divert enormous time and effort from our primary mission of education and research.

We are in the midst of an increasingly vicious cycle of congressional attack followed by intense defensive efforts by universities to create withdrawal or compromise. As we try to make our case, however, we are increasingly chided for acting like lobbyists, a role with which we are distinctly uncomfortable. Yet when push comes to shove, a common complaint by members of the Congress when an issue arises is that we haven't been paying enough attention to them. This is not a stable way to conduct federal policy. This is a time of both change and financial stress that calls for reasoned development of policy.

Universities and Industry

Just as we are in the midst of change in our relations with the federal government, so too are our relations with private industry changing. Much of this is driven by the rapid changes in industry itself. The end of the cold war, combined with the incredible rate at which electronic communication is expanding and the irreversible globalization of competitive businesses, has led to radical transformations of industries and organizations. This is accelerated by the expanding knowledge base that is giving rise to entire new industries such as biotechnology. Work is being accomplished in new ways as products are completely defined digitally before they exist physically, as so-called agile organizations are formed by electronic links among component groups throughout a company, or more likely, among large and small groups spread around the world. Although the emerging forms of organization are not yet clear, it is certain that students need different preparation to enter this new work environment.

For the research universities, this situation is full of opportunity and responsibility, but also of danger. I believe that the opportunity and responsibility greatly outweigh the danger, particularly for MIT, which was founded to create a strong, even unique, relationship with industry. The opportunities and responsibilities are clear: An exciting new intellectual and educational agenda needs to be forged, especially in engineering and management. The dangers are equally clear: Universities run the risk of assuming an overly utilitarian role, and the crucial openness of academic dialogue could be lost through ill-conceived policies regarding intellectual properties and dissemination of new knowledge.

The history of interaction of industry and academia has been mixed, and there have been major roadblocks of cultural differences and arrogance on both sides. We too often have passed as ships in the night, not really listening to or understanding each other. This is changing. Industrial issues have become intellectually challenging and exciting from the perspective of faculty and student interest, and, indeed, we need each other as never before.

The intellectual agenda of MIT and some other universities is evolving as new technological issues arise and as we attempt to understand and define new organizational structures. This can only be done by increasing the breadth and depth of dialogue and partnership with private industry, as well as with government. It can only be done if it is strongly supported both financially and intellectually.

Potential Clashes between Industrial and Academic Values
We must take great care as we develop new relations with industry, however, that universities not assume a posture that is too utilitarian. In time this would erode their intellectual independence and their ability to serve as objective critics of society. Indeed, there is a paradox in that it is this very independence and objectivity that usually attracts industry to work jointly with academia. As we work together in areas that have policy implications, such as the environment, energy, telecommunications, and productivity, we must maintain our independence and objectivity. Thus it is in the best interests of both parties that these matters be addressed carefully and resolved.

Another area of potential clashes of industrial and academic values is intellectual property. Universities hold dear their role in discovering and disseminating knowledge. The underlying assumption is that what we do on our campuses is, or should be, of general value to society and should be shared openly to advance humankind. In addition, many universities maintain unrealistic expectations about "striking it rich" through patent royalties and have tended to be overly protective and difficult when it comes to negotiating sponsored-research agreements.

Companies, on the other hand, must compete to create value for their customers and financial gain for their stockholders. Therefore they have an interest in holding closely both the knowledge and techniques that give them a competitive advantage. Patent ownership is a tool both for protection of their competitive advantage and for maximizing profits, by charging for their use, and for avoiding having to pay royalties to others, including universities.

Why has the matter of proprietary knowledge and patent rights become so controversial? First, there are simplistic understandings of what constitutes technology transfer. This has been particularly visible in debates about university interactions with non-U.S.-based companies, where it sometimes is assumed that university scientists and engineers generate highly specific devices and ideas that are the immediate "silver bullets" to create consumer products. Although this may be the case in rare instances, it generally is not. In fact, the most important mechanism for technology transfer from universities, and from companies for that matter, is educated and trained people and broad-based knowledge and know-how.

Second, the time from fundamental discovery to commercialization has decreased dramatically in many fields, and margins of competitive advantage have become very small and fleeting in many fast-paced industries. It also must be recognized that views on this topic seem to vary, largely based on the maturity and scale of the industry in question. It also generally is the case that discussions with industry leaders at the highest ranks within corporations seem to be much more flexible than with those at the operating level, who are involved with making project level decisions.

MIT's current approach to patents is designed to encourage the transfer of technology to the private sector. This requires an ability to negotiate with industrial sponsors as equals, best accomplished, in our view, by ownership of intellectual properties produced by campus researchers coupled with flexibility in reaching agreements with sponsors about licenses.

A final debate should be noted that may indeed prove to be much more complex than those discussed above—intellectual properties and copyrights in the emerging world of digital information systems. The knowledge base used for both scholarly and commercial pursuits is rapidly becoming stored, disseminated, and operated upon in digital form. Knowledge bases are increasingly created electronically by individuals and organizations dispersed both geographically and temporally. This raises very fundamental and difficult questions about ownership and access to knowledge. It is made worse because our system of copyrights and patents is an archaic one based on a world in which the printed page was the only information carrier. When coupled with the regulatory environment within which the rapidly emerging world-wide "information highway" and distributed digital library must operate, we will face some very interesting questions, that again may place universities and industries in debate.

Responses to a New Era

In an era in which economic, political, demographic, scientific, and technological changes occur at breathtaking speed, there are extraordinary opportunities for industry, government, and academia to regenerate themselves and to forge new alliances. Indeed, industry already *is* changing very rapidly; our federal government's R&D policy *will* change; and higher education, especially in engineering and management, *must* change.

Industry's Response

As American industry has faced challenges of unprecedented intensity to its ability to compete in the world marketplace, the goal of its R&D establishment has changed to concentration on relevance to commercial interests and reduction of product cycle times. The great industrial research laboratories that primarily conducted relatively basic research in areas of long-range potential to their companies have nearly disappeared. Industrial R&D groups must now clearly and continuously justify their importance to the company's business. This has had some salutary effects. After radical restructuring and clarification of missions, many industrial R&D groups are showing renewed vigor, are developing vastly improved interdisciplinary capabilities to improve goods and services, and are stimulating new commercial successes.

These changes create two potential problems. The first is a lack of investment in mid- to long-term research. The second is the danger that communication across company and campus boundaries will be choked off.

Today's technological advances are generally very complex, and we must have a broad understanding of how the entire system of research and development evolves and advances. A company that makes power generation equipment, to pick an example, depends upon an extended R&D infrastructure that, over time, has produced knowledge of combustion and fluid mechanics, computers and software for simulation and design, advanced materials, and many other techniques and entities largely developed under sponsorship by the government, often with long-range military needs in mind, or in industrial research laboratories of a type that hardly exist any longer. Much of the nation's traditional strength in industrial research that is relatively fundamental, yet has a strong potential for industrial applicability, is rapidly eroding, replaced by narrowly defined, company-specific R&D. Despite the improvements in competitiveness of individual companies that their transformed R&D organizations have greatly aided, we must recognize that a system that emphasizes short-term gain, promotes local secretiveness, and discourages open interaction across company and university boundaries, will lose the inertia needed for the long-run good of the nation.

As their economic positions improve, corporations will need to increase the fraction of earnings that is devoted to research, and they will need to direct some of this into mid- to long-term research. Once industries become productive and cost-competitive, and achieve high quality levels through concentration on process, they will enter a next round of competition that will require new levels of innovation and design. This, in turn, requires generation of, or access to, advancing scientific and technological knowledge. Companies have an obligation not only to produce some of this, but also to participate in a national, or perhaps global, R&D infrastructure. They no longer can take for granted either the extended system of federally sponsored, university-based research or the major industrial research laboratories that have provided this for the last four decades. It is essential that we experiment with substantial new forms of R&D partnerships among industry, universities, and government. Joint projects, new forms of consortia, industrial laboratories adjacent to campuses, and new research agendas will be required to create a new R&D infrastructure for the post–cold war era.

As industry establishes new research and educational partnerships with universities, "technology transfer" from universities to the private sector will continue to be an important concept. This has an honorable genesis in the land-grant universities that created agricultural experiment stations and county-agent systems for the development and dissemination of applicable scientific knowledge to the nation's farmers. Openness of agricultural research results was central to this system, but contemporary technology-based partnerships pose significant issues about dissemination of research results.

We must carefully consider the matter of patents and openness. The situation requires thought from a systemic and long-range perspective. What, in the long run, will serve all parties well? Because of the need to maintain the extended R&D infrastructure, the issue of rebalancing competition and cooperation lies at the center of consideration of policy toward patents and proprietary research on campuses. We must minimize secretiveness and overly protective patent policies on the part of companies sponsoring research or otherwise working in partnership with research universities.

Government's Response

Federal policy must respond in two ways. First, it must assure strong funding for truly fundamental research. This is the long-term investment, the patient capital that is essential for the benefit of our children and their children. Second, the government should work in partnership with private industry and academia to identify those areas of technological advancement that are most critical to the well-being of the nation. Once identified, broad goals should be set for them. Tasks must not be dictated in detail, but general strategic directions should be set and wide bands or pathways in which research scientists and engineers can pursue their efforts should be defined. There must be room for the free market of ideas.

In order to be a great nation, we must press onward with our commitment to support fundamental research and the people and institutions that enable it. History shows that advancement of knowledge, beyond its intrinsic value, does indeed lead to advances in health, productivity, learning, and quality of life. It is the foundation on which progress is built. If we in America do not pursue fundamental research along uncharted pathways, others will. Indeed, others should. All nations that aspire to excellence and advancement of the human condition should strongly support basic science.

Yet, we also know the facts. There are identifiable, strategically important areas of science and technology that we must master and advance in order to improve or even maintain our industrial competitiveness. This is true, notwithstanding the fact that with greater freedom, scientists and engineers will discover and invent new, as yet undreamed-of and even more important technologies.

It would be suicidal to dictate what all researchers should work on and to set simplistic goals for immediate commercial application of all that they do. It will not work. The futility of state planning brought down the Berlin Wall. But it is entirely appropriate to foster a new commitment to solving the problems of our era— the civilian concerns that the end of the cold war frees us to address, and that are essential to the well-being of the next generation. This is challenging and exciting. Appropriate areas are rather easy to define: the environment, energy, transportation, our telecommunications and computing infrastructure, and more livable cities, to name a few.

Research Universities' Response

The necessary response of universities lies partly in their research programs, but even more importantly in education per se. We must strive to be sure that research universities fulfill their promise as a learning environment that is remarkably well suited to the coming era—one in which undergraduates, graduate students, and faculty alike share in the discipline, joy, and continual renewal of original research and scholarship. Our research orientation enables us to lead the way in education, because society will ask much more of our graduates than that they know what others have accomplished in the past. If our students are to reach their full potential to contribute to society and, just as importantly, to enjoy fully the beauty and the adventure of creating and understanding, we have to teach them how to advance knowledge.

In addition, the increasing complexity of tasks that will face our graduates means that we must better prepare our students to understand how to draw on knowledge from many different disciplines, how to contribute as members of teams as well as individuals, and how to communicate with members of the public, government, or the business community as well as with their professional colleagues.

Beyond that, we must take greater responsibility for helping students to develop broader world views and the expertise required to live and work in a more global context. This responsibility extends beyond the classroom and laboratory to the nature of our student body and faculty itself. We must be unflagging in our efforts to be accessible and inclusive of all of our talented young men and women. Indeed, most of us can point with considerable pride to the diversity of our undergraduate student body, accomplished through a great deal of hard work in the 1970s and 1980s. Yet we still have much to do to build the diversity of our graduate student population and our faculty, and to successfully draw together the increasingly diverse talents and cultural perspectives of our faculty and students around a common set of basic values and purposes.

This need to explore and understand "real-world" complexities and organizations requires that we must work more in partnership with industry. Specifically, we need to bring engineering and management closer together in the education of industrial and societal leaders. Academia and industry should work together to bring about a greater common understanding of industry's needs and the university's educational role in fulfilling them. Of course, we should discount ideas that are relevant only to the current moment and keep focused on the long-term good.

Researchers and engineers from industry and university faculty should spend significant time in each others' domains in order to undertake cooperative projects, both basic and applied. This could become a remarkably effective mechanism for technology transfer. There are substantial roadblocks to doing so. Faculty feel that they cannot leave their posts for a year because they will not be able to maintain the momentum of their research projects. Outstanding engineers in industry believe that they will fall off their career path if they leave their current responsibilities for a year. Surely this problem is solvable if companies and government funding agencies would make a concerted effort to enable such exchanges. Let's get serious about this. Every other country in the world seems to encourage and reward first-rate engineers and scientists for spending time as visiting researchers in American universities.

Another, further, step is for colleagues in university and industry to work closely together to design the engineering and management education programs of the future and to discuss research agendas. MIT has taken a number of steps to ensure a good dialogue among faculty and industrial leaders and to complement the ongoing activities of our Industrial Liaison Program and various research consortia. In September of 1993, MIT held, in conjunction with the World Economic Forum, an industry summit that attracted over 800 high-level leaders of industry and government from around the nation and world to discuss issues facing industry and to explore solutions to them. In addition, during the past academic year, an Institute Task Force on Industry Linkages has been considering and making recommendations regarding the appropriate relationships between MIT and industry for the coming decade.

At MIT we have a special obligation to educate engineers, managers, and scientists who can lead in this changed milieu. Our greatest challenge in this regard is to develop in our students the *attitudes,* as well as the aptitudes, needed to translate new knowledge from research to practical ends.

Investing in the Future

Knowledge and a population educated and skilled in ways that permit its creative use are the capital resources of the emerging era. Knowledge, not natural resources or geographic location, will determine which nations and societies prosper. Knowledge is distributed throughout organizations and societies; we must learn to utilize it collectively and effectively. Knowledge will increasingly be gleaned by computer networks from far-flung sources, shaped by collaborative efforts, moderated by information technology. Knowledge can only be generated and wisely used by educated and inspired people. The generation of new knowledge requires commitment to, and investment in, research.

Universities are our primary vehicle for educating talented men and women and for producing new knowledge, insight, and techniques. In order to serve well, universities must balance continuity and change—continuity of their deeper values and guiding principles, and commitment to intellectual excellence and the life of the mind, are essential. Yet so is a willingness to change, experiment, and improve. America's colleges and universities are changing in response to the new era—changing too slowly, perhaps, but profoundly. A walk across MIT's campus will disclose a student body radically different from that of twenty years ago, one increasingly rich in its racial and cultural makeup, reminding us again that our country is changing rapidly and that we still are a nation of immigrants, as we always have been.

Our curricula are shifting to meet new needs, challenges, and opportunities. All MIT students must now learn cellular and molecular biology. Master's-level education in our Schools of Engineering and Management is being altered and integrated. New, international, university/government/industry partnerships are being formed to conduct objective studies of environmental issues and create sound policy alternatives. New programs are emerging—ranging from fundamental studies of mind and memory to new product development and manufacturing. New linkages to industry are forming. Yet, much more remains to be done as the intellectual agenda for the post–cold war era and a new economic citizenship emerge. We have only scratched the surface of using information technology and multi-media to create new and more effective ways of knowing and learning. We have only begun to understand what is required to prepare our students to cooperate and compete across national and cultural boundaries.

Universities like MIT must become more cost-effective and improve the quality of all that they do as organizations and learning communities. Many view us as clinging to the past, unwilling to change and improve. We must regain the public trust if we are to realize our aspirations and serve the future as we always have. This requires that we change substantively, becoming organizationally still more lean and effective. We have started to re-engineer many of our administrative and service activities to become more cost-effective, productive, and efficient. We must lead in this effort just as we lead intellectually. Only in this way will we remain financially accessible to those we must educate.

But we cannot escape the fact that the nation must continue to invest in its system of higher education and research. The federal government must stop the trend of shifting the cost of research it sponsors to tuition, gift, and endowment funds. Private industry must work with us, and invest in us, to ensure the health of the nation's research and development by supporting us intellectually and financially in new ways.

The dreams and visions of our institutions and our students will not be fully realized, and the nation and world will not fully benefit from our potential, unless a renewed commitment to education and research is forged and widely held by the public. This is not a matter of luxury—it is a matter of regaining pride and belief in our people and their future.

6

What We Don't Know
1994–1995

We must remind ourselves, and the public, that our value to practical concerns like health, economic productivity, and national security accrues ultimately from our enthusiasm for mysteries—our readiness, and that of our students, to explore the truly unknown.

Policy debates, the changing research needs of the nation, and the role of universities within the innovation system of government, industry, and academia dominated much of my thinking and writing in the first half of the 1990s, uncomfortably bypassing the most critical point of all—that scientists and research engineers are drawn to their calling and driven in their work primarily by a deep human need to understand nature. Curiosity and "big questions" attract and motivate us and drive the fundamental scholarship and research that underlie human progress. I began to realize that in the rush to explain to our governmental and industrial patrons the importance of what we in universities know, we avoided explaining that what we don't know is more important than what we do know.

Sitting on the porch of our house in New Hampshire, I sent an e-mail to several faculty leaders at MIT asking each to state two of the most important unanswered questions in their research fields—one very fundamental and the other having some apparent relevance to application. Their responses form the substance of this essay. I organized their questions and challenges as addressing the earth and its climate; human systems and organizations; information and information technology; memory, language, and thought; energy and efficient use of resources; cancer and health; and the physical universe. These questions look to the future and form wonderful foci for the MIT community and those who share our adventure. It is striking how much the meta-issue of whether some of these questions actually have obtainable answers permeates the thinking of these colleagues; equally striking is the importance to our future of the quest to answer them.

This is a period in American higher education when it is essential that research universities articulate their value to the nation and the world. We are operating in a political and economic environment that requires increased efficiency and cost-effectiveness on the part of all of its institutions, including universities. To many, being "cost-effective" implies that our education and research programs—particularly in engineering and science— must be more clearly and directly relevant to industry and other pervasive human endeavors. As a result, the discourse about our role in the community often is focused on university contributions that have obvious, widespread, and positive impact. Research universities in general, and MIT in particular, have had and will continue to have an extremely strong story to tell in this context. It is inherent in our institutional nature, and we are proud of it.

These circumstances invariably lead us to highlight our recent accomplishments, discuss current trends in education, and provide indicators of important technology transfer and medical advances—in other words, to talk about what we have already learned. Yet as we consider the nature of universities, and as we continue a dialogue with the public, we would do well to remember that the ultimate rationale for supporting a university system derives more from the unknown than the known.

It is the romance of discovery that draws young people to study and to pursue careers in science. It is the dream of creating entirely new devices, materials, and techniques that drives engineers. Humanists and social scientists look for new insights into the human psyche and social systems. Architects and planners seek new aesthetics and systems to enhance the quality of our lives. Management experts explore new principles upon which to organize institutions and the way we work.

It is a fact of modern life that research universities must increase their connections with the worlds of industry and professional practice. We must teach our students to relate analysis and theory to the practical and the concrete. However, it is the pursuit of the truly unknown—of principles, insights, materials, and organisms of which we currently have no inkling—that will yield the greatest rewards for a society that invests in education, scholarship, and research. New knowledge can advance the human spirit, strengthen the economy, and enhance the quality of life.

My annual report gives me an opportunity to reflect on the reasons why we in the academy dedicate our careers to research and education. This year, in preparing this report, I asked several members of the faculty to give me their reasons—in the form of the questions and puzzles they are seeking to solve. Their replies were illuminating both in content and in what they showed of different styles of thought. Even with their contributions, this report can offer only a tiny sampling of the countless gateways to the unknown. This sampling, however, offers more than sufficient justification for investing personal energy and public resources in building individual careers and major institutions devoted to education and research.

Interestingly, issues of what we can and cannot know or predict permeated many of the examples. Historically, we have employed science to discover basic principles on which we could then base practical predictions. Through engineering we have used basic principles and predictions to develop devices and systems to accomplish work, heal disease, travel, harness energy, communicate, learn, entertain, and create wealth. In the modern world, however, we must deal with increasingly larger and more complex issues and systems, both natural and constructed.

As we do so, we must be willing to consider the limits of our historical strategies.

The Earth and Its Climate

Such questions bear on matters of immense practical value, such as the ability to predict climate and earthquakes.

Climate can be loosely understood as the long-term average state of the weather, and results from the complex interactions among the atmosphere, biosphere, oceans, and land masses. Given the fact that there are natural variations in climate that have enormous impact on our lives, as well as the prospect that human activities, notably the burning of fossil fuels, might trigger a cascade of dangerous changes in climate beginning with "global warming," there is widespread agreement that we need to improve our capability to predict climate in order to inform public policy. This societal need has emerged as one of the greatest challenges we face in the natural sciences.

Computer modeling is one of the most valuable tools in the arsenal of scientists who study climate. However, even the most elaborate climate models, running on the most powerful computers, cannot reproduce today's climate without introducing uncomfortable levels of artificiality. Improving the computer codes may not be sufficient to answer the basic questions about the climate, because we do not know, even in principle, which aspects of climate are predictable. We must turn to other modes of analysis to address the issue of predictability.

Another tool available to scientists who work with very large, complex systems is "chaos theory," which grew out of the insights of MIT professor E. N. Lorenz. In his studies of weather, which is the short-term behavior of the atmosphere, Lorenz discovered that perturbations of a system that are so small as to be unobservable can lead to dramatically differing results over time.

Chaos is now known to have applications in areas as diverse as chemical reactions and heart disease.

Scientists are now trying to learn what elements of climate are chaotic, as well as how interactions among the subsystems of climate, such as the oceans, the polar ice caps, and the clouds that help cool the earth, will amplify or dampen the human impact on climate. They are also trying to refine precisely what we mean by prediction: what we have to know, in what detail, over what time span, in order to satisfy particular needs of society.

Many of the unknowns in our understanding of climate have parallels in the study of earthquakes, another physical system in which the ability to predict events in the short term could have tremendous benefits for individual lives and national economies. We know that earthquakes occur primarily at the boundaries of the earth's tectonic plates, and that the most active boundaries are situated in regions where the populations are increasing and mega-cities are developing most rapidly. Further, there is evidence that some large earthquakes appear to be predictable: Premonitory phenomena led to the evacuation of the Chinese city of Haicheng, for example, before it was destroyed by a magnitude 7.5 earthquake in 1975.

By contrast, sensitive instruments in place in Kobe, Japan, and Northridge, California, showed no systematic premonitory events leading up to recent earthquakes that resulted in significant suffering and property damage. The problem is that there are many types of earthquakes occurring in different geological settings, and we do not know which classes of earthquakes are predictable. We don't understand the processes that lead to ground failure, or the interactions among earthquakes and other events that occur along fault systems. We don't know with any reliability how serious an event will occur where and when, which is the level of understanding we need to protect lives and property.

Human Systems and Organizations

Understanding the behavior of physical systems like the climate, the weather, and the earth's crust is one thing; systems and organizations that involve human beings are quite another. These systems have the ability to think, communicate, adjust themselves to changing conditions, and intentionally change themselves. This lends an even greater level of complexity to understanding and prediction. Still, we know empirically that the behavior of certain aspects of such systems can be understood in an approximate sense and that there are basic principles, though of a much less deterministic nature than in the case of physical systems.

For example, we have a number of very reliable indices of national economic growth and many years of data on individual countries. We can show that for the last few decades, rapid economic growth, with an associated rise in standard of living, has occurred in a number of less-developed Asian countries, but not in many less-developed African countries. There have also been substantial variations in growth rates among the leading industrialized nations, where only Japan and Germany have approached the rapid growth rates of best-performing Asian economies in the post–World War II period. Yet we do not know why national economies grow at such different rates, either at a particular moment or over time.

We know the likely factors that affect economic growth: education, capital accumulation, national investment in research and development, tax structures, trade policies, regulation, and basic legal and political structure. The relative importance of these factors and their interactions, however, are not known with any degree of precision, yet governments continue to develop and implement economic policy. In fact, governments routinely fall because they failed to live up to public expectations for growth—a situation where lack of knowledge of what works can actually contribute to worldwide political instability.

On a smaller scale, we do not know what the successful organization of the coming decades will look like. Even the most experienced business leaders cannot predict which companies will thrive and which will go under. By drawing on such fields as coordination science, information technology, learning theory, and strategic analysis, we hope to find the principles that will provide the basis of organizations that are efficient, flexible, innovative, and successful over time.

Using Information and Information Technology

Some of the most profound and permeating changes in the nature of organizations and economies are being created by the rapidly expanding access to information. Even our largest and most dominant organizations for centuries—nations—will not be immune. We do not know what the consequences will be for the nation-state of the explosion in networked electronic communications.

The enormous collective bandwidth of the Internet makes it quite unlike the telephone, and it has the potential to create a new kind of "society," an entity in itself. We cannot predict if we will have a society of very local nets, centered around individuals and small groups, or a massive global society. We do not know the consequences in either case, nor do we know how to steer these developments even if we could determine what outcome is desirable. But clearly, the outcomes will affect the very fabric of our communities and our own daily lives. Already we are faced with the development of extragovernmental systems that are not only rich in information but that operate around the world. One need only think of the problem of organizing and operating very large-scale, integrated, international systems such as a global air-traffic control system to see the magnitude of the challenge.

And on the interface of learning and information technology, we confront the fact that we really do not know how best to use our information infrastructure and new media to promote learning among children, particularly among those children whose home and community environments do not nurture and reinforce the most positive kinds of learning. Nor have we made more than a dent in the potential of information technology to promote lifetime learning among adults.

One feature of information technology—the vast archives of information available worldwide and the rapidly proliferating tools for accessing and manipulating this information—presents us with a particularly powerful and complex set of challenges. We do not know how the vast store of instantly available information can or will be understood and used.

Access alone does not ensure that information can be located or understood. How can knowledge be gathered from disparate sources and then represented and shaped to enhance our understanding and our ability to use it productively? Can we strengthen our ability to transmit and understand concepts as well as simple facts? Can we better the odds that individuals of different age, language, experience, and culture will be able to assimilate and use the knowledge to which they now will have shared access?

These are not new problems, nor are they ones that are defined only in terms of modern information technology, but they are increasingly compelling. We need to explore the power of the human mind to better locate and use to advantage what already is known, and to take in newly available information and grasp its significance.

Memory, Language, and Thought

There is no greater mystery than how we learn, remember, think, and communicate, and there is no field in which major advances would have more profound effects for human progress and health.

The achievements of human memory are astounding. We can easily recognize thousands of faces, innumerable visual scenes, and countless melodies and familiar voices. We execute motor skills like driving a car, playing a piano, or skiing. But we do not know how we learn and remember, or how we think and communicate. We do not yet know the chemical or physical nature of storage of information in the brain. We do not know where in the brain information is stored, how we retrieve it, or whether there are limits to the amount we can store.

There is every reason to believe, however, that continued, determined investigations of the biological basis of learning and memory, coupled with computer modeling, will greatly expand our understanding of the mind in the decades ahead. Not only is this an exciting scientific frontier, but a better understanding of the brain, brain chemistry, and the role of genetics may prove the key to vastly improved diagnostic and therapeutic techniques for chemically based mental illnesses such as schizophrenia and manic-depressive syndromes. Such advances would enable us to reduce both human suffering and the staggering costs of health care.

Not only do we not understand brain function in the large, but in a more specific case, we do not understand the relationship between language and thought. Can we have thoughts that cannot be expressed in words? Can everything that can be expressed in one language be expressed in any other language as well? Cultural matters aside, linguists believe that the answer to both questions is no, but we do not know for sure. The answers are important if we are to perfect machine translation.

Another question in linguistics has even wider practical importance. All cultures have spoken language, but the discovery of written language is a historical rarity. That suggests that our biological endowment does not support reading the way it does spoken language. We do not know why or how it is that some children seem to learn to read with the ease with which all children acquire language. If we can find out, we may be able to greatly enhance our teaching of reading to every child and eventually bring down the illiteracy rate among adults as well.

No less important than cognitive science, linguistics, and biology in helping us to understand the processes of perception and thought, though from an entirely different perspective, are the disciplines of the arts—the domain of playwrights, musicians, sculptors, dancers, and their kin. They remind us that we still do not know the parameters of free will. Nor do we always know how to see through the accepted social conventions and get down to the truth beneath. How much of our lives is within our control? When does courage consist of accepting and working with our fate, and when does it consist of fighting back? Artists continually remind us that in much of human experience, questions cannot be answered just once, for all times and all places, but rather must be asked and answered by each generation, each culture, each individual. In a society and a world where rigidity of thought and inability to see another point of view constitute a deadly epidemic, that message is more crucial than ever.

Energy and the Efficient Use of Resources

As world population and industrialization expand simultaneously, issues of the efficient use of natural resources and its relation to environmental quality are becoming paramount. The underlying questions come from such disparate disciplines as engineering, chemistry, economics, political science, and materials science. They affect both developed and developing societies.

For example, although economists can show that pollution imposes real social costs, markets do a poor job of encouraging individual and organizational players to incorporate these costs into their decision making. Governments have to step in, but the approaches they have adopted to date have not, by and large, encouraged industry to be efficient and technologically innovative in solving pollution problems. We know how to design policy tools to control pollution efficiently, at least in theory. However, until recently policymakers have not relied on these policy instruments. Work is going on at MIT and other places to evaluate the potential of various "economic instruments," such as taxes on specific emissions, or tradable permits for certain effluents, to achieve both social and market goals, work that could make the policy choices more compelling.

We do not know how to produce materials with no waste by-products. In the most expansive sense, this is the objective of the emerging field of "industrial ecology," which tracks the production, use, and disposal or recycling of materials. Industrial ecologists concern themselves not only with the material inputs and outputs of a fabrication process, but with its energy requirements as well.

We do not know how to convert solar energy into practical, cost-efficient fuels for a wide variety of applications, nor do we know how to create advanced fuels for nuclear-fission reactors. Renewable, safe alternative sources of energy are critical to our ability to enhance our quality of life while sustaining the quality of our environment.

On an even more fundamental level, we do not know how to extract all the energy from existing fuel sources. We know that a certain amount of energy is stored in chemical bonds, but when we burn the fuel to break those bonds, we waste much of the energy emitted as untapped heat and chemical by-products. And as anyone who has worked on technologies from spacecraft to pacemakers can tell us, the ability to milk every unit of energy from a power source could be a breakthrough of great practical importance.

An important quest of modern chemistry that bears on the efficient use of energy and resources has to do with catalysts—substances that cause reactions to speed up but are not consumed themselves. Catalysts are at the heart of most industrial processes in the chemical, petroleum, fertilizer, pharmaceutical, and related industries. And yet, we do not know how to design catalysts for many important chemical reactions. Many of the catalysts we currently employ were discovered serendipitously; scientists then worked backward to reconstruct in each case how the reaction might work. We need to discover more about the fundamental principles governing the operations of catalysts, principles that could enable us to design new catalysts that would have a host of implications for energy, the economy, and the environment.

Similarly, superconductivity, the ability of a material to carry electric current without any loss of energy, is a phenomenon that could have almost limitless practical applications. We know how superconductivity works at low temperatures, but the applications are limited by the difficulty of holding materials at appropriate temperatures. We also know that there are materials that can superconduct at much higher temperatures, but we do not fully understand how "high-temperature superconductivity" works. An understanding of this phenomenon would open the possibility of creating new materials to take us to the next step, room temperature superconductivity, which holds out exciting promise for electric power storage and transmission, as well as ocean and rail transportation.

Cancer and Health

There was a time when the public hoped cancer might respond to an all-out attack with military singleness of purpose. We had defeated polio, ended centuries of death and disfigurement from smallpox, and created such a wealth of antibiotics that once life-threatening injuries were reduced to almost trivial annoyances.

Cancer, however, turned out not to be a single disease, in the sense of one causal agent and one set of symptoms. Rather, it is a condition of runaway cell growth triggered by the confluence of a multitude of causal factors and revealed in a multitude of physical responses. But cancer is yielding to discoveries of basic science, sometimes of quite surprising origin and nature, and cancer research has clearly demonstrated the importance of the interplay between fundamental science and applied fields like medicine and even engineering.

We still have more questions than answers, but understanding the basic cellular processes in all living organisms underlies our ability to understand and, ultimately, to prevent or treat cancer.

We now know that genes are a key to our understanding, but we do not know all the specific genes whose mutations contribute to the development and progression of cancer, nor do we understand the mechanisms by which they do it. This includes both "oncogenes," genes that can cause cancer, and "tumor-suppressor genes," genes that suppress excess growth and, if absent or damaged, allow tumors to develop. A number of genes in each category have been discovered, but many have not yet been identified, nor have all the properties of known genes been explored for their possible use in cancer treatment. For example, identification of such genes may lead to diagnostic tests that can identify high-risk individuals or identify which cancers are treatable by radiation or chemotherapy.

We also do not know how and why cells die. The suppression of normal cell death—essentially cell suicide, known as "apoptosis"—is believed to be involved in the growth of certain cancers, and promoting the controlled death of particular cells is obviously the objective of much of cancer treatment. This also has implications in the understanding of auto-immune and neurodegenerative diseases.

Yet another puzzle is this: We do not know why tumor cells migrate to new sites in the body. This question is closely related to a more general problem that arises in developmental biology: How do different cells know where to go during the development of an embryo? Here is yet another example of how studying the fundamental process can shed light on any number of related cases, such as why white blood cells home in on a site of infection or inflammation. We do know that there are areas on the cell surface (called adhesion receptors) that control how cells attach to their neighbors and whether or not they migrate. While research is far enough along that clinical trials are underway on blockers for adhesion in platelets and in white blood cells, not enough is yet known about the receptors that are actually used by the cells in spreading cancer to a new site. Once we know that, it may then be possible to inject patients with drugs that block the adhesion receptors on stray cancer cells and prevent them from binding to new sites in the body.

In the questions above, as in many others, the outline of the unknown evolved: The basic advances did not come from people looking at how to block metastasis, but from scientists trying to understand basic cell biology. Further advances in health-related fields will come from the increasing interaction of biology with other scientific and engineering disciplines.

For example, we do not know the threshold of safe exposure of living organisms to radiation. Cell biologists will be called upon to help nuclear scientists and engineers find out. We know that such a threshold exists. Cells have an inherent capacity to repair small changes caused by atomic or nuclear interaction, a capacity that allows biological life to flourish amidst the background radiation of the natural environment. Safety standards are essential for the medical use of radiation as well as in regulating emissions from industrial applications of radioactive materials. A biologically based safety standard is likely to offer far more reliable protection than our present standard, which is based on extrapolations from the effects of high levels of radiation.

The interface between biology and yet another discipline—mathematics—offers more unanswered questions. We do not know how viruses form their elegant, geometric structures from commonly occurring protein building blocks, nor do we understand the role of these structures in the infection process. By applying mathematical methods to analyze viral protein structure, we hope to gain sufficient understanding of the infection process to aid in the development of antiviral drugs for applications from HIV to influenza.

And finally: We do not know how living cells interact with molecules of nonliving materials. The answers to this question hold the promise of making great strides in the development of artificial limbs, organs, and tissues. The opportunities here have spurred cell biologists and researchers in such areas as materials and chemical engineering to work together in the emerging new field of biomaterials.

The Physical Universe

Humankind continues passionately to pursue the age-old questions about our universe. We do not know how old the universe is, what it is made of, or what its fate will be; we do not understand what mechanism generates mass in the basic building blocks of matter.

On a somewhat more modest scale, we do not know if stars other than our own sun have earthlike planets capable of sustaining life, and we do not yet have the ability to detect life, or good methods of detecting planets themselves.

Even the basic mathematics that is the language of theoretical physics must still be advanced in fundamental ways. We do not understand, in more than a limited way, three-dimensional spaces and four-dimensional geometries of space and time. Recent ideas from quantum field theory have given mathematicians novel, effective tools to help classify these spaces and perceive their shapes. New insights in these areas are expected, for example, to change our conceptions of the "big bang" and the expanding or contracting universe, which have been based, of necessity, on our present-day theories of four-dimensional geometries.

We don't know whether antimatter comes from other galaxies. The answer to that question would answer a fundamental question about the origin of the universe. Nor do we know whether the universe indeed is predominantly constituted of so-called dark matter. Most basic knowledge of the physical universe is sought by both land-based and space-based instruments. The development of such instruments is made possible by the advancing state of the art in engineering, electronics, computers, and communications technology. In turn, instrumentation development often advances our engineering capabilities. One noteworthy experiment that will address such basic issues is the antimatter spectrometer (AMS), which will be placed on the International Space Station.

Even though space-based instruments are doing much to advance our knowledge of the universe, we are still drawn by the adventure of human exploration of space. Further human exploration of the solar system presents exciting opportunities for space science and challenges for space technology, but the biggest unknown at present remains the crew itself.

We do not know how to plan a mission to Mars that would not result in a dangerously unhealthy crew. Current knowledge and experience indicate that available countermeasures such as exercise may not be adequate to offset the deconditioning effects of prolonged weightlessness. We must find ways either to dramatically shorten the journey or to develop some means of artificial gravity that will provide a more earthlike inertial environment for the long trip to and from Mars.

Conclusion

These questions—about our physical universe, our social systems, our biological systems—represent the thoughts of only a handful of faculty at one institution, albeit a faculty and an institution that are world leaders. Such questions cause us to look to the future rather than the past, a particularly appropriate focus for the MIT community and those who would share our adventure.

Being able to shape good questions is a critical capacity for every teacher and learner; it is the key to education. Unanswered questions are the single most valuable thing we lay before our graduate students. The "right thesis topic" is the question that will open not one door but many; in fact, it is a question that will lead to a whole career's worth of new questions.

Doc Edgerton once remarked that students were always coming to him worried that all the really interesting problems had been solved, that there wasn't a lot of the fun of discovery left for young scientists and technologists. Somebody had already invented the silicon chip and cloned the first gene; what was left? Doc, of course, took the opposite tack; he thought the world was a sea of wonderful puzzles. That was probably the secret of his great success, as an inventor and researcher and as a teacher: his zest for the unanswered questions.

His is a mantle the entire university community must take up. It is no redundancy to repeat the declaration with which this report opened: We must remind ourselves, and the public, that our value to practical concerns like health, economic productivity, and national security accrues ultimately from our enthusiasm for mysteries—our readiness, and that of our students, to explore the truly unknown.

7

Bold Ventures and Opportunity for All? 1995–1996

In this age, in this country, there is an opportunity for the development of [humankind's] intellectual, cultural, and spiritual potentialities that has never existed before in the history of our species. I mean not simply an opportunity for greatness for a few, but an opportunity for greatness for the many.

—Edwin H. Land

A great nation must do some bold and heroic things. Excellence in science sometimes comes from deep, focused work of an individual, but there are other scientific and technological advances that can come only from sustained efforts of large teams to accomplish bold missions of large scale and scope. Through a combination of ambivalent attitudes toward international cooperation and a congressional budgeting and electoral process that mitigates against sustained large-scale investment, America seemed to be losing its will to be bold in the pursuit of scientific excellence. We had invested $2 billion in the design and initial construction of the Superconducting Supercollider, then just dropped it, unfinished, and walked away. We were major players in the ITER (International Thermonuclear Reactor) program, and then dropped out. The Space Station, which is mostly a technological rather than a scientific project, and a step along the path to human exploration of the solar system, was increasingly vulnerable to congressional micromanagement and always under threat of cancellation. One counterexample to the trend was the Human Genome Project, which was well managed and also enjoyed the advantage that every member of Congress was aware of the importance of advancing human health.

In education as well, boldness seemed increasingly absent. From every corner we heard grand pronouncements about making our primary and secondary education world-class, but we rarely observed serious efforts to do so. Furthermore, two of the boldest concepts of American education—inclusiveness of all parts of our population, and the openness of our universities to students, faculty, and scholars from all over the world—seemed threatened. Inclusiveness, in my view, was threatened by ideologically based court challenges and voter referendums aimed at dismantling programs designed to attract underrepresented minority students to higher education and to enhance their opportunities to succeed. Attacks on the openness of our universities to those from other nations were largely driven by shortsighted assumptions that foreign students and visitors would absorb important knowledge, return to their home countries, and apply it to commercial products that in turn would be used to defeat us in the world marketplace. While people of good will can differ on how to accomplish goals like inclusiveness and national economic strength, it seemed to me that a mean and counterproductive attitude was taking root in parts of our nation. Openness, which would reappear as a far more critical issue in the decade that followed, is essential to the spirit and excellence of universities like MIT, and in our ability to serve our nation and world well.

In 1957, nearly 40 years ago, Edwin Land, the founder of Polaroid, gave the Arthur Dehon Little Memorial Lecture at MIT.[1] His address was entitled "Generation of Greatness: The Idea of a University in an Age of Science." In it, he set forth his conviction that everyone is born with the potential for greatness and that we must be far bolder in our vision and commitment to develop the full creative powers of our young.

His proposal for how universities might meet this challenge was to create within each university small communities of faculty and students who would work together as colleagues in scholarship and research—where learning would become, once again, an exciting adventure. This proposal led to the establishment in the 1960s of the Undergraduate Research Opportunities Program at MIT—still one of the strongest features of an MIT education.

But the point here is not that Land had a major influence on education at MIT, but that he had a vision of greatness and a boldness of spirit that were embraced by others. Certainly his influence can be attributed to the power of his intellect and his dream. But perhaps it also had something to do with the times, the dawn of the 1960s, when the country was ready to dream of greatness and to take bold action, and did so in many domains—in science and technology, in education, in civil rights.

Is Boldness a Thing of the Past?

Today—in 1996—we live in an age that seems to reject bold thought and bold action. This is true in America, and it is true in Europe. Why is this? Does boldness come with a price tag we can no longer afford? Does it imply excess or waste or impracticality? Are we too cynical to embrace visionary new ideas? Have we turned from boldness because such vision and action usually call for shared commitment—and we only care for what affects us personally and immediately? Is this a natural outcome of our maturation as a nation and as a society? Perhaps all of the above. Or perhaps, at century's end, we have become so concerned with eliminating the budget deficit in order to protect future generations from economic grief that we are blind to the equal importance of making the investments necessary to assure the vitality and quality of their lives.

I do not believe, however, that for most Americans, or for most people around the world for that matter, such limited vision is a conscious choice. We have slipped into complacency and self-interest, but we need not, and cannot, remain there. As a society we must once again believe that we can envision and generate greatness in our time, and build the foundation for future generations of greatness.

Science and Technology—Great Expectations?
I am not alone in this belief or desire. Take science and technology, for example.

A new national survey[2] finds that the vast majority of Americans want this country to be the world leader in scientific and technological progress as we enter the next century. They believe that public policy and federal investment should encourage education, research, and careers in science and technology, in order to build a better future for the nation as a whole and for the everyday lives of individual citizens.

And yet, we do not seem to have the will to stay on this course.

One major scientific project illustrates the point. A decade ago the United States committed itself to constructing the Superconducting Supercollider (SSC), a huge new particle accelerator that would have helped us to answer critical questions in particle physics and perhaps discover another force of nature. The frontier technology required to build this project also could have led to important technological innovations of practical benefit to the general society. We invested over $2 billion and got construction well underway. Then we simply changed our mind, walked away, and left a lifeless, partially excavated tunnel in central Texas—too expensive.[3]

But more than just expense was involved. We—the science community and the federal government—knew that this was an expensive undertaking when it was conceived and given the go-ahead. It could have been a truly international project, but it was supported in part in order to do it all ourselves, in a nationalistic spirit. Yes, the Japanese were invited to help fund it, but only after the concepts and designs were completed and construction was underway—hardly a true international undertaking.

Then there was the matter of location. The SSC was vigorously supported by Congress and by the public in several parts of the country—until it was sited. Not surprisingly, it is more attractive to support an activity in one's state or district than if it is located thousands of miles away. Yet, in reality, facilities like the SSC would be shared by researchers—faculty and graduate students from all around the nation and the world.

My purpose here is not to argue that the SSC should have been built; many good people disagreed about that. My point is to ask why we cannot conceive and carry through such bold ventures— why our commitments have no staying power.

Other science and technology programs also illustrate the point. Take, for example, our nation's magnetic fusion program. As the trauma of the 1970s' oil embargo and other "wakeup calls" regarding worldwide energy needs have receded in our memories, we have ceased to think much about the future of energy supplies and use. The most conservative analyses indicate that we will need at least to double worldwide energy production by 2050 if nations around the world are going to have the opportunity to become industrialized and improve their standards of living. At the same time, doing this in a way that does not degrade the earth's atmosphere to an intolerable extent represents a major challenge. Just consider one country, China, with a population of 1.2 billion people, which is developing its industrial base and meeting its heating needs primarily by burning coal. Meeting the demand for energy throughout the world will require new technologies for large-scale generation of heat and electricity that are relatively environmentally benign and that employ readily available fuels. It is difficult, if not impossible, to construct a scenario that does not involve substantial use of thermonuclear fusion reactors for this purpose. They offer the potential of using essentially inexhaustible fuel, producing very little radioactivity and releasing no carbon dioxide into the atmosphere.

The problem is that fusion science and technology are very complex and the state of the art must be advanced considerably over the next few decades. A great deal has been learned, but much remains to be done. In 1995, the U.S. magnetic-fusion program was funded at a level of $375 million and scheduled to increase substantially in the years ahead, in large part to meet our obligations to the International Thermonuclear Experimental Reactor (ITER) project. ITER is a large joint undertaking of the United States, Europe, Russia, and Japan. In 1996, however, funding for the U.S. magnetic-fusion program has been cut to $244 million—and is headed toward a still lower level in 1997. In order to maintain a viable program in the most essential basic fusion science and technology, the United States will likely need to drop its commitment to ITER. Reducing our overall fusion program to such levels decreases the probability that our companies will be major players in the provision of power generation plants in the expanding world markets as we approach the middle of the next century. Furthermore, we greatly increase the risk that no acceptable means of meeting world energy needs will be available.

Now let us turn to two bold ventures that, in fact, appear to be moving toward realization: the Space Station and the Human Genome Project.

The Space Station is primarily a technology, rather than a science, project. To a far greater extent, however, it is about humans in space. I believe that reaching beyond the boundaries of earth has an intrinsic value—it is as surely a part of the ongoing human adventure as Hillary and Norgay's ascent of Mount Everest, the Lewis and Clark expedition, the sixteenth-century explorations of Vasco da Gama, or the fifth-century Polynesian expeditions across 2,300 miles of open ocean to Hawaii.

Some of the most wondrous and important explorations of space have been made remotely, by spacecraft with no crews aboard: the Hubble Telescope's observations of the Shoemaker-Levy Comet collision with the planet Jupiter, or the Galileo Space Probe's magnificent exploration of Europa, Ganymede, and other Jovian moons. Remote exploration through technology should continue to expand our understanding and sense of wonder about the universe.

Still, the human presence in space captures the imagination of most people. The realization that in the entire sweep of human history, my generation was the first to go beyond the bounds of the earth is both a marvel and an inspiration. Children, in particular, remain entranced by this adventure—always a sure sign that something is worthwhile.

Now, fundamentally, the Space Station can do only two things that cannot be done in other ways. It can put humans into a microgravity environment for very long periods of time, and it can put very massive objects into orbit for very long periods of time. Why should we want to do this? For one thing, we will be able to perform empirical medical studies that are necessary preludes to future interplanetary flights.

And while the Space Station is basically a technology project, the ability to place massive objects in orbit for sustained periods of time appears to be leading to an important, though initially unintended, role for the station in fundamental science. The Alpha Magnetic Spectrometer, conceived by MIT/CERN physicist Samuel Ting, will be placed on the station. There the device, which will weigh two tons and be about a meter high and a meter in diameter, will allow us to study the properties and origin of cosmic particles and nuclei, including antimatter and dark matter. Discovering the presence of either material will increase our understanding of the early universe and could potentially lead to a clearer understanding of the actual origin of the universe and to the discovery of antimatter stars and galaxies.

The Space Station, whose history and congressional support is checkered, to say the least, appears to be moving toward reality for two reasons. First, it is an international project that overtly became a tool of U.S. foreign policy. Second, there is broad public enthusiasm for human space travel.

The Human Genome Project is the one bold, high-profile, large-scale science project that appears to be moving at a direct, determined pace toward its intended goal. The idea is to tap our newly discovered knowledge of the structure of genes and chromosomes in order to improve our understanding of the physical structure of human life, and, ultimately, to make possible dramatic advances in medical science and health care. Originally, it was thought that a map of the entire human genome could be completed by 1998. In fact, this program has been so successful that the mapping was completed in 1996, and work has now begun on the vastly larger task of sequencing the human genome.

The pace of success has been so rapid because project leaders such as Eric Lander and his team at MIT/Whitehead Institute recognized early on that this was not a task for thousands of biologists and technicians working ploddingly with micropipettes. Rather, it was a problem to be solved through the creative and careful application of combinatorial mathematics, computer science, and robotic automation. Technological innovation, combined with human imagination, made the difference.

In addition, this project has been able to proceed on course because Congress and the public understand that the medical advances so important to all of us spring from such basic biomedical research. They are willing to support the necessary investment in this area because they share the vision and can understand the potential for dramatic returns—in the form of better health and improved quality of life.

It is much more difficult, however, to generate such shared vision for basic research that does not hold such immediately recognizable benefits. We have a quandary. Most Americans, when asked, say that they expect science and technology to solve some or most of the problems faced by our society, and that in order for that to happen, we should invest in research and put more emphasis on science in our schools. But at the moment, at least as far as the long-term prospects for research funding go, we seem to be moving in the opposite direction.

Somehow, as a nation, we are unable or unwilling to make the sustained investment or have the confidence that will ensure the kind of future we want—a future made brighter by cures for cancer and mental illness; by clean, renewable energy; by sustainable industrial development; by broadly accessible transportation and information systems; by affordable food and shelter; and by expanded horizons.

There is legitimate concern about how much we can afford to do. We need to balance the national budget so that future generations will not be burdened with our debt. Fair enough. But we need to distinguish between spending for the moment and investing in the future. Just as we cannot saddle the coming generations with our financial debt, neither can we saddle them with our societal debt through lack of concern for the future. We must invest in that future—through education, through research, and through attaining common purpose.

Education—Pass, Fail, or Excel?

The American educational system certainly developed through a series of bold assertions and actions. It is an essential part of our national heritage. What assertion could have been more bold in the eighteenth and nineteenth centuries than the belief that for a democracy to function and a nation to thrive, education must be the universal right of our young? What action could have been more bold than the passage of the Morrill Act, providing a large grant of land to each state to enable the establishment of universities that would provide higher education to vast numbers of young men and women, mostly of modest means? And, in our own century, what step could have been more dramatic, or have better provided for our future, than the establishment of the GI Bill? This is the stuff of greatness, nation building, and empowerment.

Today, however, we have evolved into a truly paradoxical situation. We have, by a huge margin, the greatest and most effective system of higher education in the world—in terms of quality, accessibility, and creation of new knowledge. At the same time, we have a system of primary and secondary education that is a national shame, one that is a surefire determinant of national decline if it is not corrected.

Repeatedly we have set national goals to be met by our schools by the year 2000—just four years hence: goals that call for our students to be first in the world in science and mathematics achievement, and for every school to be free of drugs and violence. But few seem serious about accomplishing such goals. Too ambitious.

Our schools, especially in large cities, have had thrust upon them social ills with which they are not prepared to deal—parental indifference, students with low expectations, outmoded and decaying infrastructure, political infighting, misplaced ideology, meaningless bureaucracies, and insufficient financial support. But these are symptoms. They are symptoms of a loss of national will and vision, uncertain or nonexistent values, and lack of respect for our most important profession—the profession of teaching our children.

I do not profess to know the answer to improving America's public schools, but it must begin with a bold reassertion that nothing is more important than preparing our young to face the future.

To do that, I suggest that we must give our students the ability to live, act, and contribute meaningfully in a world that is ever changing. This will require far more than simple mastery over a body of knowledge. We need to prepare our students with a solid foundation in the sciences, social sciences, and the humanities to appreciate what they encounter, and we need to do so in ways that will provide them with the skills to negotiate the unknown. To be prepared for the future, our students must be intellectually adventurous.

This is not the place to lay out a set of educational goals for our schools, but I would suggest that there is much to be learned from a set of national standards for science education recently developed by the National Research Council.[4] These standards are based on principles that could apply to many fields. They are based on studying the changing needs of our populace, the changing nature of science itself, and successful educational practices. The standards promote science as discovery, rather than science as a collection of facts to be memorized and accepted. Students are encouraged to develop skills of analysis and synthesis and perspective. Our educators should explore these standards as well as the associated pedagogical techniques. If they were to be adopted, we would see some fundamental changes in the way we assess the progress and preparation of our students. There is much to be learned that could inspire a whole new generation of students and teachers.

Setting ambitious educational goals is one thing. But we will not attain them unless there is broad societal recognition of the importance of the teaching profession. We must support our committed teachers, and we must create a new generation of teachers who are well educated, future-oriented, technologically literate, willing to be accountable, and excited to explore new ways of teaching and learning.

This is only the necessary condition, however; it is far from sufficient. These teachers must be supported by our citizenry of all ages, by government at all levels, by the mass media and the entertainment industry, by sports figures, by the criminal justice system, and, above all, by the parents and guardians of the young. They must be provided with the tools, the resources, the financial rewards, and the respect to do the job that must be done.

There is progress on at least one of these fronts. There appears to be enthusiasm and action at both federal and state levels, and within the private sector, for connecting all of our schools to the Internet by the end of the decade. This is a bold move, and it is appropriate. But the technical and financial requirements and capabilities must be thought through with great care, though expeditiously. Then the real question must be addressed: How can this new technology enhance learning?

First, of course, teachers must have the necessary understanding of and access to computers and information systems. But beyond that, the community of educators must become a learning and sharing organization. Herein lies the promise: There must be ways of sharing and learning from each other's experiences. The theory and practice of learning organizations must be tapped for techniques applicable to our educational system in the large.

The use of the World Wide Web and related tools holds huge promise for sharing learning resources. In the hands of skilled educators networked across the country, one school can produce a small, effective video, text, or other segment on, say, basic cell biology. Another school can produce brief segments about elementary algebra, another can address instruction in Spanish, and yet another may develop an exciting history unit. Individual teachers can then pull different units together to form coherent learning tools for the use of each class or student. By making all of these units available through the World Wide Web, it will be possible to share expertise, and achieve savings, on an unprecedented scale. There is no reason that this kind of collaboration need be restricted to the United States. The opportunities to share and work in education across national boundaries should be seriously explored; they will serve future generations well.

Are We Still a Land of Opportunity?

When we think of the future, scientific and technological innovations often come to mind. But the quality of our future will have even more to do with human relations than it does with science and technology. If this nation is to thrive—economically, socially, politically—we must do all we can to ensure that all of our citizens are able to reach their full potential. Only then will we realize the full benefits to be found in a society peopled with different cultures, races, and nationalities.

Race and Society—One Nation or Many?

In the 1950s and 1960s, we as a nation determined that we would build a racially integrated, nondiscriminatory society, and we recognized that various interim commitments and corrective actions would be required until we reached that goal. Full attainment of that goal has proved more elusive than most anticipated. We now seem to be backing off in many ways—too ideological; too uncomfortable; too difficult.

Educational institutions have had central roles in both the action and debate throughout this period. Fundamentally, this is because of our special responsibility to prepare young people to take their full place in our society. Indeed, America's course in these matters was largely set by the 1954 Supreme Court decision in *Brown* v. *Board of Education* that laid the foundation for the affirmative-action initiatives of the 1960s by ordering racial integration of public schools with all deliberate speed.

Today, more than forty years after *Brown* v. *Board of Education*, we still find ourselves at the center of discussion, evaluation, and legal decisions about race and diversity. Largely because of explicit actions to increase access to our colleges and universities, most have become much more diverse racially, culturally, and economically. The presence and role of women on our campuses have improved dramatically. Still, most campuses cannot be judged to be broadly representative of the makeup of contemporary America. Statistics regarding most measures of academic success and access of young people to career, professional, and leadership tracks tell us that the goals set in the 1950s and 1960s have not yet been achieved. My sense is that we are losing will, ignoring realities, falling into political partisanship, and, not infrequently, introducing mean-spiritedness into the national debate on these matters.

Effectively addressing issues of race and diversity is too essential to the future of the United States to allow it to be dissipated in partisan rhetoric. Maintaining our momentum is too urgent to allow it to be defined away through narrow, technical judicial decisions. Reinvigorating a national commitment is too demanding to allow it to drown in a sea of red tape. We need both idealism and pragmatism, but we cannot, through what Father Theodore Hesburgh refers to as "combat fatigue," enter the next century without making real progress toward broad equality.

It astounds me how frequently the issue of diversity is addressed as if it were an abstract concept. Racial diversity is a reality of American life in 1996, and we know with certainty that it will be an even more dominant reality in, say, 2015, when the children being born this year are of college age. In 2015, the college-age population of the United States will be 16 percent African-American and 19 percent Hispanic-American, and the mix of new immigrants to our shores, especially from Asia and Southeast Asia, also will contribute more substantially to the makeup of our citizenry.

By the year 2015, the work force will be one-third white male, one-third white female, and one-third people of color. All these workers will be toiling to support not only themselves, but all of us who, as retirees, will be dependent upon them—and they will constitute a much smaller proportion of our population. (In 2015, there will be only half as many people working and supporting the retired population as there were in 1960.) If they do not form a cohesive, productive society, the future will indeed be bleak. This prognostication is truly daunting, especially when combined with the fact that we will need to compete in a marketplace and economy that will be even more globalized and integrated than today.

Thus, even if we are willing to ignore the historical imperative and noble goal of equality and true integration, we must be problem solvers and set a sound course for our rapidly changing nation.

It is sorely tempting to declare victory and turn our back on affirmative action and related processes in America. How pleased I would be if we could legitimately assume that all of our citizens have reached a sufficient state of actual equality of opportunity and access that we could adopt simple, race-blind approaches to all that we do. That, of course, is the goal. But is it an honest evaluation of the situation today? One need only peruse the extensive tabulations of national statistics regarding wages, crime, education, health, and many other parameters in Andrew Hacker's book *Two Nations: Black and White, Separate, Hostile, Unequal* to know that we have not achieved anything approaching equality across the racial boundaries of our society. If that is not convincing, read the front page of any urban newspaper on any given day.

Yet we are retreating. The federal district court ruling in *Hopwood* v. *University of Texas* has already had repercussions around the country—as organized efforts to end affirmative action continue to grow. The actions of the University of California's Board of Regents are well known; and in Colorado, the governing board of the university system has cut back on affirmative action programs. Other efforts include legislative moves in Pennsylvania and Arizona to outlaw affirmative action, and more than a dozen campaigns to amend the constitutions of various states.

In this context, I use the term *affirmative action* rather broadly to refer to programs or actions that specifically foster access or participation of minority groups or women in educational programs or jobs. This breadth seems appropriate in discussing universities in light of recent court decisions. MIT's admissions process is consistent with the Supreme Court's 1978 *Bakke* decision that universities may consider race "as one factor among many" in making admissions decisions. We build our admitted class to bring together students from diverse geographic, economic, cultural, racial, and experiential backgrounds, all of whom have exhibited the intellectual capacity, achievement, and motivation that are needed to succeed and benefit from MIT. Furthermore, our undergraduate financial aid is awarded solely on the basis of demonstrated financial need.

Yet in 1996, in *Hopwood* v. *University of Texas*, the Fifth Circuit Court of Appeals effectively reversed the *Bakke* decision for public institutions in Texas, Mississippi, and Louisiana, by declaring that "*any* consideration of race or ethnicity by the law school for the purpose of achieving a diverse student body is not a compelling interest" and therefore is not permitted.

I do not wish to defend across the board all federal affirmative action laws and set-aside policies, with their attendant red tape, cumbersome bureaucracies, and often artificial metrics. But I do want to defend the core concept that determined, often race-specific consideration and effort are still essential to move us toward the integrated, cohesive society we will need in the years ahead. The society I believe we will need is one in which individuals can realize their potential, and in which we can draw effectively on the individual and collective strengths and talents of our citizens of all colors and ethnicities. We cannot command, decree, or wish into existence such a nation. Rather we must work proactively to build it through the environments and opportunities we create for learning and working.

The idea that affirmative action programs are unnecessary or even unconstitutional is gaining momentum just at a time when we in science, engineering, and higher education are beginning to see some real results from these programs.

Last summer, the American Council on Education released its study on minorities in higher education,[5] and reported a record number of PhD's awarded to black graduate students in 1995. And over the past eight years, the National Science Foundation reports,[6] there has been a 75-percent increase in the number of science and engineering doctorates awarded to black graduate students—from 319 in 1987 to 557 in 1995. The media and others have hailed this as a dramatic increase. It is, indeed, real progress; nonetheless, the absolute numbers are stunningly small. Last year, for example, the number of blacks receiving the doctorate in electrical engineering in the United States rose 40 percent over the previous year—to twenty-four. Yet this is out of a total of 966 doctorates awarded in that field.

And yet there are arguments over the reasons for this progress. Supporters of affirmative action claim the increase as evidence of the programs' effectiveness, while critics argue that it is the result of increased educational opportunities, and that any benefits of affirmative action are offset by the negative effects of what they regard as preferential treatment of minorities.

Did "affirmative action" play a role in this modest success? It should not be a difficult matter to assess how many of these new PhD graduates were definitely encouraged or enabled to reach this high level of attainment by specific programs or support. It should not be a matter of guesswork; the data should be obtained and affirmative action and outreach programs should be objectively evaluated on the basis of outcomes over time. It should not be a matter of ideology of the left or of the right. We should assess where we are, demonstrate what does and doesn't work, and get on with the job.

In the current legal environment, attorneys are recommending to organizations that were established specifically to promote educational opportunity for minority students that they modify their eligibility criteria to indicate that they will review applications without regard to the applicant's ethnicity. Frankly, this strikes me as a strange and artificial approach.

My own view is that we must hold to our principles if our nation is to benefit from the full range of talent needed to meet the challenges of a changing world. Our journey is not over. Our goal is not attained.

I believe that the time will come when affirmative action programs will no longer be necessary, but for now, we still have a compelling need for proactive efforts, despite calls by some that what is needed instead is simply stronger enforcement of antidiscrimination laws. Indeed, as Tom Wicker put it in his recent book, *Tragic Failure*: "If enforcement of antidiscrimination laws is the alternative to affirmative action, race, sex, and ethnic discrimination will be with us for a long time."

An Open Society—to Whom?

Race is not the only focus of the argument about how open our society should be. These are economically difficult times in America—at least relative to our aspirations and to the postwar boom years. And as times get tight, there is a natural tendency to turn inward. So once again, we hear concerns that we should not be educating so many foreign graduate students. We hear that immigrants are a major cause of our woes. And we keep pulling apart into homogeneous groupings of one sort or another. But just because these are natural or understandable tendencies does not make them right.

America has always been a nation of immigrants and we have always been a land of opportunity. These statements perhaps sound quaint or old-fashioned, but they are true, and we must retain their spirit.

Each year my wife, Becky, and I host a dinner in our home for the men and women who are retiring from the tenured faculty ranks of MIT. These are always extraordinary assemblages of talented and accomplished colleagues—people who have defined MIT and who have defined their professional and scholarly fields. No lack of bold thought there!

Yet, as I survey that room each spring, I realize how much MIT and indeed America have benefited from our being open to those from other countries, and how wise has been our tradition of selecting and advancing people on the basis of their talent and accomplishment rather than their wealth or nationality. Now, some might say that this represents a passing era, that what I am observing has its origins in the intellectual migrations from Europe associated with the turmoil of the World War II era. Or it might even represent the vestiges of the times during which the leading universities in science and engineering were in Germany and England.

No, it is an ongoing fact that the excellence of our institutions is due in very large measure to our openness to international scholars. MIT faculty who have received the Nobel Prize include individuals who were born in Japan, India, Italy, and Mexico. Our provost was born in Israel. We have deans who were born in Canada and Australia. Almost all came to the United States as graduate students.

In fact, about one-third of all PhD degrees in science and engineering earned in U.S. universities are awarded to foreign citizens. (In engineering alone, half of the PhD's are earned by foreign citizens.) Many of these doctoral recipients initially pursue their careers in the United States, and about 40 percent of them appear to remain here permanently. What a magnificent resource for our industries, universities, and government laboratories! Openness and meritoc-racy are what have made our universities great, and we must con-tinue that spirit and philosophy in our national endeavors.

At the same time, we should concentrate on improving both science education and general education in this country's K–12 system in order to increase the number of motivated, well-prepared students entering universities and colleges. We should more highly value intellectual pursuits and celebrate the accom-plishments of those who contribute to our health and quality of life by advancing science and technology. This is the way to ensure that, in the long run, our graduate programs have a larger, more stable base of U.S. students.

We must, however, continue to provide access, opportunity, and welcome to the brilliant immigrants who contribute so much to our society—people like Institute Professor Hermann Haus, who received the National Medal of Science this year. Recollecting the call from John Gibbons, the President's Science Advisor, Professor Haus said, "I did not trust my senses, at first. After the news sunk in, the thoughts that came to my mind were that I was grateful to my fate for having come to the U.S., a victim of the 1945 ethnic cleansing in Yugoslavia; for becoming a citizen; and for the recognition I received on account of work I thoroughly enjoyed and for the privilege of association with outstanding students and colleagues."

I can think of no more eloquent description of what it means for this country to be the land of opportunity. We must retain our commitment to this bold dream.

A Closing Note

Boldness and openness are qualities that we as a nation must seek to preserve and advance. We in America's research univer-sities have a particular duty to do so.

Boldness flows from a spirit of adventure and a "can-do" attitude long associated with America. These characteristics must again be dominant. To be effective, however, we must remember that boldness must be accompanied by staying power. Staying power is waning. We are increasingly better at starting things than at carrying them through. Contemporary politics demands "change" and new vision at least every two to four years. Our budget cycles cause us to be unreliable international partners as we start and stop projects. Staying power does not mean stagnation, it permits the fulfillment of bold ideas, with plenty of correction, evolution, and adaptation along the way.

Openness flows from a spirit of generosity that has long characterized America, but which today appears to be in peril under the stresses of change, slow economic growth, and increasing uncertainty of the future. We must not allow this to happen, for openness and generosity can only be replaced by narrow expectations and selfishness.

We must, instead, choose to be bold and to be generous of spirit. We must believe in the possibility of greatness, for our society today and for the generations to come.

Notes

1. Edwin H. Land, "Generation of Greatness: The Idea of University in an Age of Science," Ninth Annual Arthur Dehon Little Memorial Lecture, delivered at the Massachusetts Institute of Technology, Cambridge, Massachusetts, May 22, 1957.

2. A description of the project appeared at that time on the Web: "The Texas Supercollider was to be 87 km long in an oval with major axis of 30 km and minor axis of 24 km. It was being driven by four TBMs which were erecting a 4.27 m internal diameter concrete segmental lining, when funding was withdrawn by the U.S. government. Some 37 shafts and 25 km of utility adits were also cancelled at various stages of construction. The ring was located in the Austin Chalk, the perfect TBM medium with ucs of 14,250 kPa, and advances of 80 m/shift were

regularly recorded. The TBMs were withdrawn and the shafts capped. The final bill was not disclosed."

3. National survey on public opinion of science and technology, commissioned by the National Science and Technology Medals Foundation, and conducted in June 1996 by the Roper Center for Public Opinion Research at the University of Connecticut.

4. *National Science Education Standards* (Washington, D.C.: National Academy Press, 1996).

5. Reginald Wilson and Deborah Carter, "Minorities in Higher Education 1995–96: 14th Annual Status Report," American Council on Education, June 1996.

6. *Selected Data on Science and Engineering Doctorate Awards, 1995*, Division of Science Resource Studies, Directorate for Social, Behavioral and Economic Sciences, National Science Foundation (NSF 96-303).

8

Stewards of the Future: The Evolving Roles of Academia, Industry, and Government

1996–1997

The future is not some place we are going to, but one we are creating. The paths are not to be found, but made, and the activity of making them changes both the maker and the destination.
—John Schaar

In this period I returned to expand on themes sketched in my 1993–1994 report. The relative roles of the public and private sector seemed to be shifting in fundamental ways, with the themes of privatization and economic competition dominating public discourse. It seemed that industry would increasingly shoulder responsibility for certain social goods such as environmental quality. The widespread availability of the Internet, and later the World Wide Web, created new modalities for producing and sharing knowledge. At MIT we established a Council on Industry Relations, a Council on the Environment, and a Council on Educational Technology to analyze the changing situation and guide the evolution of our institutional role.

The idea of a national innovation system—a loosely coupled collaboration of universities, industry, and government to generate new knowledge and technology, and to educate men and women to use it wisely to create new products, processes, and services and move them into the marketplace—seemed increasingly to be the dominant framework for thinking about our roles in the American economy. Indeed, MIT in partnership with the Council on Competitiveness began planning a National Innovation Summit that would bring leaders of government, industry, labor, and academia at the highest levels to our campus the following year for a seminal discussion of these matters.

I believed that MIT should lead certain changes in education, especially in engineering and management—retaining the underlying scientific rigor, but anchored more firmly to modern industry; deemphasizing narrow disciplinary approaches; increasing team experiences; giving more attention to living and working in an international environment; and making better use of the Internet and World Wide Web. We were increasingly working in partnership with industry on global environmental problems and to flesh out the concept of sustainable development: working toward a framework and scientific and technical knowledge base for synergy between economic development and sound environmental stewardship. All of this needed to be built on a substrate of solid federal and industrial support for long-term, fundamental research in universities so that an openly shared base of scientific and technological knowledge would be established. In the fast-paced, market-driven world of contemporary industry, companies had come to contribute very little to this shared base.

As we approach the twenty-first century, we will be overwhelmed by the rhetoric of change. Though often overblown, this rhetoric stems from a human tendency to mark passages. Such observances can serve us well if they result in introspection, recognition of new realities, and thoughtful planning for the future. Change, whether or not associated with the approach of the new millennium, is a reality. And change brings with it new opportunities and responsibilities, many derived from advances in science and technology, and from the concomitant globalization of our communications, economies, and politics.

Much of the change we are currently experiencing seems to be bringing with it a substantial rebalancing of social responsibilities among the private and public sectors, especially in the United States. It remains to be seen how deep and long-lived this rebalancing is. To some extent, it is a matter of politics, in the narrow sense of the word, but to a greater extent this rebalancing of responsibilities is likely to flow from the deeper forces bringing about such change in our society.

What do I mean by rebalancing the roles of the private and public sectors? Two major themes of the current decade are economic competition and privatization. There is less trust in governments, and increased trust in business and market efficiency. Central planning generally has been found to fail, crumbling away with the destruction of the Berlin Wall and the Soviet State. Entrepreneurial activity is increasingly valued.

In the United States, with Congress and the administration having pledged to balance the federal budget, many long-standing federal programs will be reduced or eliminated. For the most part, however, the needs that gave rise to those programs will not disappear, and the private sector will find itself with some new or expanded responsibilities.

Increasingly, industry will be called on to address issues of common good that extend beyond the traditional principles of market-driven efficiency and shareholder value. Industry may need to write with a more visible hand than that memorialized by Adam Smith in the days when pin factories epitomized high technology and the latest in management theory.

Research universities, too, are affected by these changing circumstances. Today, many of our faculty are developing educational and research programs based on a more direct engagement with national and international priorities. More than ever, we in the universities will be called on to create—and share—scientific and technical knowledge for the common good, and to work in new ways with industry and government in so doing.

In this report, I will trace the changing roles of industry, government, and academia in generating and sharing knowledge, particularly as they bear on two areas essential to our future: a vital economy and a healthy environment.

Creating and Sharing Knowledge

Our nation and world are the beneficiaries of an unprecedented reservoir of knowledge about science and technology. This reservoir has been developed and continually replenished largely by two sources—federally supported university research and education, and research conducted in the national and corporate laboratories. Federal support of university research—the keystone of the nation's ability to advance and use new knowledge—is waning, however. Government investment in research in engineering and the physical sciences is being eroded by inflationary pressures, and even support for biomedical research has slowed to little better than the rate of inflation. There have been significant changes, as well, in the nature of corporate research. Indeed, no more profound change has occurred in large U.S. companies during this decade than the change in their R&D function, and its relation to the creation of products.

Both of these developments have deep implications for education and research in our universities. The new modes of conceiving and producing products and services must be reflected in the education of our students, especially in engineering and management. At the same time, responsibility for fundamental scientific inquiry and basic technological innovation will rest in even larger measure with our research universities.

Changes in Corporate Research and Development
For decades, most large U.S. corporations maintained a central corporate laboratory. These usually had a campuslike environment and encouraged wide-ranging thought and exploration. Scientists and engineers in these laboratories were encouraged to play strong roles in professional societies and scientific conferences, and to publish their research findings in the professional journals. A process essentially like university tenure was followed in selecting and maintaining the senior scientific staff. Most interactions between industry and universities were channeled through the central research laboratories, creating a flow of people and ideas.

Nobel laureate Arno Penzias, then director of Bell Labs, summarized the value of the Labs to AT&T in the early 1980s when he said "Bell Labs' value comes from the fact that we allow enormous freedom of exploration in scientific fields as long as there is a potential application to telecommunications in the long run."

In other words, the best corporate laboratories—Bell, IBM, GE, Xerox, Exxon, and so forth—advanced science and technology, shared most of their discoveries through the scientific literature, and also established technological advances that ultimately manifested themselves in products and processes for the company. Such laboratories gave rise to a remarkable array of transforming innovations, including the transistor, high-temperature superconductivity, the laser printer, and a host of synthetic materials.

Central laboratories also provided in-house consultation for operating divisions, which themselves often undertook research and development, with the clear emphasis on development. Indeed, some laboratories like Bell had different elements that worked directly on product development.

Most of this changed in the late 1980s and early 1990s as corporations adjusted to the new realities of global competition. Increased attention had to be paid to manufacturing processes, which in turn had to be far better integrated with design. More emphasis was placed on reducing costs, addressing customer needs and expectations, reducing product cycle times, addressing new environmental concerns, and manufacturing and selling on a global basis. The demands of meeting these new realities caused a deeper integration of the work of corporate researchers into the specific, more immediate goals of the company. This interweaving of technical and commercial activities changed the nature of R&D. The corporate laboratory often disappeared or was altered so as to be almost unrecognizable.

These changes have been exciting and productive. New intellectual challenges have been established and met. The integration
of researchers into cross-functional teams has created a new style
of fast-paced, complex, and challenging work. Product development began to emerge as a new professional discipline. Most
R&D that continues to be carried out in industrial laboratories
is aimed more directly and strategically at enhancing companies'
product lines. New styles of targeted, and very efficient, scientific
inquiry began to emerge, notably "discovery science," whereby
chemical and pharmaceutical companies, for example, attempt
to optimize the search for medicines, reactions, or products with
prescribed properties.

No corporation can be competitive today without the kind of
focused, integrated R&D described above. However, there may be
a price to be paid. Now that many of their problems in manufacturing and product development have been solved, they can compete well. The strong U.S. economy and low unemployment rate
presumably stem in part from these changes. Indeed, even the Holy
Grail of a balanced federal budget probably owes much more to
this improvement of U.S. industries than to federal policies.

But the next round of competition is likely to be won by those
who innovate, that is, those who create new ideas, products, and
services, those who solve new human problems and create new
commerce. There is a danger that wider-ranging research has
been cut back too far to sustain industrial leadership in the long
run. So much local optimization by individual companies may
leave the larger innovation system impoverished by lack of
broader-based research whose results are shared broadly.

Implications for Universities
In my view, these changes in the corporate world leave universities with dual increases in responsibility. First, we must alter our
education in engineering, management, and, to a lesser extent, in

science as well—in order to prepare our graduates to work and lead in the new industrial world. Second, universities will have an even greater responsibility for conducting broad, basic research. Some might argue that these two responsibilities are incompatible. I do not believe that is the case, however, as long as we draw from our special strengths and work with others to address our common challenges and opportunities.

As we move ahead, I believe that there are a number of features that should be incorporated into our educational programs, particularly (but not exclusively) those in engineering:

• We must begin with the sine qua non that we are going to retain the rigor and the scientific basis that underlies engineering education and practice. Having said this, I believe it is time that we anchor ourselves somewhat more firmly with industry. "Anchor" may not be the right term, because we are hooking onto something that is moving in new directions very rapidly. Still, we do need to maintain much closer contact with industry as it is evolving.

• We have to deemphasize narrow disciplinary approaches, particularly in the structure of our curricula and in the way we help students learn to think. We need to pay more attention to the context in which engineering is practiced. This sounds simple, but we are finding it very challenging. We need to give students more hands-on engineering experience, or grounding in how to "design-build-operate," as we like to call it.

• We need to educate students to work better in teams. Do not misunderstand: Ultimately, the most important strength we have is individuals and their capacity for innovation. However, every organization that I know about accomplishes most of its work in teams because of the complexity of today's tasks. Indeed, many teams in business and engineering today are in fact world-wide electronic communities, linked by a variety of telecommunications channels.

• We need to become more adept at preparing our students for living and working in an international environment. Globalization is not something that is coming, it is something that has already happened. Academic institutions are behind the curve somewhat in bringing this reality into our educational programs. My guess is that the key is going to be engagement—engagement by U.S. universities with organizations, governments, and industries operating in other countries. We tend to work best and learn the most when we're actively engaged in partnerships of one sort or another.

• We have to continue developing and using information technologies in education, no matter how rapidly they advance. At MIT and elsewhere, books are published and courses taught on the World Wide Web. Nonetheless, I continue to believe that we have just scratched the surface of what the new technologies make available to us in education and learning. This is a time for experimenting. It is a time for networking among U.S. universities to learn which new approaches to learning are working well and which are not.

All these changes, and others that will follow, require thought and development by dedicated faculty, but they also may require conscious involvement and support on the part of industry.

As noted earlier, the changes in the nature of research within industry will place an even larger responsibility for conducting broad, basic research with our universities. Since we generally do this very well, that is fine. However, who will be our patron? First and foremost, the federal government. There seems to be general agreement on this point across the political spectrum. Indeed, formal statements by large numbers of industry CEOs, chambers of commerce, state governors and legislators, members of Congress, and university leaders seem to indicate an effective national consensus on the importance of strong federal

investment in university research. However, despite the committed leadership of key members of Congress on behalf of science and engineering research, that agreement is not translating
into the increased levels of support needed to sustain this effort
in the long run. Furthermore, many in the government ask the
legitimate question, If industry ultimately benefits from university research, then why are they not paying for more of it?

This is closely related to the question, Why doesn't industry
itself increase the long-term, basic research it conducts and contribute more to the commonly shared base of scientific and technological knowledge? The answer generally is that, in the short
term, the market doesn't demand it. Furthermore, the value
derived from such endeavors does not necessarily accrue to the
organization that conducts research that is not directly applicable to its product line.

How do we resolve this conundrum? We might start by considering our national innovation system—and how it depends
on academia, industry, and government working together in new
ways to sustain a vital economy.

Sustaining America's Innovation System

The health of our economy depends on a vigorous system for
supporting innovation. America's innovation system consists of
academic, industrial, and governmental institutions working
together to support and generate new ideas, to educate the next
generation of innovators and entrepreneurs, and to transfer the
practical benefits of new scientific and technological knowledge
to society.

The great public and private research universities that are spread
across our land play an indispensable role in this system. Their faculties conceive and conduct the research that generates a great deal
of our new knowledge, and in the process they educate the young

men and women who will become the inventors, innovators, industrial leaders, company founders, teachers, and doctors of the future. Their graduate students, carrying new ideas from their research experiences as they enter the workforce, are the primary means of technology transfer from academia to industry.

This has been possible in large measure because of wise investment by the federal government in higher education and research. Every federal dollar spent to support university research does double duty. Not only does it pay for the conduct of the research, it simultaneously supports the education of graduate students who learn as they work together with faculty on research in science, engineering, medicine, and business.

I believe we must give the highest priority to maintaining our nation's world leadership in science and technology. We must sustain the vitality of university research and education as the foundation of America's innovation system. Beyond this, we must support an innovation system that is not bound by one-size-fits-all government regulations, but thrives on a mixture of creativity, competition, and cooperation.

Meeting such a challenge holds implications for the responsibilities of both the public and private sectors. The private sector will need to take increased responsibility for contributing more to the base of shared knowledge and to better define its role in the long-term sustaining of technological leadership. The public sector must more effectively recognize both the underlying support it must provide for research and education and its responsibility to provide a business-friendly and research-friendly tax and regulatory environment.

The Importance of New Partnerships
Beyond that, we must even more effectively couple university research to industry and business by building partnerships. Yet we must do so without destroying the fundamental values and

culture that allow universities to serve society over the centuries, and not just at the moment.

During the last year, the Council on Competitiveness, a nonprofit group of industry, labor, and university leaders, has convened a series of bipartisan, multisector meetings across the country. These have brought state governors, CEOs of large corporations, university leaders, representatives of Congress and the Clinton administration, entrepreneurs, labor leaders, directors of federal laboratories, and venture capitalists together for intense discussions about strengthening and sustaining our innovation system.

One of the most pervasive and widely accepted conclusions of these discussions is that the greatest opportunity to strengthen the U.S. system of innovation lies in an improved synergy among industry, universities, and the federal research apparatus.[1] Creating a policy environment that encourages partnerships across sectors seems to be essential. This will require attitudinal changes, mutual respect, a greater degree of openness, and purposeful dialogue. It will work only when projects and programs are seen as mutually beneficial and when all parties are genuinely interested in the problem at hand. This generally argues that such partnerships will deal with moderate to long-term issues, and with sorting out emerging new principles underlying contemporary industrial operations and organizations.

A ground-breaking new partnership of this type is MIT's Center for Innovation in Product Development. The establishment of this center was motivated by the enormous intellectual challenge of identifying the basic principles of effective product development, and the need to better educate engineers and managers to undertake the development of new products in today's fast-paced, competitive, and complex and globalized industrial world. The center's existence was greatly facilitated and accelerated by the National Science Foundation's Engineering

Research Center program. In the end, however, without the shared perception of need and opportunity among MIT and several companies, large and small, the center would not have been possible.

Working closely with a consortium of high-level managers from Xerox, Ford, ITT, and other leading corporations, the center will draw on MIT's unique combination of strengths in both engineering and management to conduct cutting-edge research in such topics as the better matching of technology development to the timing of market opportunities, the alignment of product development risks with corporate capabilities, and the translation of consumer preferences into technical specifications. The center will also develop texts and course offerings for both graduate and undergraduate students, and will make these materials available to engineers and managers working in industry.

Other emerging partnerships at MIT involve direct scientific collaboration with companies such as Amgen and Merck. These partnerships involve no federal component. They support mutually agreed-upon basic research problems at the cutting edge of modern biology and biotechnology, and encourage intellectual synergy and sustained dialogue among company and academic scientists. They, too, have a strong emphasis on supporting education, at both the graduate and postdoctoral levels.

Finally, any discussion of America's innovation system must recognize the central importance of entrepreneurship and the establishment of small companies. In this era, it is such "start-up" companies that have created expanding employment. It has been the opportunity to be entrepreneurial that has allowed the U.S. economy to rapidly restructure in the wake of corporate downsizing and international pressures. Finding better ways for large companies, the government, and research universities to work with such emerging companies is the key to strong innovation and its translation into economic and social progress.

In the end, however, the single most important contribution of research universities to our innovation system is the education of men and women with an understanding of emerging new science and technology and the creativity, mindset, and skills to apply them wisely.

A Sound Environment in a Sound Economy

Another domain in which we all have a vital stake and an inescapable responsibility is the global environment. The growth of human population and activity has fouled the air, depleted the soils, diminished the forests, and degraded our fresh waters. The consequences are immense: Three and a half million people die each year from diseases borne by unsanitary water; hunger is a fact of life for countless more; the damage to the ozone layer threatens us all; and we face the annual loss of thousands of species.

Stewarding the earth's environment will require industry, universities, and government to assume new responsibilities and to join forces in new ways.

For the past thirty years or so, environmental concerns in this country have been dominated by a mentality of government regulation and remediation. At its best, this has dramatically improved our health and quality of life. At its worst, it has led to unreasonable legalistic resolutions, adversarial decision processes, and priorities set without sound scientific or economic bases. Perhaps this was inevitable as our understanding of the issues developed within the context of a high-consumption economy and mature industrial infrastructure. Many current industrial processes were developed in an age when resources seemed inexhaustible, and when it seemed incomprehensible that the day might come when humankind's influence might substantially threaten the balance of the global environment.

Today, however, we understand that many resources are finite, that industrial development affects our air and water and perhaps our climate, and that the green revolution in agriculture has its price. What is new in all of this is our awareness of the enormous complexity of the problems and of their possible solutions. Understanding and analysis of environmental issues, and the development of innovative solutions, require a complicated interaction of basic science, engineering, economics, politics, social theory, and education.

I am optimistic that in the long run we will make great progress. Why? Because we all cherish good health and the beauty of our earth, and because this is extraordinarily rich and fertile territory for academic investigation and industry problem-solving. Furthermore, many aspects of good environmental stewardship at heart involve increasing efficiency—efficiency of energy conversion, efficiency in the use and processing of materials, efficiency in transporting people and goods, and efficiency in the use of financial resources. Engineers, economists, organizational experts, and managers all value good efficiency on some plane, so working to reduce waste and environmental damage has an innate appeal to many of the key disciplines.

However, there are counterforces:

• Our political and journalistic systems are susceptible to nearly random inputs. Hence we tend to develop "issues of the day" rather than to analyze and prioritize problems to the best of our ability.

• The pressures of intense competition coupled with the regulatory systems do not always lead to optimal strategies for cleaner operations and environmental improvements. Hence the investments in research and industrial infrastructure or cooperative activities that are needed for the long haul are not always made.

• Commitment at the top of organizations sometimes flags at lower levels where day-to-day pressures dominate.

• Our political system mitigates against the flow of large financial and technical resources across national boundaries for the solution of environmental problems. As a result, the disparities between the north and south, between the developed and the developing worlds, remain serious impediments to a healthy environment.

New Roles and Responsibilities

Industry and academia must play increasingly important and synergistic roles in establishing environmental responsibility and developing effective solutions. We at MIT are working hard to establish this new paradigm—by educating engineers, managers, scientists, economists, and policy experts to analyze environmental issues and synthesize sound solutions. This does not mean only that we need to educate more environmental experts, it means that sound thinking about, and commitment to, sustainable development and environmental stewardship must be an integral part of the education and practice of engineers and managers.

Equally important is the emerging role of MIT and some other leading research universities in convening disparate parties for serious dialogue. Such discourse can help identify the key research issues, improve understanding of how governmental and industrial decisions can be informed by scientific knowledge, and make resource distribution more effective.

This approach has been enthusiastically welcomed by the corporate world, which is finding that sound environmentalism and an anticipation of its requirements is good business.

The growing commitment to a healthy environment on the part of both industry and academia is setting the stage for new partnerships between the public and private sectors. Take, for example, the Montreal Protocols on the reduction of chlorofluorocarbons in the atmosphere in order to halt the damage these do to the earth's protective ozone layer.

These protocols are based on the fundamental scientific work of MIT's Nobel laureate and Institute Professor Mario Molina and his scientific colleagues, including Sherwood Rowland of the University of California at Irvine and Paul Crutzen of the Max Planck Institute for Chemistry in Germany. It is an agreement that rests not only on sound science, but on determined and thoughtful work across complicated political and geographic boundaries to ensure that all the citizens of the world benefit, whether they reside in rich nations or poor ones. The genealogy of the protocols begins with atmospheric chemistry research funded by the federal government, which led to a solid understanding among knowledgeable industry leaders, which in turn led to a political will to execute a thoughtful international agreement. In sum, three sectors played appropriate and highly interacting roles that led to improvements for all.

At MIT we are wrestling with various organizational issues to best approach these matters. As is appropriate in our intellectually diverse and entrepreneurial institution, many efforts have grown somewhat independently and are now interacting with each other.

A particularly effective example of this new approach is the MIT Joint Program on the Science and Policy of Global Change. This program has brought together the talents of faculty, research staff, and students from several disciplines, forming an integrated approach to analysis of global climate change. It is sponsored in a consortial manner by a large number of U.S. and international companies aided by governmental research support, and governmental and public group participation. Central to the program's mission and effectiveness has been the Global

Change Forum, which has become a very well-attended ongoing seminar among high-level scientists, executives, and decision makers from industry and government. It has met twelve times in seven years, generally alternating between MIT and a location in another country. The program participants are working from a common understanding and set of goals, proceeding not from the emotion that has driven much of the environmental debate and decision making in the past, but from a base of mutual learning, research, policy analysis, and public education.

This is not to say that matters of environmental stewardship can or should be approached in a manner devoid of emotion. Emotion has a legitimate role in environmental matters. It is our ability to experience and envision the benefits of a healthy environment that signals to us the importance of environmental stewardship. And it is our ability to envision potential degradation and its effects that leads us to understand the critical necessity for preemptive action. Rational policy analysis, objective science, and sound technology, however, are the extensions of human thought and physical capability that will enable us collectively to establish and accomplish our environmental goals. In other words, *mens et manus*, MIT's mind-and-hand philosophy, is precisely what is called for.

Similarly, we cannot progress by ignoring economic and social realities any more than we can ignore scientific and engineering principles and realities. These provide the framework in which the new responsibilities and opportunities for business and industry emerge. On one plane, business exists to create wealth and to provide for the financial advancement of its shareholders. Of course, on a deeper plane, business exists to advance the human condition. These enterprises produce clothing, shelter, and food, and provide health care, entertainment, and all manner of services. The markets distribute our wealth, provide incentives for productive activity, and, to a significant extent, influence how we interact with our environment and use the resources of the earth.

Unfortunately, markets and businesses, as conceived within the dominant value and social systems, tend to be too dominated by short-term thought and goals to create capital flows from rich to poor and north to south. There arguably is too much local and near-term optimization. But this situation can be improved. Indeed, in my view many leaders of industry are beginning to work toward long-term solutions to environmental and economic problems, and many scholars are working on new constructions that will support this, and that will work with, rather than against, markets.

Sustainable Development

The concept of sustainable development is emerging as a framework for these efforts. Much of the original thinking about this concept has come from business leaders, particularly the Swiss industrialist Stephan Schmidheiny. As he wrote in a declaration prepared for the Business Council for Sustainable Development,

> The world is moving toward deregulation, private initiatives, and global markets. This requires corporations to assume more social, economic and environmental responsibility in defining their roles. We must expand our concept of those who have a stake in our operations to include not only employees and shareholders but also suppliers, customers, neighbors, citizens' groups, and others. . . . Progress toward sustainable development makes good business sense because it can create competitive advantages and new opportunities. But it requires far-reaching shifts in corporate attitudes and new ways of doing business.[2]

Sustainable development sets as a goal providing for the needs of the present generation, including the right to advance economically, while minimizing the risk to future generations' abilities to enjoy the same provision and right. It requires of us a more cooperative, interactive approach, a much longer time horizon in our thinking, a responsibility to educate ourselves about risk and efficiency, and an obligation to develop technologies that are more efficient in their overall use of resources.

Is a world of continual economic development absolutely sustainable? In the sense that this implies total and continual renewal of all resources, clearly not. Both the laws of physical nature and of economics deny us that ideal. However, we should strive to understand what levels of sustainability may be achievable, and strive to approach them in our industrial practices.

This leads to the concept of eco-efficiency. Admittedly it is a vague concept, but it is very important, nonetheless. It requires an awareness of how our systems for generating energy, producing food and goods, or transporting people and materials are intimately linked to environmental quality and sound economies. It requires examining the total flow of materials through the processes of production, use, and reuse. Such an approach could lead, for example, to locating industrial plants in such a way that the "waste" or by-products of one may be used as the resource or raw material of another. Eco-efficiency requires a significant base of research, development, and innovation. Above all, it requires a longer vision and a more integrative style of thought and analysis than we are used to.

This vision and style must be driven not only by concern for our fellow humans, present and future, but by pragmatism and hard-nosed analysis. As environmental awareness and concern become more prevalent, increased efficiency and improvements in "cradle-to-grave" employment of natural materials is becoming good business. If the importance of sustainable development becomes increasingly influential in setting our societal goals, sound environmental stewardship will become even better business.

Indeed, I believe that business and industry are likely to lead our movement toward more sustainable development and improved environmental stewardship. We are beginning to see the necessary proactive yet pragmatic business leadership emerging in several global corporations.

Education and understanding are key to setting and effecting such an agenda. If the world's educational institutions, and particularly our research universities, increasingly focus on the issues of sustainability and resource management, we can ensure that more knowledge is gathered, developed, and shared about these issues. MIT, the University of Tokyo, and the Swiss Federal Institutes of Technology in Zurich have joined together for just that purpose by forming an Alliance for Global Sustainability. We do so in the conviction that universities around the world can make a profound difference in how their societies think and act on the question of global sustainability. The result will be better business and a better environment.

In Conclusion

Ours is a dynamic society, continually redefining its agenda and the relative roles of its players. But some things are so basic to our welfare as to transcend temporal shifts in priorities. A vital economy and a healthy environment are two such fundamentals. They are not incompatible. Working together, universities, industry, and governments can find ways to sustain a sound environment *and* a sound economy.

For universities, this is an exciting time—a time of rapidly expanding knowledge, of engaging even more directly with activities that are vital to the common good, and of working in new ways with industry and government to achieve these goals. We are creating new paths as our relative responsibilities come into a new balance, but one thing is clear: We are all stewards of the future.

Acknowledgments

I would like to recognize the work of MIT's Council on Industry Relations and Council on the Environment, whose work and interviews with leaders from all sectors have been most helpful in forming my personal views on these subjects.

Notes

1. *A Call to Action—1997 Regional Summits on American Innovation*, Council on Competitiveness, 1401 H Street, NW, Washington, DC 20005.

2. Schmidheiny, Stephan, *Changing Course: A Global Business Perspective on Development and the Environment* (Cambridge, Mass.: MIT Press, 1992), p. xii.

9

MIT: The Path to Our Future
1997–1998

This report, as implied by its title, "MIT: The Path to Our Future," was different from those that preceded it: It was focused solely on MIT. This was a time of enormous optimism and opportunity. I believed that MIT was poised to be the preeminent university in shaping and serving an emerging new age. We believed we were entering into a period of change unprecedented since the post–World War II years, when the modern MIT was shaped. The U.S. economy was strengthening, federal research funding had maintained greater strength than had been anticipated, and public understanding of the essential role of research universities had improved. Our partnerships with industry were generally successful, and we were about to launch a campaign to raise more than $1 billion. Above all we were in the most exciting period in history with respect to science and technology, and MIT's strengths seemed well suited to the emerging frontiers. A successful and well-received program of retirement incentives had created opportunities to renew our faculty through hiring an unusual number of new professors. The role of residential campuses in the information age needed to be refined and articulated. We needed to accelerate the shift away from overdependence on federal support to a greater use of private support. It was time to renew our campus through greater investment in maintenance and renovation, and through new construction to set a bold new standard of architecture as we approached the new century. Through both programmatic change and improved infrastructure, we needed to enhance the quality of the overall experience of MIT students, using as a guide the thoughtful and well-grounded report of the Task Force on Student Life and Learning.

The Path to Our Future served as a broad vision and plan—intellectual, programmatic, and financial—that reflected the thinking of many

*faculty and administrative leaders. A congruent ten-year, dynamic
financial plan was crafted by the senior MIT administration working
together with the MIT Corporation's Executive Committee. Annual
budgets were set against the financial plan, and progress toward meeting the goals of The Path to Our Future would be reviewed each
October with the full Corporation.*

At this time during each year of my tenure as president, I have
written an essay of relevance to MIT, but speaking as well to a
larger audience beyond our campus. This year my report is
directly addressed to the MIT community alone, because I
believe that we have reached a watershed and must craft a more
explicit vision of our future and an intellectual and financial plan
for realizing it. What follows is a personal statement and framework, yet one that is informed and influenced by many others.
The work of many of my faculty, administration, and corporation colleagues is embedded within it. I hope it is useful.

MIT is the quintessential American research university, and
the world's preeminent institution focused primarily, though not
exclusively, on science and engineering. We are dedicated to serving our nation and world by discovering fundamental knowledge of the natural, social, economic, and aesthetic realms; by
working in concert with others to bring this knowledge to bear
on the world's great challenges; and by preparing a highly talented and diverse group of students to deeply understand science
and engineering and developing their ability, values, and passion
to apply this knowledge wisely and creatively to the betterment
of humankind.

We can take great pride in our accomplishments, and we do.
Yet this is precisely the moment when we must reach for our
promise. The times and the needs of the world are changing
rapidly, and in the years ahead MIT must redefine itself and the
very nature of the research university if we are to best serve our
students, our nation, and the global society of which we are a part.

The cold war era has receded into history, and we find ourselves in a new, fast-paced, globally interconnected, knowledge-driven age. This age presents its own instabilities and dangers, but it also is rich in promise and opportunity driven by an unprecedented acceleration of knowledge, understanding, and technology. In the coming century, as the information and genetic revolutions gather momentum, and great environmental challenges loom ever larger, society will, as always, look to MIT graduates, faculty, and staff for fundamental research, and for creative understanding and application of science and engineering. But society also will expect MIT and its people to play an increasingly important leadership role in many dimensions of world affairs. We have begun to prepare for this by increasing our understanding of, and partnership with, business, industry, and governments in new endeavors of learning, research, and problem solving. This will be an important element of the research university of the future. It is an exciting moment for us.

Looking to the Future

MIT is uniquely poised to be the preeminent university in shaping and serving an emerging new age. We are blessed with an intellectual environment of remarkable creativity—generated by the synergy among world-class programs in science, engineering, and management together with extraordinary programs in the arts, humanities, architecture, and the social sciences. This provides an ideal educational setting at the dawn of the twenty-first century. Our faculty, students, staff, and graduates will make breakthrough discoveries and redraw the intellectual map in areas that will define the quality of our future. We will bring our talents to bear on the toughest challenges and most exciting opportunities before us. We will reinvent ourselves and our institutions along the way.

Our plans rest on several assumptions about the future—of science, society, and universities themselves. What are some of these assumptions?

First, the end of science is nowhere in sight. Indeed, we stand at the brink of many new scientific adventures. Understanding the brain and the mind, for instance, will be one of the most profound and productive scientific ventures in the next century—one that will have great implications for maximizing human potential and for living long and living well.

The strength of economies, regions, and nations will be determined in large measure by technological and organizational innovation. This innovation must be built upon a foundation of new research in science, engineering, and management.

Humankind's advances will depend increasingly on new integrative approaches to complex systems, problems, and structures. Design, synthesis, and synergy across traditional disciplinary boundaries will be essential elements of both education and research. Engineering, for example, will provide instruments and techniques to facilitate the rapid advancement of the biological and physical sciences. Biology and physics, in turn, will create revolutionary new approaches to engineering and production, as well as to health care.

Research universities will grow in importance as the primary source of fundamental research and scholarship in the United States.

The need for leaders to solve the complex problems of the modern world requires a new paradigm for the research university itself—one in which industry, academia, and governments work together in effective partnership. For example, the quality of our environment, the sustainability of economies, and the efficient use of our material and energy resources, will depend upon sound scientific and engineering knowledge leading to action by all three partners.

The flow of information will be instantaneous and ubiquitous, as the technology, applications, and benefits of computer, information, and intelligence sciences evolve, expand, and become more central still to human activities.

Information technology will dramatically alter learning and working. Many faculty will change their teaching role from one of lecturing to one of shaping and guiding the use of electronically available information. They will lead team efforts in both campus-based and electronic communities.

Still, the residential campus experience will remain the best and most important form of education of our most talented youth.

Our security and quality of life will require that all people work together to form a coherent, productive society, built on common values as well as rich diversity. This will not occur unless it is fostered within our schools and universities.

Finally, the future will demand new leaders—leaders with a deep understanding of science and engineering who possess the ability, values, and desire to apply their knowledge wisely and creatively to the betterment of humankind.

A Vision for MIT

Upon the strong foundation of our institutional heritage, but informed by these assumptions about the future, we can build a vision—a set of defining goals—for MIT. MIT can and must:

• attract the best and brightest students and faculty and support them with a stimulating and effective living and learning environment;

• be committed to excellence, yet thrive on change;

• be steeped in fundamental scientific inquiry, yet lead the new, integrative modes of scholarship, learning, and action;

• be dedicated to scholarship, inquiry, and criticism, yet be adept at bringing together industry, government, and academe to explore and solve major problems facing the world;

• recognize that its educational, scholarly, and leadership goals, as well as the quality and effectiveness of its intellectual dialogue, require the continued presence and engagement of strong programs in the arts, humanities, and social sciences;

• be dedicated to expanding technological and organizational capabilities, yet be concerned with exploration of attendant moral and ethical issues; and

• serve our nation first and foremost, yet recognize that to do so now requires substantial global engagement and cooperation as well as competition.

These, I believe, are the essential goals that will enable MIT to be the quintessential research university of the next century, as it has been in the past.

MIT in the 1980s and 1990s—Strengths to Build On

The 1980s were a decade of remarkable accomplishments at MIT: We developed an exceptionally diverse student body; maintained and strengthened the excellence of our programs across all five schools; continued a deep, though often insufficiently recognized, commitment to undergraduate education; led American academia in internationalization, through such activities as the MIT Japan Program; established a new paradigm of education, research, and industrial interaction through the Leaders for Manufacturing Program; launched Project Athena, the first really large-scale academic computing environment; embarked on an unusual and highly successful venture with a newly created, affiliated research organization—the Whitehead Institute; entered a new level of private fund-raising through the successful Campaign for the Future; and realized one of the very best investment performances among university endowments.

Our path through the 1990s has been marked by exciting progress in numerous aspects of education, research, and campus development, despite the pressures of shifts in federal research funding policy, the world economy, and public support of higher education and research.

The following highlights offer a picture of an energetic, dynamic institution oriented toward and investing in the future.

Science

MIT's excellence in mathematics and the basic sciences is a defining strength of our institution. In the 1990s, the life sciences have continued and expanded their world-class excellence and now play a major role in the education of all MIT students. The emergence of neuroscience and the study of the mind and brain as major new intellectual arenas is reflected in the establishment of the Center for Learning and Memory and the reorganization of Brain and Cognitive Science as a department in the School of Science. The development last year of the "atom laser" is yet another example of how faculty at MIT are inventing the future.

Engineering

At the same time, we have initiated a second revolution in engineering education, characterized by increased emphasis on integrative aspects of engineering and real-world considerations involving production, process, and design. We continue to be at the heart of the information-technology revolution through many endeavors, such as the leadership and management of the World Wide Web. Of particular note is the establishment of the new Division of Bioengineering and Environmental Health, which organizes faculty, research, and education outside of traditional disciplines in recognition of the future role of cell and molecular biology in engineering.

Management
The MIT Sloan School of Management now is clearly recognized as being in the first rank of business schools. It has astutely built synergy with many other schools at MIT, totally redesigned and expanded its MBA program, emphasized entrepreneurship in new ways, and established coherent new international initiatives, such as the World Business Curriculum project with Tsinghua and Fudan Universities in China. Its eminence in quantitative and international matters and its strong interfaces to technology are excellent comparative advantages today.

Humanities, Arts, and Social Sciences
The role of the humanities, arts, and social sciences has expanded in recognition that these are essential intellectual and cultural components of the creative spirit and ethos of education and scholarship at MIT. The humanities and social science faculty have played leadership roles in extending the global reach of many of our programs and in broadening the perspectives and expertise needed to engineer, manage, and set policy. MIT's world-renowned strengths in economics and linguistics continues to build and evolve. Writing and the performing arts have continually expanded their importance and, in addition, have played a notable role in developing an appreciation of the role of diversity in living and learning. The visual arts have evolved in new directions and have expanded their strength and centrality in our institution.

Architecture and Planning
The School of Architecture and Planning has undergone a renaissance, as it has begun to define the new technology-based modes of practice and education. There is a rededicated emphasis on

design in Architecture; Urban Studies and Planning is at the fore-front of using technology to inform the planning, management, and delivery of services in urban settings; the Media Laboratory is better integrated into the activities of the School; and the School has established new and increasingly important links to other elements of MIT.

Interdisciplinary Programs
A number of large, highly interdisciplinary programs have been formed across the Institute, many of which focus on the environment. The Center for the Science and Policy of Global Change, the Alliance for Global Sustainability, and other activities have set new standards of effectiveness in bringing sound scientific understanding and more effective policy contributions to important discourse among industry, government, and academia on a national and international basis. Educational and research programs requiring effective partnership between the School of Engineering and the Sloan School of Management have emerged as a nearly unique comparative advantage of MIT. We have made progress toward more efficiently and effectively realizing our full potential in bringing new scientific and engineering techniques to the practice of human medicine, but more remains to be done in this regard.

Student Support
The office and role of the dean of students and undergraduate education was dramatically changed by combining all elements of service for our students: Academic support, admissions, athletics, bursar, career planning, counseling, dining, financial aid, housing, and student records were combined into a single, more integrated organization. Through this change and through substantial process reengineering, we are establishing an organization to support the improvements in the quality of student

experience that will be important to accomplish in the years immediately ahead.

Campus Development

Over the years, MIT's physical plant has evolved through a combination of new construction, periodic major renovations, and rework of existing buildings. During the 1990s, we constructed the Biology Building, widely regarded as the best facility for biological research and education in the world; completely renovated Buildings 16 and 56; rebuilt the interior of our oldest residence hall, Senior House; constructed the Tang Center for Management Education; and carried out a prudent schedule of maintenance and reuse. There is much to be proud of on our campus, but much remains to be done if our campus in toto is to inspire, reflect, and support the excellence and creativity of MIT and function better as a means for enhancing the student experience and building a sense of community and pride of place.

Challenges

Our greatest challenge is to bring to MIT the best students and the best faculty, and the people and infrastructure to support them. And we must provide the physical facilities and information infrastructure that enable them to live, learn, and work within an effective and inspirational environment. Increasingly, we must compete with other, often more heavily endowed, institutions for these students and faculty. We must make continued investments in people and facilities in order to remain great, yet our financial underpinnings and opportunities are changing rapidly.

MIT, more than any other university in America, built its financial structure on the foundation of federal support. In the early 1990s, federal support for our universities in general, and

MIT in particular, began to erode. Despite this, the MIT faculty succeeded in maintaining strong research support. However, a series of changes in federal cost reimbursement policy, including the reduction of financial support of graduate students, and other mechanisms for shifting costs of research from the federal government to universities, seriously reduced our operating revenues. Financing MIT's future requires a rebalancing of public and private support.

There were other sea changes during the decade as well. The pressures of world economic competition shortened both vision and time horizons in research and development. The public became deeply concerned about rising costs of education, both real and perceived. The arts and humanities were devalued. Continuing racial and economic schisms in our society, together with failures in many elements of American primary and secondary education, reduced educational opportunity for many and thereby deprived society of their full talents. The costs of continuing our deeply-held commitment to need-blind admissions and need-based financial aid grew.

The support, authority, and convening power of MIT must be continuously earned, and this requires that we recognize and address these realities as we strike out on the path to our future.

The Path to the Future

Our path to the future will be guided by our vision and assumptions. We will chart a course to meet the priorities established by our academic leadership and will address the challenges and obstacles before us. In so doing, we also will be informed by various task forces and councils that have worked throughout the past two years to chart our course and to outline the principles and directions that will lead to an enhanced campus environment for learning, working, and living.

Academic Priorities

As always, the new intellectual directions of the Institute will be determined by the faculty. Our institutional goal is to create the infrastructure of services, facilities, and support to enable them to pursue their ideas and activities in as vigorous a manner as possible.

Even though evolving faculty pursuits will drive our intellectual future, there is a clear sense of several overarching themes that characterize much of the Institute's emerging research and educational agendas. It is clear, for example, that our faculty have every intention of leading the continuing revolutions in information technology and the intelligence sciences; in the study of neuroscience, the brain, and the mind; in basic biology and its application to engineering and medicine; in the environment and sustainable development; in twenty-first-century business practice and entrepreneurship; in understanding the nature and social impact of new digital media; in visual and performing arts; in the understanding, design, and operation of large-scale, complex systems; in blending technology, management, economics, and policy; and in the development of new modes of teaching and new uses of technology to enhance learning.

Our faculty's commitment to deep, fundamental research and scholarship is matched by a desire to transfer new knowledge, insights, and technologies into the world in important and positive ways. We will pursue a number of strategic educational and research initiatives that will create a new paradigm for the research university—one dedicated to bettering the human condition through partnerships among industry, government, and academia. These partnerships will have the goals of improving our environment, advancing health, creating new products and services, and enhancing productivity. Many of these initiatives will be global in scope and will increase the exposure of our students to different modes of thought and activity throughout the world.

We must clearly define our place in the changing galaxy of educational institutions, activities, and alliances. There can be no doubt that emerging information technologies with enormous storage, bandwidth, and display capabilities will profoundly affect the way we all work, live, and learn. Institutions and groups of institutions will provide various educational services, from specific training and the updating of skills to high-quality degree programs. MIT will define an appropriate balance between using these new capabilities to help educate those beyond our campus and bringing a wealth of information and interaction to those on our campus. We will do both, but likely will emphasize the latter. We must be certain that we define the most advanced concepts and operate at the cutting edge of new learning modalities.

Above all, MIT wants to make it possible for its remarkable students to achieve their full potential as scholars, innovators, and leaders. The residential campus will remain the best environment for the education of the most talented young men and women, and it is they we must continue to attract.

The Learning Environment
We will take a number of steps to enhance the quality of life for students, faculty, and staff, recognizing the Task Force on Student Life and Learning's formulation of an MIT education built on a triad of academics, research, and community. The learning environment will be enhanced by specific commitments of resources to improving the freshman year, expanding and improving housing for undergraduate and graduate students, enhancing our athletic facilities, and establishing a cutting-edge computing and digital media environment as well as state-of-the-art library/information facilities. The arts will further strengthen their place in MIT culture and experience. We will raise a major endowment for enhancing undergraduate education and student life, create new alternative pathways through

the MIT undergraduate curriculum, and increase opportunities for leadership training and experiences.

Residential Campus Life

The magic and synergy established by bringing together bright, motivated, interesting, and dedicated young men and women in a residential campus is the essence of the best in American higher education. To do so within an intense research university that additionally enables them to be part of many electronically extended learning communities, both within the campus and throughout the world, creates the potential for an unparalleled social and educational experience. Yet student years remain times of intense personal development, value formation, and individual exploration and growth.

We will draw on the many strengths of our diverse housing opportunities in campus residence halls, fraternities, sororities, and independent living groups to create a diverse yet enhanced and better-integrated residence system. The living experience must simultaneously nurture and support individual needs and build an extraordinary common experience that defines MIT and bonds all to it. Students, faculty, alumni/ae, and administrators will work intensely to forge this system and its detailed objectives as we move toward fall 2001. From that year forward, greater coherence of purpose and community for our students' years here will be manifest, with all MIT undergraduates sharing the experience of residing on campus during their first year.

The distance between living and learning at MIT has become too great. For many, the components of education have become too compartmentalized. Building on the foundation of the report of the Task Force on Student Life and Learning, we must assure every student of personal engagement with scholars and advisors, and with more inherent avenues for serious dialogue and mutual learning. Residential and dining experiences must contribute to this.

Building the Infrastructure

Even as we forge these exciting new pathways, we must overcome serious practical obstacles. We must improve our ability to adequately fund the education of graduate students, particularly in our doctoral programs. We must be able to maintain the levels of compensation, start-up expenses, and flexibility to explore new areas and seed new programs that are required to attract and retain the very best faculty. We must keep an MIT education affordable by moderating the growth of tuition, strengthening financial aid, and attenuating self-help levels. And while some might not think of this as infrastructure, we must continue to build a diverse student body, faculty, and staff in order to educate our students effectively and prepare them for leadership in our increasingly diverse society—a society that must function more cohesively and productively in the future.

Finally, we must place emphasis on improvement of our physical campus. We propose major enhancements of our facilities and infrastructure that will be efficient and functional, yet will generate a greater sense of community and pride in MIT and what it stands for. These developments will be guided by our desire to enhance the quality of student life and learning, but they also are congruent with our vision of the key areas of research and education in the coming decades.

The Strategy

Meeting our challenges and advancing along the path to our future requires a three-element strategy of building public understanding and support, managing our assets well, and developing new financial resources. Our strategy has been consistent for the last several years, and will continue to be so.

Advocacy

In order to keep the nation on a course toward a vibrant future, and to create an environment in which MIT can flourish, we have worked vigorously to increase public, federal, and business understanding and support of science, technology, research, and advanced education. We have delivered a consistent message centered on the importance of investing in the future through support of research and education. To do so, we have built national coalitions, worked with all branches of the federal government, worked with the traditional scientific and educational organizations, and engaged the business communities, state governors, and the media. Critical to our effectiveness has been our practice of bringing MIT faculty expertise to bear on the problems and challenges faced by leaders in government and business, and of convening serious interactions across these sectors.

Our advocacy efforts are helping to create new understanding and support in industry for university research and education, and they have had a significant influence on the federal government's stance as well. There is a growing recognition, stimulated in part by MIT-based efforts, that the future strength of America's economy and quality of life depend on our ability to innovate, and that innovation in large measure depends on investment in research and education. After six years of essentially level funding, both the administration and Congress, in an increasingly bipartisan manner, now are supporting stronger research budgets. The issue of federal entitlements, however, still threatens these budgets in the ensuing years.

Fiscal Discipline and Management Improvements

The quality and dedication of our administrative and support staff are vital elements in our ability to realize our vision of excellence and effectiveness in education, research, and service to society. In the last several years, staff throughout the Institute have worked to rein in costs and provide more effective services. We have reengineered several of our administrative services, outsourced many functions, cut back some administrative paper flow, and reconfigured many of our operations. Fiscal discipline and our efforts to gain administrative efficiency have had positive results, involving and affecting the entire institution. This has been difficult and controversial. Much has been accomplished, but more remains to be done, and it is a tribute to MIT's staff that they continue to develop better ways to support our education and research programs.

Management improvements are but one of the ways in which we have made major adjustments to new financial realities. Others include absorbing very large costs associated with sponsored research that used to be paid for by the federal government; using Institute funds to support the full academic year salaries of almost all faculty; and reducing the size of the staff as employees leave or retire. (The retirement incentive program also enabled us to open many positions for new faculty, primarily in the junior ranks, allowing us to renew the Institute's most critical resource—its intellectual capital.) We are nearing completion of the installation of a modern financial and management information system, thereby increasing our potential for efficiency, and avoiding the costs of solving the "Year 2000 problem" in our primary systems.

We also have been moderate in tuition increases, have reduced operating budgets, have reduced our energy costs (through conservation and the construction of a modern cogeneration plant), and have extended the life of our physical plant through major renovation of existing buildings.

Increasing Private Support
Increased private support is a dominant and absolutely critical component of our strategy. Simply put, the financial structure of

MIT must change substantially. This requires that our support from traditional constituencies such as alumni and alumnae, other individual donors, and foundations must grow substantially. Happily, our intellectual agenda in many areas of research and education requires deeper partnership with industry and greater global interaction, both of which also open new avenues of financial support. We have made a good start in gaining increased financial commitment by donors to MIT, and by forging innovative new partnerships with business and industry, but this is just the beginning of the road.

The outlook is good. We have set three consecutive record years for private fund-raising at MIT, with cash received reaching $137 million in fiscal year 1998. With the addition of generous contributions and skillful investment in strong financial markets, MIT's endowment has more than doubled in recent years, growing from $1.40 billion in 1990 to $3.68 billion in June 1998. Industrial support of research at MIT has grown from 15 percent of our research volume in 1990 to almost 20 percent of our research volume in 1998. This growth is the result in part of newly conceived strategic partnerships with industry.

Funding Our Future: MIT's Financial Plan

Realizing our vision of the future also requires a new financial plan. During the last nine months, we have worked with the Executive and Investment Committees of the MIT Corporation to develop a new vision and plan for deployment of our financial resources. This plan is evolving, but its broad aspects, assumptions, and goals are clear.

The costs of our operations, facilities, and infrastructure are funded by three sources of revenue: tuition, externally-sponsored research, and gifts and endowment income.

We have projected the expenses of realizing our goals and vision. They include funding for core needs, programmatic initiatives and improvements, and extensions of physical plant and infrastructure. They commit us to certain specific strategic directions, yet allow for some increase in the freedom, flexibility, and intellectual entrepreneurism that must characterize a great university.

The financial structure of MIT must evolve rapidly to meet the new realities of changing federal support, increased competition from our peers, and deterioration of our physical facilities. Simply put, we will become more dependent upon private resources. This raises profound policy issues about our operating budget, our capital budget, and, particularly, the long-term development and deployment of our asset base, especially our endowment.

MIT must increase its expenditures from earnings on its endowment and other invested assets, as well as from newly raised funds for both non-recurring and recurring purposes. We are confident that MIT faculty will conceive and find support for the great new ventures of the future if we continue to provide a conducive environment and infrastructure to support them.

The key factors in our financial planning fall into two categories: essential baseline parameters, and the incremental expenditures needed to maintain and expand our areas of excellence.

Background Facts

Before presenting these factors, it is useful to review a few background facts.

Approximately 85 percent of what MIT does is engineering and science, requiring highly-compensated faculty and staff, and necessitating a continually changing physical and informational infrastructure. Unlike most of our peer institutions, we have no large academic programs with low intrinsic and infrastructure costs.

MIT has been highly dependent on federal research support through almost four decades in which federal policy favored us both implicitly and explicitly. Faculty salaries, graduate student support, and funding of research-related construction and renewal all have been funded (appropriately) in very substantial measure by sponsors as direct and indirect costs of research. In 1980 federally sponsored research revenues paid for 56 percent of our campus operating budget; by 1995 that figure had dropped to 44 percent. Further changes in federal policy have now made even this level untenable in the absence of increased private support.

MIT is unique in its practices of charging full tuition to most graduate students during their research and study for 12 months per year, rather than the 9 months per year that is the practice at our peer institutions.

During the last six years we have made a number of major transitions in our funding sources. MIT resources, rather than sponsored research, now fund 96 percent of faculty salaries during the academic year. MIT now expends $56 million annually from private resources to meet costs that the federal government used to fund as legitimate, audited costs of research. We have made substantial, though not sufficient, progress toward the government-mandated shift of tuition support for graduate research- and teaching-assistants from the employee benefit pool to a combination of direct charges to grants and to Institute funds.

Essential Baseline Parameters
Student tuition accounts for about a quarter of our campus revenue. The largest component of our operating expenses is salaries and wages. Our commitment to strong undergraduate student

aid programs is fundamental. In addition, MIT's finances and our faculty's ability to compete for grants and contracts are very sensitive to the indirect cost rate charged to our sponsors. The plan must begin with assumptions about these four parameters.

Tuition: For the last five years, we have held the annual increases in the cost of education (tuition, room, and board) to approximately 1.5 percent above the Consumer Price Index. Our tuition alone has grown at about 5 percent per year. We are now in a time of very low inflation, and of strong competitive, social, and political pressures to restrain the cost of education to students and their families. It is appropriate and prudent that we continue to hold tuition growth to modest levels.

Salaries and Wages: Competitive pressures on compensation are strong. This reflects pent-up demand, increased resources for faculty compensation at peer institutions, and the tight labor market in technical and administrative positions. Compensation must continue to rise at reasonable real rates.

Undergraduate Financial Aid: MIT is deeply committed to its excellent, diverse, and often financially needy undergraduates. We must continue our commitment to the important principle of need-blind admission, and therefore must maintain strong programs of need-based financial aid. We intend to meet the cost of remaining competitive in undergraduate financial aid.

Indirect Cost (F&A) Rate: The indirect cost rate charged to research sponsors, under new federal guidelines, is known as the Facilities and Administration (F&A) Rate. The magnitude of this rate and the details of its accounting have been contentious issues between universities and the federal government. F&A costs are increasingly a competitive factor in attracting and retaining faculty at MIT. Our goal is to restrain the growth of F&A rates through prudent management and increased private support for facilities and infrastructure.

New Expenditures to Achieve Excellence

Recruiting and retaining the very best faculty remains one of our greatest challenges. To do so, we must be able to offer competitive salaries, state-of-the-art research and teaching facilities, and opportunities to work with the very best students. Faculty salaries are included in the baseline budget parameters discussed above. In addition to these parameters, there are three major incremental expenditures that we believe will position MIT for greatness in the coming decades.

Graduate Student Support: We must take bold action to substantially reduce the price of graduate education, or, equivalently, the cost felt by programs and research projects. This will substantially enhance our ability to attract the most promising graduate students to MIT, make our research proposals more competitive, and assist those programs that have limited access to sponsored research. To accomplish this, we intend to eliminate summer tuition for research-based graduate students, and to create a large number of graduate fellowships to support recruitment of the very best graduate students to MIT.

Facility Maintenance and Renewal: MIT has a strong record of maintaining and renewing its facilities, and of adapting them to changing purposes over time. Nonetheless, we have identified very substantial deferred maintenance across our physical plant. We will undertake a broad program to upgrade existing facilities and infrastructure, especially where it will support innovation in teaching and research and enhance the quality of campus life.

New Construction: A great university requires sound, attractive, and efficient buildings and spaces for world-class teaching, research, and student life. We are establishing priorities, schedules, and private funding goals for new construction during the next ten years. Our plan also clearly recognizes the increase of the operating costs which new construction brings. Fund raising for new facilities is off to a strong beginning, but we are just starting down the road.

Funding the Plan

Meeting MIT's goals will require new revenues, new approaches to use of our resources, and revised processes and procedures in our operations. Increased dependence on gifts and investment earnings requires a dynamic adjustment to economic conditions and greater control over some aspects of budgeting and expenditures.

Capital Campaign: MIT must embark on a new capital campaign with a fund-raising goal in excess of $1 billion during a seven-year period. We have every reason to believe that this goal is attainable. Indeed, during the last year MIT has received several gifts of $15 million and above. Substantial planning and preparation for the campaign has already been accomplished, and in the months ahead we will be working with the community to refine and articulate its goals and priorities.

Return on Invested Assets: MIT can support operating and capital budgets that achieve our vision, but only if policies regarding allocation of investment returns are modified. Our endowment and other invested assets have been managed extremely well, and have benefited from the extraordinary performance of the stock market during recent years. This provides optimism regarding distributions from the endowment during the next few years. Going forward, we plan to provide at least the normal rate of growth of distributions to Pool A funds; however, a portion of the earnings above that, together with some earnings on unrestricted funds, will be allocated to Institute-wide improvements—primarily to the support of graduate education, to our program of renewal of facilities and infrastructure, and to our program of new construction.

Control of Budgeting and Expenditure: MIT will establish and adhere to a dynamic ten-year financial plan covering operating and capital expenses. It will achieve our essential goals of modest real tuition growth, real growth of compensation, restrained growth of F&A (indirect cost) rates of research, and maintained commitment to need-based financial aid and need-blind admissions.

Our ability to achieve our goals for graduate education, facility maintenance and renewal, and major construction will depend to some extent on the performance of the economy and the financial markets. Increased expenditures require improved control. We will fulfill legal and moral obligations to maintain the purchasing power of our endowment. Projects and expenditures will be prioritized and paced throughout the next decade. Our spending plans at all times will be keyed in part to investment performance during the preceding three years and to the growth of other resources. We will be prepared to suspend some of these expenditures in a pre-planned manner if our financial performance decreases dramatically.

Finally, our ability to realize our vision necessitates internal budgetary simplification and continued commitment to the quality and efficiency of services. We will improve and simplify our system of funds, budgets, and plans. We will make budgeting a clearer and more direct process for meeting our academic goals. We also will remain dedicated to improvement of our financial and management systems and processes.

A Final, or Beginning, Word

Together, we have the opportunity to lead the most intense period of change and redefinition of MIT since the post-war years. Now is the time. I hope that this document will provide a useful framework and agenda for this task. It is about ideas, buildings, finances, opportunities, and responsibilities. But it really is about something even more important—it is about people.

MIT—its past, present and future—is defined by people. It is the dedication, ability, and effort of our faculty, staff, students, trustees, and alumni and alumnae that have brought us to our current extraordinary position on the world stage. It will be your vision, creativity, abilities, values, sense of mission, and will to excel that will create the MIT of the twenty-first century. It will be a grand adventure. I am grateful for your service, support, and accomplishments, and I look forward to working with each and every one of you to make this vision of the future a reality.

10

Three Questions in Search of Answers
1998–1999

During this year I traveled around the country to consult with alumni and friends about MIT's directions as it prepared to enter its capital campaign. These consultations caused me to focus on three often-raised issues. The first had to do with the continuing appropriateness of MIT's longstanding commitment to admit students solely on the basis of merit and to distribute our undergraduate financial aid only on the basis of financial need. As we had predicted at the time we battled with the Justice Department in court over this matter, the system that, in my view, had long served the country well was spinning out of control as more and more colleges and universities focused on "enrollment management" and "merit-based aid" and transformed financial aid into a quantity for which families increasingly shopped and bargained. I believed then, as I do now, that this trend shifts scarce resources away from those who need it most to many who do not.

The second issue had to do with the collective responsibilities of faculties to students—in how we provide for their experience and learning outside the formal classroom, and how we teach implicitly through our own moral and ethical actions and decisions. I was led to these considerations largely because of the complex and widespread reactions to my decision that all undergraduates at MIT would live their first year in campus residential halls, rather than having the option of living as freshmen in fraternities or independent living groups. Addressing the issue of faculty responsibility was further stimulated by reflecting on the Report of the MIT Task Force on Student Life and Learning.

The third issue addressed the widespread concern around the country that increasing interaction of universities with industry would improperly distort their academic mission and thus reduce their ultimate value to society. Conflicts of corporate and academic goals, and conflicts of financial interest and of commitment of time by faculty entrepreneurs, presented real and present dangers. But I strongly believed that these matters could be managed and that carefully constructed partnerships among universities, industry, and government were not only desirable, but also essential for our future economic vitality, security, health, and quality of life.

During the last year I have traveled across the country to consult with a large number of MIT alumni and friends about the future of MIT and its responses to a rapidly changing world. In these discussions, many questions of fundamental importance have been raised. Additionally, issues and experiences in campus life, and interactions with government and industry have also raised a number of questions. In this report, I offer a few thoughts and opinions on three such important questions:

• Does merit-based financial aid serve the common good?
• What is the faculty's collective responsibility to our students?
• Will industry sponsorship of research distort our mission?

Each of these questions deserves deeper analysis than is presented here. Nonetheless, I hope that these thoughts will stimulate further consideration of these matters.

Does Merit-Based Financial Aid Serve the Common Good?

For about fifty years, MIT, the Ivy League universities, and many other outstanding private colleges and universities adhered to principles known as need-blind admission and need-based distribution of financial aid. "Need-blind" means that those making admissions decisions do not know the financial status of the applicants. "Need-based" means simply that we expect admitted students and their families to pay what they reasonably can of the cost of education, and we will make up the difference. These policies enable the institution to do the greatest good by distributing finite resources to those most in need.

Why did these colleges and universities follow the principles of need-blind admission and need-based distribution of financial aid?

First, they believed that they should select students from the richly talented pool of applicants on the basis of their capability, accomplishment, talents, fit to the institution, and contribution to the characteristics of the class as a whole. No preference would be given to wealthier students, and no discouragement would be given to needy students.

Second, the policies worked. Institutions like ours have been able not only to attract absolutely remarkable young men and women, but also to help them financially to pursue their education. Fortunately, by employing a combination of institutional and federal scholarships, loans, and remuneration for work, we have had sufficient financial resources to implement these idealistic policies.

There is a third motivation. Financial aid to undergraduate students in private universities largely comes from alumni donations. Almost all such donors to our financial aid programs tell me, often with considerable emotion, that they would not have been able to attend MIT if they had not been helped financially. They want to be sure that other bright but needy young people will be able to attend, just as they did.

During this same period, and today, public universities generally have taken a different approach. Most public institutions have less per student available through endowments to use as financial aid, and they encounter a wider range of talent among the students who apply. They try to be sure that any state resident admitted to their campus can somehow afford it, usually through charging relatively low tuition and offering scholarships and loans. Nonresident students usually are charged a much higher tuition. In an effort to increase the quality of the student body, public universities frequently use a part of their scholarship funds to create "merit-based financial aid." Merit-based aid is made available to students judged to have unusually high academic qualifications, and may well go to a student who has no strong need for financial assistance. Frequently it is targeted at bright nonresident students.

A Changing Environment for Financial Aid

During the past several years, the picture I have sketched here has begun to change, largely because of financial pressures on the institutions. Some colleges and universities that believed in need-blind admission and need-based distribution of financial aid were increasingly unable to afford the system, especially as they strove to restrain increases in tuition. Many families also felt increasing pressure, and the range of students needing financial assistance began to rise up well into the middle class.

Federal policy also is a large driver of the changing financial pressures and of the broad shift of financial aid away from the neediest families and toward those of somewhat greater means. The federal government is a major player in the financing of students' education. Thirty years ago, the government primarily provided need-based grants, that is, scholarships, to assist students and their families. In more recent years, the government has cut back dramatically on outright grants and moved toward federal loans, to be paid back with reasonable interest after graduation. In the last few years, government programs have begun to provide tax credit and deductions for educational expenses. These provisions do little to help those at the bottom of the economic scale, but are helpful to those in middle-income ranges. They accrue to those in high tax brackets as well.

The result of these various pressures has been twofold. First there has been a substantial increase in the awarding of merit aid. Second, throughout higher education, there has been a substantial drift of financial resources away from the most needy students and families and into families who have less need.[1]

But the picture is a bit more complicated than this. In addition to some shifting from need-based to merit-based aid, there has been a clear increase in bargaining between schools and families on a case-by-case basis. The squeaky wheel increasingly gets the financial oil, in the form of "discounting" for individual students and families. Discounting simply means charging less than the advertised price of tuition, room, and board. To be sure, all financial aid is a form of discounting, but it has traditionally been applied across the board in accordance with guiding principles and rules. Discounting as overt bargaining or matching of offers from other schools is a relatively new phenomenon.

In some institutions all of this has been taken to an extreme through the application of so-called "enrollment management." Enrollment management basically is an optimization process, in which a school tries to maximize the quality of its student body given the fixed amount of funds available for financial aid or discounts. Enrollment management involves a combination of merit aid, a conscious attempt to attract a certain number of wealthy students, and a certain pot of money with which to conduct bargaining and discounting. Indeed, there now is a web-based, for-profit company that intends to bargain among schools to drive the best financial deal for its clients.

A Primer on the Finances of Higher Education

Before addressing my own view of all of this, let me state some basics of the financing of private higher education that are so obvious that they are often not discussed.

If higher education is a business, it is a very strange business. The reason is bound up in the concept of *subsidy*. As Professor Gordon Winston of Williams College[2] points out: In the world of business, companies produce a product at a cost and sell it for a price. If the price is less than the cost, the business does not survive for long. Colleges and universities are a different kettle of fish. Our "product" is education. The cost of that product is determined by the expenses of faculty and staff salaries, buildings, laboratories, equipment, computers, and services that support the learning environment inside and outside the classroom. The price of the product is called tuition, and it is invariably lower than the cost. The difference between tuition and the cost of education is made up by a subsidy. In a private college or university the subsidy is paid for by returns on an invested endowment and by annual gifts from alumni and other supporters. In the case of public institutions, the subsidy largely comes from funds allocated by the state legislature.

At MIT we calculate that tuition covers about 50 percent of the actual cost of educating a student. This is rather typical among private universities. Thus, as we contemplate the issue of financial aid, the context of a high-quality, *subsidized* undergraduate education must be kept in mind. The tuition, or "sticker price," is substantially less than the actual cost, so financial aid or any form of discounting is simply a variation in the level of subsidy the institution and its trustees believe they can afford.

What about MIT?
Given the great variety of public and private colleges and universities in this country, there is room and logic for many different approaches to financial aid. One shoe does not fit all, and I do not presume to know what is best for any other college or university. But I do have a strong view about MIT and other universities that share many of our characteristics.

The commitment of our most competitive private colleges and universities to need-blind admission and need-based distribution of financial aid served the nation and the world very well for several decades, and I believe continuation of such policies will serve us well. These policies open up our institutions to a broad range of bright students in a competitive and meritocratic context. As students choose among such universities, these policies enable them to base their decision primarily on what they believe to be the best fit in terms of their needs and aspirations, rather than simply where the best financial deal can be struck. This approach also enables us to maximize the good done with finite resources. I believe that our continued adherence to these principles will, at least in part, help to stem the flow of financial aid away from those who truly need it toward many who do not. And I believe that it honors the wishes of most donors to our financial aid coffers.

But why wouldn't MIT want to optimize the quality of its student body by providing extra financial incentives to the very best students to attend?

First, through the quality of our programs, our reputation, and our recruiting efforts, we are able to admit and enroll classes of truly exceptional students. Indeed, it would be very difficult to differentiate among them in terms of talent, accomplishment, and promise. We educators are notoriously inept at actually predicting which individual students will end up with the highest grades, make the greatest contributions to our intellectual community, be the most inventive, or be the most successful in life.

MIT's dean of admissions, Marilee Jones, has said, "A lot of schools offer merit awards, but we'd have to pay every kid who walked in the door. There is no Top 20. How would you pick 20? By what criteria? There are more than 20 gold medalists on the International Physics Olympiad alone in this pool. Three percent of the class we just admitted has 800s on every single test—in all that's five tests. Sixty percent of the class has at least one 800. By every measure we use, a full third of the entering class will have either national or international distinction in something. So that's hundreds of kids. How do you pick the Top 20?"

Second, if such a talented class is divided into merit aid "haves" and "have-nots," it creates unnecessary social tensions. Some of those deemed to be less meritorious when they are admitted would inevitably end up outperforming some of those who had achieved special status and financial reward based on high-school achievements. The meritocracy we value so highly is based on accomplishments here at MIT, not on a prediction.

In summary, as long as we can garner the level of gifts and endowment to make it possible, we should remain true to our principles of need-blind admission and need-based distribution of financial aid. MIT has long been a place that attracts the best and brightest and is accessible to them regardless of their financial status. This should continue to be our goal.

What Is the Faculty's Collective Responsibility to Our Students?

The answer to this question may vary in detail, or even in the large, from campus to campus throughout the cornucopia of U.S. colleges and universities. This probably is good—particularly if the fit of individual students to the institution at which they study is good.

At MIT the faculty defines admission philosophy, criteria, and procedures. They alone determine the curricular requirements for the various degrees, and they are responsible for the development and implementation of individual subjects. Few would wish it to be any other way.

But when we consider life beyond the formal classrooms and laboratories, the debate begins.

I recently had a discussion with an accomplished and respected young MIT alumnus about a somewhat controversial change in the residential options available to our students. I noted that the change had important origins in discussions and debates among our faculty. His reply was that such matters should be of no concern to the faculty, who have no relevant basis of experience or understanding to address them. I was told the same thing last spring by a group of eighty students who camped for a period in the hallway outside my office.

The 1998 Report of the Task Force on Student Life and Learning[3] takes a diametrically opposite view. This group of faculty and students proposes that MIT's educational philosophy be explicitly based on a triad of academics, research, and community. They state that "the ultimate goal is to bring students, faculty, and staff together in the pursuit of the common educational enterprise, and doing so entails recognizing the relationship between what happens within the classroom or laboratory and the informal learning that takes place outside."

More bluntly, the Task Force called for a cultural shift "*from* demanding separation of student life and learning *to* demanding they be inseparable; *from* focusing on formal education *to* emphasizing learning in both formal and informal settings; *from* a community divided by place, field, and status *to* a community unified by its commitment to learning; *from* keeping research, academics, and community apart *to* unifying the educational value each provides."

Such notions are hardly radical, but the term "cultural shift" makes it clear that as life in our universities has become increasingly complex, intense, and demanding, some ideas of the collective responsibility of faculties have changed as well. Any exploration of this matter must begin with an understanding that the deepest commitment of faculty members in research universities is to maintain an environment of academic excellence, and that their most precious resource is time.

American universities grew rapidly in size, scope, and accessibility during the two decades following World War II. They were transformed further during the last three decades as their student bodies became enormously diversified in every dimension—by gender, age, economic status, geographical origin, life goals, race, religion, culture, experience, and so forth. These developments, as well as changes in societal expectations, funding patterns, legal requirements, and so forth, have resulted in a shift of many duties from faculty members to professional staff and administrators.

Indeed, the modern university is in many ways a modest-sized city. In addition to its core mission of teaching and research, it provides housing, food services, medical care, counseling, financial services, a police force, transportation, computers and telecommunications, aid to individuals with disabilities, and much more. Although we may dream of a simpler time, the reality is that the demand for all of these services beyond the classroom continues to grow.

As a result, student-services professionals have taken on many duties once performed by faculty—including aspects of personal, career, and even academic counseling. Generally, this is more efficient and in many dimensions more effective. Still, the nagging internal voice suggests that the balance may have swung too far.

Not only has the balance shifted, but roles and responsibilities have become unclear. Indeed, the MIT Residence System Steering Committee,[4] composed of students, faculty, and alumni, recently stated, "In our many discussions with hundreds of students, faculty, staff, and alumni/ae about our residence system, a fundamental issue is always one of authority, responsibility, and accountability. Not only are our students unclear on these matters, so too are our staff and faculty. . . . This must change."

I suspect that this appropriately characterizes many other campuses as well.

My view is that faculty do have certain collective responsibilities to our students beyond their core duties in the formal classroom and laboratory. I suggest three critical duties—to visibly engage in responsible, moral, and ethical action and decision making; to recognize the cumulative effect of incremental decisions; and to work toward better integration of life and learning within our campus community. I offer these views in full recognition of the demands on faculty time, and of the interaction between such duties and the quality of their personal and professional lives. Of course, many professors at MIT do far more than meet the minimum set of obligations I suggest below.

Responsible, Moral, and Ethical Actions and Decisions

Colleges and universities teach by their actions as well as through their curricula. Faculties and administrations alike owe it to their students to visibly deal with important discussions and decisions in a way that displays a conscious effort to act responsibly, morally, and ethically. Much of the lesson will be contained in what we choose to think about, to do, and not to do. We owe our students open discussion, serious consideration of various points of view, and clear explanations of decisions made. All must realize, however, that timely and clear decisions are necessary.

MIT has an interesting advantage in this regard, because our institution rests so firmly on the strong foundation of science. Integrity is the only possible substrate upon which science can be built. In teaching, demonstrating, and guiding our research by the rigorous methods of scientific inquiry, we set a tone of action and decision making that is very important. But this is not enough.

Let me cite a powerful example of appropriate decision making. In 1974, Professor David Baltimore and his colleagues on biology faculties here and in other universities led a national moratorium on the use of recombinant DNA technologies in their research. This very new, and obviously important, research tool struck an uneasy chord with the public. Were there terrible dangers of unleashing strange, unnatural mutants or new diseases into the human environment? Did we really understand the procedures needed to avoid contamination of the environment or gene pool? Rather than dismiss such concerns, they engaged the broader community, including scholars from nonscience disciplines and political and religious leaders, in intense discourse and analysis of the issue. In a relatively short time, these discussions led to both increased understanding and broad consensus.

Although some others may disagree, I believe that our institution has worked hard to act in a responsible, ethical, and moral manner in many other important though controversial instances: in acting to build the diversity of our community, in battling the Justice Department over the matter of implementing need-based financial aid, and, quite recently, in engaging students, faculty, and alumni/ae in the redesign of our residential system.

In any event, it is incumbent upon us to act responsibly, ethically, and morally, and to maintain an environment in which responsibility and accountability accompany the considerable freedom accorded to us.

Cumulative Effects of Incremental Decisions and Actions

Campuses are complicated systems. People and actions are interrelated in many ways. There is continual opportunity to make decisions or take actions without considering, or even recognizing how, in the aggregate, they affect our students.

A simple but important example is the set of guidelines established by the faculty for examinations or reports due at the end of each academic term. Each term the chair of the faculty receives many complaints from students about individual professors who have deviated from these rules. I suspect that in most cases, the faculty member's decision was made in order to reflect some particular element of the subject's nature or content. Nonetheless, such locally sensible changes can cause irresolvable conflicts for students who are balancing the demands of several subjects. This type of regulation is made collectively by the faculty and should be adhered to.

A more complex example of collective responsibility is that discussed in the Report on the Status of Women Faculty in Science at MIT.[5] This important report was authored by a group of distinguished women and men on the faculty of our School of Science. It portrayed a long-term pattern of bias or discrimination against senior women in the school, and also noted recent steps that had been taken by the school, and especially by Dean Robert Birgeneau, to address the situation.

This report, and a more detailed, confidential document that supports it, presented many facts and figures, to be sure. But note how they described the essence of the matter:

> While the reasons for discrimination are complex, a critical part of the explanation lies in our *collective ignorance.* . . . [The tenured women faculty] identified the forms that gender "discrimination" takes in this post–Civil Rights era. They found that discrimination consists of powerful, but unrecognized assumptions and attitudes that work *systematically* against women faculty *even in light of obvious goodwill.* Like many discoveries, at first it is startling and unexpected.

The italics are mine; they emphasize that here again is an example of why we must understand the cumulative effects of individual decisions and actions. Furthermore, the ways in which we at MIT collectively think about and extend the work of this group and address the issues it raises and the recommendations it makes will be an implicit lesson to our students, as well as a determinant of our future excellence.

An Integrated Approach to Life and Learning in a Residential University

In a residential research university such as MIT, many dimensions must be integrated—teaching, research, and living—so that the total experience of our students far exceeds the simple sum of their involvement in each individual element.

The MIT faculty has long been deeply dedicated to integrating the education of undergraduates with the superb research activity that surrounds them. They do this by continually renewing and enlivening undergraduate subjects with methods and results from their own and their colleagues' research. In an even more explicit manner, they provide, through the Undergraduate Research Opportunity Program (UROP), a direct involvement of undergraduates in research.

But—as noted by the Task Force on Student Life and Learning—the third element of the living environment and experience of our students needs to be better integrated. The concept of a true community of scholars adds an extra dimension to faculty life and goals. By engaging with students beyond the formal classroom and laboratory we can help to develop wisdom and understanding as well as knowledge and skill. We can display and enhance our humanity as well as intellectual expertise. I believe that students and faculty can benefit dramatically just from understanding more about each other's lives. Virtually all of us can point to encounters with specific faculty members that had a profound influence on the fulfillment of our potential in our personal and professional life.

Change need not be dramatic, but it needs to be systemic. A modest involvement with living groups, a few evenings or lunches spent in discussion with undergraduates, holding seminars in residence halls, teaching a freshman advising seminar, creating exciting field trips or other off-campus experiences for students, participating in a preterm orientation program, conducting an informal IAP class, talking with students on the Net, or simply stopping to chat in the hallway can have an amazingly positive influence on students. Many of these things happen quite naturally in graduate education, but not always for our undergraduates.

A number of our faculty colleagues shoulder massive amounts of this responsibility, such as those who serve as housemasters in our residence halls. But each of us has a role. Our students came to MIT to engage with world-class professors. If we all devote ourselves to building campus community, the incremental time involved can be modest, but the consequent enhancement of our already vital and exciting student experience will be great. It is our responsibility to do so.

In sum, my response to the second question is that faculty, and administrators and staff as well, have a collective responsibility to our students that extends beyond meeting our basic duties in the classroom and laboratory. We must build community by integrating student life and learning into a more coherent whole. We must not only teach, but exemplify moral, ethical, and responsible behavior. And we must understand the cumulative effects of our individual actions on our students, colleagues, and others, and act accordingly. This is particularly important at MIT because of our strong tradition of being a single faculty—we are of a whole cloth, dedicated to the Institute, not just to our individual departments or schools. This is an important value in and of itself.

Will Industry Sponsorship of Research Distort Our Mission?

Research universities are supported by society in a variety of ways because of the common good they serve: educating young men and women for responsible, productive lives, and generating new, fundamental knowledge that expands the human spirit and increases our collective understanding of the physical, biological, social, and artistic aspects of our world. But increasingly, much of the knowledge generated through university research has quite immediate practical and economic value. This complicates the mechanisms by which the common good is promoted.

Since the close of World War II, the federal government has been the primary supporter of university research in the United States, and universities have become nation's primary research. This relationship stemmed from recognition of the contributions that science and technology had made to the defense effort and of the promise that they held, in President Roosevelt's words, "for the improvement of the national health, the creation of new enterprises bringing new jobs, and the betterment of the national standard of living." The principles underlying this relationship were articulated by MIT's Vannevar Bush, then director of the Office of Scientific Research and Development, in his report, *Science—The Endless Frontier.*[6]

In short, these principles are that it is in the nation's long-term interest for the federal government to support scientific research and advanced education conducted in universities, and that the nature of such research should be determined by the scientists themselves and not guided toward particular applications. The assumption was that in due course, the new knowledge would find its way to improve our industry, commerce, medical practice, and national defense.

The quality, vigor, and societal contributions of the great research universities of this country are directly linked to the adoption of these principles by the federal government. This is certainly the case for MIT, which was able to leverage this support to build its world-class faculty and research enterprise.

Our reliance has been great: In 1965, sponsored research support, predominantly federal, accounted for over 60 percent of all of MIT's campus operating revenues. But now things are changing, as they should. Some would argue, and I am one, that MIT became overdependent on federal support. While the federal government will—properly in my view—remain the dominant source of research support, industry is starting to play a more substantial role at MIT. By Fiscal Year 1999, sponsored research had dropped to 45 percent of our campus operating revenues. Of this, approximately 70 percent came from the federal government, 20 percent from industry, and the remainder from private foundations and other sources. This is the age of the private sector, and such change is appropriate and, indeed, necessary.

A Changing Scene
MIT has worked hard during the last few years to develop strong and appropriate research relations with private industry for three reasons: to improve our education; to diversify our sources of financial support; and to create new pathways for contributing to the common good.

The world of commerce and industry that our graduates now enter is very different than it was even a few years ago. Contemporary industry is fast-paced, knowledge-based, global, electronically interconnected, and often created by entrepreneurs. It thrives on innovation. As a consequence, I believe that, especially in engineering and management, our education must change to better serve our students and their future employers. To accomplish this, some of our faculty and research students need to be engaged with contemporary industrial problems and environments. Such engagement will generate not only new types of academic research, but improvements in our curricula.

Conflicts and Responsibilities
Interactions with industry create new pathways to serve society. However, as with all paradigmatic change, questions of appropriateness and mission are properly raised. Faculty members

interact with industry in a variety of ways. They do so as educators, as leaders of research programs, as consultants, as generators of intellectual property, and as entrepreneurs. In each of these possible roles, money crosses boundaries and missions and objectives become intertwined. Thus we must examine the implications of these new relationships, raise questions, and set policies to address them.

With regard to any non-MIT activities, faculty, officers, and staff have an obligation to avoid ethical, legal, or other conflicts of interest and to ensure that their activities do not conflict with their obligations to the Institute or its welfare.

The ability of professors to spend up to a day a week as consultants to business, government, or industry has long been accepted as a valuable way of gaining new experience, which can lead to increased curricular vitality and can open new areas of research. MIT monitors consulting only to the extent necessary to ensure that there is no conflict of commitment—that consulting faculty adhere to the time limits and that their outside activities do not interfere with meeting their professorial duties and responsibilities.

When faculty act as entrepreneurs, or when the intellectual property they generate is otherwise commercialized, further considerations and policies come into force—for them and for MIT as an institution. Our conflict-of-interest policies have two basic objectives—to ensure openness of information flow in our classrooms and laboratories, and to keep research agendas in our laboratories from being improperly affected by the personal financial interests of faculty or staff.

In today's world, we pay particular attention to the issues associated with ownership of intellectual properties and to potential conflicts arising from ownership of equity in companies. We have recently established new guidelines for avoiding and managing such conflicts. These guidelines are basically clear, but the complexity and pace of commercialization today require that we all be vigilant and thoughtful in this regard. Common sense, foresight, and thoughtful consultation are the most important vehicles for avoiding conflicts of interest and commitment.

Entrepreneurship

One of the most direct ways in which research-intensive universities serve the greater society is by moving new ideas and technologies into the commercial sector, thereby building wealth and creating jobs. Indeed, a now well-known 1997 study showed that MIT graduates had founded or cofounded over 4,000 companies employing over 1.1 million people and having annual world sales of $232 billion. Other leading universities could tell similar positive stories. This represents a huge return on the investment made by the federal government through its sponsorship of research and graduate education, and by individuals and foundations that have helped support universities and students over the years.

Today, the movement of ideas, technologies, and graduates from universities to the world of commerce occurs at a blinding speed. And the rapidity at which money can be made in conjunction with this movement is sometimes astounding. Entrepreneurial activities have always been a very important part of the culture of MIT, but their roles and importance have accelerated dramatically.

We foster this aspect of our culture in many ways. We have, for example, a growing Center for Entrepreneurship, located at the Sloan School of Management, that engages students and faculty from throughout the Institute; research and educational programs in electronic commerce and in new product and venture formation; and a variety of programs for mentoring students and alumni who are interested in starting new businesses.

These activities demonstrate an important aspect of MIT's nimbleness in responding to a rapidly and fundamentally changing world. I would have it no other way. It is exciting and important. Some people question whether this new strength of entrepreneurship and electronic commerce are fundamental transformations, or are a modern version of the tulip craze of early seventeenth-century Holland. I believe that they are fundamental transformations, and that it is important for universities to play a major, though properly balanced, role in their development, and in preparing our students to participate.

However, there are three dangers, in my view:

• First, the rapidity and high stakes of entrepreneurial activities in Internet, software, and biotechnology startup companies require special vigilance regarding conflicts of interest and commitment.

• Second, overemphasis on the possibility of great personal gain can erode the very teamwork and collective spirit that must increasingly drive excellence, innovation, and effectiveness in our laboratories and departments.

• Third, students can easily lose a sense of balance and perspective about what aspects of university experience are of fundamental, long-term value to their lives. There is unquestionably a great appeal to the prospect of a great personal fortune, but we must help our students understand that there is more to life than maximizing net worth. We must stimulate them to be idealistic, to recognize the value of public service, and to undertake the challenges that will make the world a better place, no matter what professional path they pursue.

Thus, we should vigorously develop our programs and contributions to this new world of innovation and commerce, but do so in the context of our fundamental values in scholarship and education.

Interaction with Companies

Research universities have a dual responsibility in relationship to contemporary industry, especially in the fields of engineering, management, and, to a lesser extent, science.

To fulfill our educational mission we must bring some fraction of what we do closer to the contemporary and future world of industry. We need to teach new skills of collaboration and teamwork, a more integrated approach to design projects, a deeper involvement with multiple disciplines, and a better understanding of process, production, and economic factors. In order to do so, some of our faculty members must be deeply engaged with industry in research and educational activities, because it is faculty interests, insights, and experience that ultimately drive the learning experience of our students.

But we have an even greater responsibility for research that is, in a sense, at the opposite end of the spectrum. During the last fifteen years or so, large companies have adapted to a dramatically changing world market by increasing productivity and quality while reducing product cycle times and costs. This required a major reorientation of corporate research toward product development and production. As a result, relatively little corporate research is now fundamental and long-term in nature and shared openly and broadly with the scientific community. Increasingly, universities are the only game in town when it comes to developing fundamental knowledge through research.

During the past few years, MIT has worked at both ends of this spectrum of research and education by forming new partnerships, alliances, consortia, and centers involving industry collaboration and funding. Examples of path-breaking collaborations between the Institute and consortia of sponsoring industries include the Systems Design and Management Program, the Lean Aerospace Program, and the Center for Innovation in Product Development. These programs seek to discover new principles of industrial practice and build them into engineering and management education. There are numerous other exciting industry-sponsored consortia for precompetitive research throughout the Institute.

In addition, we recently have pioneered a number of industry partnerships with individual corporations. These are major undertakings, funded at a substantial level for a period of at least five years. The research agendas of the partnerships have been hammered out by teams consisting of MIT faculty and research or technology leaders from the companies. For the most part, these partnerships explore advanced research into fundamental topics of strategic interest to the company and to MIT faculty. Examples of partnership topics include environmental research, fundamental biology, biotechnology, the uses of future information technologies, the engineering function in global corporations, improved information technology infrastructure and practice in higher education, and emerging financial technologies.

All of the partnerships include a strong component of support for graduate education. For the most part, they deal with long time-horizon research. All result in open publication of research results after the usual modest period of time for review by the sponsoring company. Intellectual property agreements are fairly standard, with MIT owning the rights to most discoveries, and with clearly specified ground rules for the partner company to negotiate for exclusive or non-exclusive patent rights, depending on the royalty situation.

There is another form of exclusivity that is important to contemplate. Companies that engage with us at the partnership level should not be the sole company in their industry or sector to have a presence at MIT. So far, this has not emerged as a problem. Indeed, in some instances our partners have actively worked to engage other companies in the research efforts.

The most important characteristic of the industry partnerships is that they truly are partnerships. There is strong and essential intellectual involvement of industrial scientists, engineers, and managers. They thrive only through trust, mutual respect, and increased understanding of each others' cultures and working time-scales. Both organizations expect to receive substantial intellectual value from the undertakings. All recognize that producing innovative, well-educated students who are knowledgeable about future-oriented fields, especially those that combine or cross traditional disciplines, is a key goal of the partnership.

My view on the third question: Increased industry sponsorship of university research does not distort our mission; it widens and enables it. Indeed, done properly, it broadens the scope of our scholarship, improves education, creates opportunity, expands our infrastructure, diversifies our portfolio of revenue sources, and contributes to society in new ways. However, as with any other partner or patron, there are risks and potential conflicts to be directly confronted, especially when, as at MIT, we take bold new approaches. Above all, we must protect the overall freedom and flexibility of our faculty and students to pursue research and scholarship wherever it leads, and to serve society as objective critics.

In Conclusion

The issues I have raised in this report—financial aid, the collective responsibility of our faculty, and our relations with industry—may still hold more questions than answers. I offer my views here in the hope of stimulating an ongoing discussion of matters that I believe to be of fundamental importance as MIT responds to a rapidly changing world.

They speak to the questions of who we educate, how we do so, and what principles we rely on to guide our future. They are quite interrelated.

We attract remarkably talented students to MIT. Through our financial-aid policies, we seek to ensure that they are selected because of their talent, accomplishments, and potential for benefiting from an MIT education and contributing to our academic endeavors—with no regard to their financial status. While they are here, we as faculty have a growing obligation not only to provide them with an excellent and rigorous formal education, but also to create a more holistic experience of living and growth within a dedicated learning community. This community will increasingly interact with private industry, thereby expanding the scope of our scholarship and creating new pathways for the knowledge we generate to benefit society. In these interactions, as in those with our government patrons and partners, we must carefully avoid inappropriate conflicts of interest and commitment and remain true to our fundamental mission and values.

The future is bright and challenging for MIT, and for our sister research universities. Our opportunities to contribute greatly to the common good in the century ahead are unlimited. I hope that this modest exploration of three issues we all must face will contribute to meeting our opportunities and responsibilities.

Notes

1. Michael S. McPherson and Morton Owen Schapiro, *The Student Aid Game* (Princeton: Princeton University Press, 1998).

2. Gordon Winston, "College Costs: Subsidies, Intuition and Policy," Williams Project on the Economics of Higher Education. Discussion Paper 45, Williams College, Williamstown, Massachusetts, 1997.

3. Report of the Task Force on Student Life and Learning, Massachusetts Institute of Technology, Cambridge, Massachusetts, 1998.

4. Report of the Residence System Steering Committee, Massachusetts Institute of Technology, Cambridge, Massachusetts, 1999.

5. Report on the Status of Women Faculty in Science at MIT, Massachusetts Institute of Technology, Cambridge, Massachusetts, 1999.

6. Vannevar Bush, *Science—The Endless Frontier: A Report to the President* (Washington, D.C.: United States Printing Office, 1945).

11

Disturbing the Educational Universe: Universities in the Digital Age— Dinosaurs or Prometheans? 2000–2001

This essay about the role of information technology in university education was particularly rewarding to write. Every institution needed to address the question of how it was going to use information technology in teaching, learning, and discovery; virtually none could ask the question of whether to use it, because its role is clearly fundamental to what we do and will be increasingly so in the future. In general, MIT faculty undertook many experiments in educational technology, and this essay was a welcome opportunity to display our experience with some of them.

But the real joy in this essay was to showcase the MIT faculty's remarkable answer to the question, "How is the Internet going to be used in education, and what is your university going to do about it?" Their answer was to use it to provide access to the primary teaching materials for virtually all of our courses, about two thousand in number, to teachers and learners anywhere in the world, at any time, and free. This MIT Open-CourseWare initiative is in the great tradition of the Institute's broadly sharing its knowledge and pedagogy, and builds on the fundamental nature of the Internet as an enabling, liberating technology.

My conclusion in all of this is that the essential human quality of teaching and learning in a residential setting will never lose its importance; indeed, information technology will bring the world into the campus in important ways. But we also will find new ways to improve how students learn, and to raise the quality of education around the world.

Taking the Fork in the Road

If there is one experience common to every university president in the United States during the past decade or so, it is being accused of leading institutional dinosaurs down a path to rapid extinction in a digital age. Peter Drucker has decreed it. Editorial writers have shouted about it. Alumni and trustees have stated it. Some of our own colleagues agree.

The issue is simply stated. Does the future of education, learning, and training belong to a new machine-based digital environment, or will the best learning remain a deeply human endeavor conducted person-to-person in a residential campus setting? I believe the answer is "Yes"—to both.

We are at the proverbial fork in the road where we should, and will, take both paths.

There is not an ounce of doubt in my mind that the way we learn throughout our lives is and will continue to be profoundly influenced by the use of digital media, the Internet, the World Wide Web, and devices and systems yet to be developed.

We will inhabit continually evolving electronic learning communities in which amazing new technologies will help us learn. Cognitive science, virtual environments, and new modes of interacting will all come into play in powerful ways. We will extend educational opportunities to people throughout the world in a more cost-effective manner. On-the-job, just-in-time learning will become the norm in many industries. And there will be new players in both the for-profit and nonprofit educational domains.

But there is even less doubt in my mind that the residential university will remain an essential element of our society, providing the most intense, advanced, and effective education. Machines cannot replace the magic that occurs when bright, creative young people live and learn together in the company of highly dedicated faculty.

The residential research-intensive university will not only survive, it will prosper. If anything, its importance will grow as we continue to provide access to the brightest young men and women regardless of their social and economic backgrounds.

However, the residential university also will be enhanced by wise use of the new technologies. But every institution—new and old—must make some choices about the tactical and strategic role it will play in the digital age. There is not one grand solution. Indeed, I believe that it is too early to declare comprehensive positions and strategies. Rather, it is a time for substantial experimentation and calculated risks that will help us sort out opportunities and find effective paths.

I ask only two things as universities find their way in the digital age. First, our emphasis should be on one thing—the enhancement of learning. Second, from Day One we must build serious evaluation of educational effectiveness into our experiments.

As we undertake our experiments and developments, we must have some guiding visions. At MIT we have decided that one of our dominant visions is that of openness.

The Principle of Openness

OpenCourseWare

Consider the direct question, "How is the Internet going to be used in education, and what is your university going to do about it?"

An answer from the MIT faculty is this: Use it to provide free access to the primary materials for virtually all our courses. We are going to make our educational material available to students, faculty, and other learners, anywhere in the world, at any time, for free.

Why are we doing this?

The glory of American higher education is its democratizing reach. Its great landmarks—the establishment of land-grant universities in the mid-nineteenth century and the GI Bill at the close of World War II—spread knowledge and opportunity across our landscape on an unprecedented scale. As we have progressed from World War II to the age of the World Wide Web, we have built a system of higher education that is the envy of the world, and we have developed the Internet as a universal medium for rapidly distributing and accessing information. These forces must now combine to raise educational opportunity throughout the world.

The Internet will revolutionize all kinds of teaching and learning, and some of that will necessarily and appropriately be done in the for-profit world. But inherent in the Internet and the Web is a force for openness and opportunity that should be the bedrock of its use by universities.

Think about what a professor at a research university does. She works with her students and colleagues to discover new knowledge, shares those discoveries with the professional community through papers, seminars, and conferences, and brings it to the students in her classes. She is not only discovering the future through her research, she is bringing it right into the classroom and using these new findings and insights to develop and refine the courses she teaches. The resulting course notes and outlines, reading lists, demonstrations, and assignments become the educational content that undergirds the actual pathways to learning—the discussions, debates, and discoveries that faculty and students engage in together.

We now have a powerful opportunity to use the Internet to enhance this process of conceiving, shaping, and organizing knowledge for use in teaching. In so doing, we can raise the quality of education everywhere.

The quality of education in universities and colleges across America has grown dramatically over the past fifty years, aided by outstanding textbooks and other formal educational materials produced by the faculty. In this century, a similar role will be played by sophisticated educational materials that will be commercially available in electronic form.

But the positive transformation of our universities came about even more through the young men and women who studied at our most cutting-edge institutions and went on to become faculty members at other schools across the land. They took with them the class notes, syllabi, and other materials they used as students and based their teaching on these materials—sampling, shaping, expanding, and improving them to fit their new contexts and students.

At MIT, we plan to speed this process to Internet time, by making the primary materials for nearly all of our 2,000 courses available on the World Wide Web, for use by anyone anywhere in the world. A new engineering university in Ghana, a precocious high school biology student in New Mexico, an architect in Madrid, a history professor in Chicago, or an executive in a management seminar down the hall at MIT, will all find these materials freely and instantly available. Together they will build a web of knowledge that will enhance human learning worldwide.

The computer industry learned the hard way that closed software systems—based on a framework of proprietary knowledge—did not fit the world they themselves had created; the organic world of open software and open systems was the true wave of the future. Higher education must learn from this. We must create open knowledge systems as the new framework for teaching and learning.

In this spirit, MIT has asked itself, in the words of T. S. Eliot, "Do I dare/Disturb the universe?"

Our answer is yes. We call this project MIT OpenCourseWare (OCW). We see it as opening a new door to the powerful, democratizing, and transforming power of education.

We are pleased to have been joined by the Andrew W. Mellon Foundation and the William and Flora Hewlett Foundation in a partnership to launch MIT OCW.

Even as we gird our institutional loins to undertake this great adventure, the reaction to its announcement has been astounding. Some have likened it to the Gutenberg printing press and to the Great Library at Alexandria. This is a bit hyperbolic for my taste, but even as clear-eyed an observer as IBM's CEO, Lou Gerstner, recently stated to Wall Street analysts: "What do you think happened when MIT put its entire course catalog on the Net, for free? If that didn't send a shiver through the higher education system in the world, I don't know what will."

We have received messages and letters from all over the world. One writer, a faculty member at another U.S. university, said: "As a boy, I used to get up early in the morning to watch "Mr. Wizard" on television, and I dreamed of a day when all university courses would be available on television for interested students. That day never came, but today I am delighted to learn that my vision was too limited and that MIT is at the vanguard of a new era in education."

Another message sums the dominant international reaction well:

What I saw from your initiative is the possibility of a major global upgrade of education—professors in the U.S. and around the whole world, including those in little Uganda where I am from, will be inspired and motivated to be on par with MIT standards. The students will demand it because they will have access to high-end quality education, giving them opportunities for a better life and better access to other opportunities. . . . This is global, and I would like to thank you for your generosity, for your commitment to education and not just to quality content but to designing an environment that fosters curiosity and joy in learning.

MIT's opportunity to serve society in this new way is immense, and we are organizing the systems and the services to the faculty that will be required to meet these high expectations.

It is very important to note that the radical concept of MIT OCW evolved through the deliberations of a faculty-led study of MIT's role in Internet-based education. As we rolled out the idea and discussed it with the faculty, we encountered some unexpected reactions and learned some important lessons.

There had been some apprehension that many would argue that we would be giving away too much potential intellectual property revenue. In fact, this argument was voiced by only a few. Almost all of our faculty saw it as a way to enhance our service to society and to improve education worldwide, goals they considered to be more important than revenue possibilities.

In those discussions, however, there were other strong concerns that any university undertaking such a project must recognize. First, the undertaking should not detract from resources and innovation in our on-campus education. (Indeed, I believe that MIT OCW will lead to enhancement of on-campus education.) Second, we must generate sufficient funding to provide a high level of service, making it as easy as possible for faculty members to convert their materials to a high-quality Web format. Together with our foundation partners, we are committed to meeting these important criteria, and also to developing concepts and systems that will aid other universities who may join in the open courseware movement.

Open Systems
Much of the discussion and prognostication about the future of education has been based on "distance education," thought of as a form or analog of business-to-consumer electronic commerce. In such a model, lectures would be delivered to large numbers of students over the Internet, or through some variant of video-conferencing. The idea of MIT OCW is different. It is more related to business-to-business commerce. It is a form of sharing among institutions. It is a form of academic publishing more than of teaching. It puts materials in the hands of others to use as they see fit.

If sharing and pedagogical openness are to become major forces, there must be systems and platforms to support it. Here too, I believe that the spirit of open systems and of LINUX should prevail.

MIT and Stanford, together with partners that to date include the Mellon Foundation, Dartmouth College, North Carolina State University, the University of Pennsylvania, and the University of Wisconsin, are undertaking the Open Knowledge Initiative (OKI). This is a project to create an open-source system of Web-based environments to support pedagogical sharing and the management of educational systems.

The project leader, Vijay Kumar of MIT, indicates that the primary goal of OKI is to design and develop an open and extensible architecture for learning management systems. OKI has other goals, but this is the foundation from which everything else springs. We intend OKI to become a community, a process, and an evolving open-source set of tools that will be of service to a very wide range of educational environments. If OKI is successful as an architecture, then it will inspire contributors to help us realize these other goals. It is ambitious and important.

Outward and Inward

The new media enable us to reach out to the world and extend our learning community by teaching at a distance. They also enable us to bring the world in to our students on campus. Often, we arrive at an amalgam of the two.

MIT has for some time been engaged in so-called distance education. For example, our Sloan School of Management conducts ongoing seminars with management faculty in leading Chinese universities, and our System Design and Management program uses advanced videoconferencing and the Web to teach master's-level students in their workplaces around the country.

Last year, Andrew Lo of the Sloan School taught his popular course on investments to twenty-eight Merrill Lynch directors, vice presidents, analysts, and associates in offices in Japan, Hong Kong, and Australia. With students with very busy professional schedules located in several countries, it would have been nearly impossible to conduct the classes and discussions simultaneously. Instead, Lo's formal lectures were made available on CD-ROM, which the students could use anywhere—on commutes, at home, or during nontrading hours at work. Faculty provoked discussions and answered questions, and students "met" with each other and the teaching staff at all hours—by e-mail, on the Web, and through a more primitive technology: the telephone. Despite their demanding schedules, the students committed themselves to fourteen weeks of very hard work; what they got in return was an immersion course in global business as well as financial engineering.

The largest MIT experiment in distance education is the Singapore-MIT Alliance (SMA). MIT has worked since 1998 in partnership with the National University of Singapore (NUS) and the Nanyang Technological University (NTU) to develop world-class, research-based, highly interactive graduate engineering education across national and institutional boundaries. Students earn SMA-based graduate degrees from NUS or NTU through access to exceptional faculty and superior research facilities in all three institutions.

Walk into one of MIT's state-of-the-art classrooms at 8:00 A.M., or at 8:00 P.M. this fall, and you will find students engaged in classes together with their counterparts in Singapore. Indeed, we are planning to beam 540 hours of instruction in twelve subjects to a total of 155 students. SMA subject areas range from advanced materials for micro- and nano-systems to manufacturing systems and technology to molecular engineering of biological and chemical systems. We believe that SMA, which is supported by a 155-megabytes-per-second Internet-2 line, is the world's most technologically advanced point-to-point synchronous educational program. It uses a dual-screen delivery technology that enables students to view simultaneously camera images from the classrooms and a computer screen for displaying PowerPoint presentations. This technology also makes it possible for MIT faculty to hold help sessions for the students and conduct oral examinations of doctoral students in Singapore.

Learning—not technology—is the goal of SMA. How is it going? Singapore and MIT students enrolled in the same classes are performing at comparable levels, but professors do report that there is a very steep learning curve for preparing and presenting lectures across these boundaries. Fortunately, however, they also report that in a modest amount of time they reach a point at which the technology ceases to dominate their planning and they are able to concentrate on educational quality.

Through these and many other experiments, we are extending our learning community by teaching outward from our campus in both synchronous and asynchronous modes—carrying MIT to the world.

But what about bringing the world inward to our primary students—those in residence on our own campus? Interesting examples have been developed in our School of Architecture and Planning, where our students use technology to interact with people and projects around the world. For example, student design projects are routinely evaluated by juries of distinguished architects on several continents, whose schedules would not allow them to convene here in Cambridge. They have monitored the progress of large international construction projects such as the new Hong Kong Airport. One term, a class was team-taught by Professor Bill Mitchell at MIT and architect Frank Gehry in Santa Monica, with Mayor Jerry Brown of Oakland, California, serving as the client for a project to design a reuse of an abandoned naval base.

Many other examples could be found throughout the Institute and across academia.

Sharing Laboratories, Libraries, and Lectures

Scientists and engineers learn in laboratories as well as in classrooms. MIT professor Jesús del Alamo has developed WebLab, a novel on-line laboratory for conducting experiments to test microelectronic devices—a lab that is available to students 24 hours a day from their dorm rooms or elsewhere. Last fall, 120 students at MIT enrolled in three different courses and twenty students in Singapore performed remote measurements in real time on state-of-the-art devices located at MIT and at Compaq's development laboratories. At its busiest hour, WebLab handled thirteen users running ninety-nine different experiments.

WebLab has nucleated the development of a broader tool, I-Lab, which will ultimately be used for experiments in many different fields of study. "Bringing the lab to the student" has proved to be a great way for students to explore theory versus experiment as they study.

In the same spirit, the World Wide Web increasingly brings library resources to users wherever and whenever they need them. Some of this has become simply routine, but other aspects are in a fascinating stage of development.

Welcome to DSpace: an effort to capture, archive, and distribute much of the intellectual output of MIT in the form of durable digital documents. It sounds simple. It is not, because while libraries know well how to manage books and papers, they are just starting to learn how to create and maintain digital libraries. Some of the challenges are technological, but the most difficult challenges derive from the profoundly different copyright environment that is emerging in the digital world. More about that later.

A more common vision is that of bringing a high-quality learning experience to students wherever and whenever they need it. There are many activities of this kind around the country, but a major effort at MIT has been directed to the development of PIVOT, the Physics Interactive Video Tutor. PIVOT enables students to adapt the use of course materials to their own learning styles. It includes the video segments that comprise the entire lecture set of our introductory physics course, a complete textbook, and a set of linked demonstrations and practice problems.

Students can readily navigate through the material by selecting topics or key words. A "personal tutor" monitors the student's path through the material and his or her performance on problems in order to make suggestions about areas to investigate or reinforce. Early indications are that the use of PIVOT does not lead to higher scores on basic tests, but appreciably improves conceptual understanding.

The level of expense and effort to develop such a tool, however, reminds us that in the long run we will need to find ways to share resources among institutions and rely on appropriate commercial development as well.

So much for laboratories and libraries. What about lectures? University campuses are replete with stunning lectures, performances, and events that should be shared beyond our boundaries. In our case, the demand for such access is especially strong among our alumni/ae and among engineers and managers in industry. To begin to bring such events to these and other constituencies, our Center for Advanced Educational Services (CAES) has joined forces with our Alumni Association and our Industrial Liaison Program to establish MIT World.

MIT World is a website (http://mitworld.mit.edu) that makes available on-demand videos of events on our campus. Indeed, our intent is for it to evolve into a 24-hour-a-day TV station on the World Wide Web. Currently it contains such events as lectures by linguist Noam Chomsky; economists Paul Samuelson, Bob Solow, and Franco Modigliani; physicist Frank Wilczek; biologist Eric Lander; planetary scientist Maria Zuber; space scientist Claude Canizares; and many others. Like MIT OCW, this is a means of sharing our intellectual largess with a broader community, and is an example of what we believe many universities will develop as well.

Improving Education on Our Campus—Fueling Innovation

Despite our status as a research university with global reach, our first duty is to the education of the students on our campus, and it is to this that the vast majority of our energy, resources, time, and innovation are directed. Technology has an increasingly important role in this core endeavor. In addition to bringing the world and its information resources to the desktop of each student, it makes possible new methods of teaching and learning.

Does the shibboleth that we should "replace the sage on the stage with the guide on the side" point to the future of university education? The jury is still out, but I believe that, by and large, that is the case. Prudent use of technology enables faculty to concentrate more on the learning process and less on the direct transmission of information. We are proud of the many exceptional lecturers on our campus. They inspire students and organize knowledge wonderfully. But there is increasing evidence that other, more flexible modes of teaching can better stimulate discovery and improve understanding of conceptual material.

A major endeavor in the use of studio learning at MIT is spearheaded by TEAL/Physics, led by Professor John Belcher. TEAL stands for "Technology Enabled Active Learning," and it will be used this fall to teach our electricity and magnetism course. Taught in newly designed facilities, its first goal is to reintroduce hands-on experiments into the large freshman introductory subjects; its second goal is to more fully and actively engage students in the introductory courses than is possible with a strict lecture format. This concept was pioneered at Rensselaer Polytechnic Institute and at North Carolina State University.

In studio teaching, lectures, recitations, and hands-on laboratories are merged into a single experience. Students work together in groups of nine per table in a specially equipped classroom. They make heavy use of computer simulations and visualizations. Whiteboards are always available for impromptu discussions or explanations. Video projection screens make it possible to present and share materials in both impromptu and formal ways.

We will carefully evaluate performance in these classrooms and compare it with how students do in traditional lecture courses.

How does an institution foster and support major innovations like this? The answer is simple: Make funds available to those faculty members who want to reform or improve education and who have good ideas they want to try out. Our experience is that such funding will catalyze rapid progress, even in an institution with a long-standing commitment to teaching and learning.

We are fortunate to have established two such funds in addition to the resources that individual schools and departments provide. The first is a generous endowment established by Alex and Brit d'Arbeloff to promote excellence in MIT education. The second is a major program called I-Campus established by MIT in partnership with Microsoft. Both programs enable faculty, students, and staff to submit proposals that are judged by a committee of educators. Ten percent of the budget for each d'Arbeloff-funded project must be set aside to support careful evaluation of its effectiveness, and all I-Campus projects must have an assessment component in order to receive funding.

Currently the d'Arbeloff Fund supports fifteen projects, most associated with improvements of the freshman-year experience. They range from TEAL/Physics to a freshman project in solving complex problems. Last year, the freshman project—Mars 2000—explored the design of a mission to Mars to determine whether life exists there, drawing on many experts from outside MIT who acted as mentors and resources to the student teams. The results—in terms of intensity, engagement, and learning— appear to have been spectacular. Other funded projects ranged from pedagogical initiatives in basic mathematics to innovative advising and tutoring systems. Note that not all of these initiatives involve new uses of technology. The emphasis is on learning and on improving the student experience.

Similarly, the Microsoft I-Campus program currently funds thirteen projects that utilize computer technology to enhance learning or to effectively manage educational systems. These projects run the gamut from on-line teaching modules in electrical engineering, computer science, and fluid mechanics to collaboration at a distance in aerospace design courses. It funds work on cross-media archives to be used in teaching Shakespeare studies, and has enabled students to develop a wireless system for instantaneous interaction and feedback in the classroom, including real-time assessment of understanding.

The Legal Environment and Intellectual Property Issues

As higher education—and the world at large—begins to develop new tools for the digital age, it encounters many unanticipated obstacles, mostly stemming from our litigious society and regulators straining to regulate something quite new and different.

For example, one large corporation recognized that the tools embodied in PIVOT could be used to help pass along hard-earned "know-how" to new generations of engineers and managers. The idea was simple: to establish a tutorial web site on which experienced "masters" would record their experiences, approaches, and life lessons regarding engineering and managerial problems. Newer staff could then gain an in-depth understanding of the craft through this professional "oral history."

This concept is excellent, and the goal is important in an age when fewer people devote long careers to a specific company or industry. In the end, however, it didn't fly very well. Why? The senior people were afraid that they would be the subjects of lawsuits if they honestly recounted mistakes of the past.

Or consider the issues associated with a library archive project like DSpace. If a traditional library owns a book, it can make that book available to anyone it chooses—library subscribers, students of the university, or anyone it lets enter its building. A library can do this because, as owner of that book, it has "first copy rights": it can not only read the ideas contained in the book, it can offer them to anyone else.

However, today's digital materials do not generally afford such "first copy rights." Instead of "subscribing" to an electronic database, we "license" access to it. The original owner thus has far more control than with the traditional printed book. For example, a publisher can tell the library to whom it must restrict access. This flies in the face of the traditional openness of academic libraries.

How did this state arise? It is simple—the entertainment industry and its interests have guided the development of legislation that governs electronic media. A meaningful set of changes and exemptions must be worked out in Washington if digital libraries are to realize their promise for research, scholarship, and education.

Of course, one of the hottest questions in academia is who owns the intellectual property when a faculty member produces electronic teaching materials. We are all struggling with this, and certainly no uniform approach has evolved across U.S. colleges and universities. The question is complex because the potential forms of electronic teaching materials are complex. At MIT our policies are evolving, but are becoming more concrete.

Normally when a faculty member writes a book, he or she simply owns the copyright and can independently assign it to a publisher. The institution plays no role in this. But electronic educational materials may well not be simply a book in digital form. They may capture the essence of our classroom or laboratory experience. They may be highly interactive. It may be unclear whether they comprise teaching or publishing. They may be very time consuming and expensive to produce. How do we resolve this?

Insofar as possible, we are building our policies on the foundation of the basic mission of the institution, and what we expect of a faculty member in pursuit of that mission. We exist to discover and teach and to enable our faculty to achieve full, unfettered dissemination of their intellectual property. But we also expect their appropriate commitment of time and effort to this mission. We have long-standing processes for avoiding conflicts of commitment. Faculty should not enter into contracts with outside parties that would constrain their teaching or scholarly responsibilities at MIT. They also cannot disseminate intellectual property that impairs the rights of others associated with it.

The *Policies and Procedures* of MIT basically indicate that MIT owns intellectual property if "substantial" MIT resources were used to generate it. This will frequently be the case when sophisticated digital teaching materials are developed. But by no means is the matter cut and dried. Time and experience will be required to establish sound understanding and application of these policies.

The Spectrum of Educational Technology: What's Next?

In this essay I have tried to portray some of my views on the nature of research universities in the digital age. I find it to be a time in which educational experiments large and small must progress, and sense that it is a time in which a deep recommitment to effective teaching and learning is evolving. I have illustrated some of the phenomena by citing a few of the activities underway at MIT.

It seems to me that the vector of these activities points to what we should expect during the next decade or so: increasing collaborative activities and electronic learning communities, on both national and international scales; the development of tutorial and studio teaching, enhanced by digital tools; production of advanced simulations and visualizations; the development of sophisticated platforms for sharing Web-based materials and for managing the educational enterprise; a myriad of devices and programs for interaction; and, I very much hope, the establishment of an OpenCourseWare movement to enhance education around the world. It must be a time of experimentation and risk-taking. We must conceive and implement some very large-scale projects, and also make modest modifications to existing ways of teaching.

This is a picture of somewhat chaotic, intellectually entrepreneurial evolution, as opposed to overwhelming revolution. That is in the spirit of the Internet and the World Wide Web, which are the bases of much of the opportunity before us. But it is important to note that the technology must serve us as educators and learners, not the other way around. The concept of appropriate technology holds. It runs from a simple wireless Personal Response System (PRS) that allows students in a lecture hall to respond to a faculty member's query about their understanding of a concept to the Internet-2 connection that makes it possible for students in MIT and Singapore to have a shared, simultaneous learning experience.

Indeed, our rather revolutionary MIT OpenCourseWare initiative is based on relatively straightforward technology. The users of MIT OCW, for the foreseeable future, will mostly reduce its content to paper form, or use it as the foundation of lectures and seminars.

Looking beyond the relatively near horizon, however, is difficult. Why? Largely because the technological platforms will continue to evolve at blinding speed, and there will inevitably be discontinuous changes and surprises.

I would particularly look to the use of new interfaces and means of human-computer interaction, which can take simulation and interactive learning to the next level. This is part of the goal of Professor Hiroshi Ishii's "Tangible Bits" group in the MIT Media Lab. Their goal is to communicate digitally mediated senses of activity and presence at the periphery of human awareness. For example, they are developing workbenches, walls, and rooms in which ambient light, sound, airflow, and water movement can display information.

Through these and other advances, the learner's interactions with his or her surroundings will soon involve all five senses, as the environment itself displays, receives, and conveys information in a myriad of forms. As they strive to understand basic concepts and learn to design or synthesize information in new ways, students will navigate virtual space and time.

Dinosaurs or Prometheans?

Now I return to the central question.

I believe that universities like MIT are making steady progress in using emerging electronic technologies to enhance and extend learning. But we must separate the wheat from the chaff, and we can only do this by keeping focused on the real objective—learning. We should not use these technologies just because they are there, or only because we see some potential revenues associated with them.

Above all, we must evaluate our educational experiments and new approaches in order to understand whether they improve learning. Evaluation is key. Understanding what doesn't work is as important as recognizing success.

Some of our experiences with long-distance collaborative design and mentoring were not successful. This was because we had not invested sufficiently in the use of expert technical operators of the videoconferencing systems. On the other hand, the simple Personal Response System has been used very effectively.

Two years ago, when Alex and Brit d'Arbeloff established their extraordinary fund to support improvements in the excellence of education at MIT, we held a daylong program of talks, proposals, and brainstorming about teaching, expecting that people would focus on advances that could come from the use of digital media. Interestingly, digital media received almost no attention that day; the faculty and students were concerned about more fundamental goals and concepts. Nonetheless, in due course, many good proposals were made to this fund, and also to the Microsoft I-Campus initiative, which uses electronic media and devices to improve pedagogy.

The real lesson of the MIT experience with educational technology, in my mind, is that it has forced us to rethink the educational process. Faculty engaged in these new approaches do believe that they have become better teachers—but not so much because of the technological extensions of their capability but because the process of designing the programs forces them to think in fresh ways about ancient techniques.

Thus we come full circle to the essential human quality of teaching and learning. It is our minds, our sharing spirits, our insights into our students, our quest to improve what we do, and our passion to explore new horizons that drive the quality of teaching and learning in a research university.

But we can do better in the future than in the past. That is the simple definition of progress, and this progress will be driven in part by new technological possibilities.

We are not dinosaurs. We are Prometheans.

Our progress will be driven by competition as well. Others, driven by emerging technological and market forces, will increasingly challenge our leadership in education. I welcome this, because a healthy mix of competition and cooperation fuels excellence.

We have new opportunities to form educational alliances across distance, time, institutions, and nations—alliances that will expand opportunity, learning, and understanding. This, too, I celebrate, because we and our students must be citizens of the world as well as of our own countries.

However, the energy, passion, and inventiveness of our residential students, together with an environment that combines research, scholarship, and teaching, is our greatest source of renewal and our greatest strength.

12

Response and Responsibility: Balancing Security and Openness in Research and Education 2001–2002

The scale and nature of the ongoing revolution in science and technology, and what it implies for the quality of human capital in the 21st century, pose critical national security challenges for the United States. Second only to a weapon of mass destruction detonating in an American city, we can think of nothing more dangerous than a failure to manage properly science, technology, and education for the common good over the next quarter century.

—U.S. Commission on National Security in the 21st Century, March 15, 2001

On September 11, 2001, three thousand innocent people died in the murderous attacks on the World Trade Center, the Pentagon, and in Pennsylvania. The federal government thus had thrust upon it a daunting responsibility to protect the lives of people in the United States— but to do so within a new, complicated environment far different from that of the cold-war years during which our national defense was shaped. Protecting us is, of course, a fundamental responsibility of our government.

This new world of homeland and international security presented opportunities to the research university community to serve through security-related R&D. But the academic community also recognized very quickly that reactions to these all-too-real dangers would inevitably pose conflicts with some of our most deeply held values, and indeed with the fundamental methodology of science. Immigration policy and access of international students and scholars to our campuses and to scientific meetings would come into question; restrictions on publication and open scientific dialog about topics of potential use by terrorists would be proposed; and safeguards and restrictions on the use in our laboratories of potentially dangerous materials, especially biological agents, would be established.

This essay was an exploration of these critically important issues. It concluded that we must maintain the openness of our campuses to students, faculty, and scholars from around the world, or else we will lose an essential element of our greatness, and of our citizenship in the world. We also need to be vigilant to safeguard the openness of scientific inquiry and communication, or else we could inadvertently weaken the conduct of science and its application to creating a better world. All of this requires that the academic and scientific communities establish a respectful and cooperative dialogue with the federal government. Unnecessary damage to our nation, our institutions, and to the respect with which the world views both, are most likely to arise as unintended consequences of risk-averse decisions made in the absence of high-level policy. The academic community must shoulder part of the responsibility of avoiding these outcomes.

Openness and Security

The ability of our nation to remain secure in the face of both traditional military threats and international terrorism while maintaining the excellence and pace of American science and technology requires a delicate balance. It depends first and foremost on effective dialogue and joint problem solving by those responsible for maintaining our security and those who lead our scientific, engineering, and higher-education communities.

Our immediate impulse when threatened is to wall ourselves off and to regulate the release of information of potential use to our enemies. This is understandable, and frequently justified, but in today's complicated world, the security issues raised regarding research and education do not lend themselves to simple responses—especially when long-term consequences are considered. Why?

The future health, economic strength, and quality of life in America, and indeed the world, depend on the continued rapid advance of science and technology, and on the education of scientists and engineers at the most advanced levels. The rapid progress of science and technology, and the advanced education of scientists and engineers, in turn, depends critically on openness of process, openness of publication, and openness of participation within our institutions and across national boundaries.

Historically, our nation and world have faced many challenges to peace and security. Now we face a constant threat by determined terrorists. Their immediate objectives are to kill large numbers of people, or to cause terror, panic, or disruptions of our lives and economy.

As we respond to the reality of terrorism, we must not unintentionally disable the quality and rapid evolution of American science and technology, or of advanced education, by closing their various boundaries. For if we did, the irony is that over time this would achieve in substantial measure the objectives of those who disdain our society and would do us harm by disrupting our economy and quality of life.

Americans are learning that the balance between protection of our lives and of our liberties is as difficult to strike as it is essential that we do so. I believe that it is equally imperative that we strike the right balance between security and the openness of our scientific research and education. But I conclude that we must rely very heavily on maintaining that openness.

In the year since the murderous attacks in New York, Washington, and Pennsylvania, the experience of MIT and other leading research-intensive universities has been primarily one of calm and reasoned interaction and consultation with the federal government on such matters as the admission of international students and scholars, the openness of scientific research, and the control of dangerous chemical and biological agents.

However, the discussion of these issues and the establishment of a regulatory environment associated with homeland security are far from over. It therefore seems timely to address some of the fundamental issues and long-term consequences of our decisions.

Before doing so, let me make clear that, although it is not the topic of this essay, MIT and our sister institutions take very seriously our responsibility to serve our nation by applying our talents and capabilities to the protection of human life and infrastructure in our homeland and throughout the world. (See, for example, our website on MIT research and education on homeland and global security: http://web.mit.edu/homeland/index.html.)

International Students

A matter of current debate, legislation, and policy implementation is the degree to which our university campuses should remain open to international students and scholars. Who should receive student visas? Should there be limitations on what foreign-born students can study? What criteria should be applied when answering such questions?

American research universities hold deep and long-standing values of openness in scientific research and education. Yet we must test these values and their implications against the realities of the catastrophic terrorist acts that left 3,000 dead within our borders in a single, horrific day. The fact is that an environment requiring careful evaluation of these values and their security implications had developed well before September 11, 2001.

For decades, the outward diffusion of people, ideas, and collaboration from our universities has been celebrated as important and timely. This diffusion has been accelerated by the Internet and the World Wide Web, and by the rapid evolution of globalization and internationalization. These forces of openness and outward pull are now opposed by concerns about their possible implications for our vulnerability to terrorism and for the nation's broader posture regarding export controls on certain technologies and information.

Clearly, the resolution of these issues requires an ongoing, substantive dialogue between the academic community and the federal government. In my view, during the past twelve months, such a dialogue has begun and in general has proceeded well toward a reasoned resolution of several core issues. Nonetheless, the underlying sense of partnership is fragile and is vulnerable to political winds that can shift in a moment. It would be devastating to our long-term national interest if substantive dialogue and mutual problem solving were not continued.

The MIT Context

Let me begin with the MIT context. Approximately 9 percent of our undergraduate students are international; they come from eighty-eight countries. About 37 percent of our graduate students are international; they come from ninety-one countries. Across our institution, there is a deep belief that these young men and women contribute immensely to MIT's educational environment—one in which all students are exposed to a variety of cultures, personal experiences, and worldviews.

These international students are the best and brightest from their nations and they strongly enhance the excellence of learning and research at MIT. They are not some spice added to the mix; rather, they are an integral and valued part of what makes MIT great. Furthermore, the industries and institutions in which our graduates will live and work are highly globalized, so that even from a purely pragmatic perspective, cross-cultural and cross-national learning and experience are valuable and in our national interest.

MIT has a long tradition of educating not only citizens, often the first in their families to go to college, but also immigrants. Although we maintain no data to confirm it, my impression is that many of our students are U.S. citizens whose parents came to this country from elsewhere. Engineering and science in this country have traditionally been pathways up the ladder to economic success and productive contribution to our society.

If ever there were a meritocracy, it is the MIT faculty, which has selected many in its ranks from those who have come to this country from elsewhere. The recent Nobel laureates on the MIT faculty include people born in Japan, India, Mexico, Italy, and Germany, as well as the United States. Most of them came to this country as graduate students. Or consider our Institute Professors, the dozen or so faculty members who have achieved the highest faculty rank at MIT. They were born in the United States *and* in Belgium, Italy, Mexico, Israel, and China. Any of our great universities would offer similar lessons.

The preponderance of our graduates appear to have remained in this country, contributing to the ranks of other faculties and the leadership of our high-tech industries, and participating broadly in our ongoing civic enterprise. Today, it is widely assumed, though not well documented, that as economies have improved around the world, especially around the Pacific Rim, more graduates are returning home than has previously been the case.

And those who have returned to their native countries have frequently contributed greatly to their leadership and to their industries. They take to their nations new knowledge and training that can grow strong economies and attenuate the inequities that are at the core of world strife. MIT's Department of Economics has graduated many PhD's who went on to become economic ministers or other high-level officials around the world. The Sloan Fellows Program of advanced executive education has had a large international enrollment from its inception. Sloan Fellows are found all over the world in leadership roles. A visitor to practically any country will find MIT-educated engineers and scientists leading faculties and industries. The vast majority carry with them an understanding of and respect for our institutions and for many of our national values and characteristics.

Have MIT graduates returned to other countries and worked against the interests of the United States? There are undoubtedly a few such instances, given the large numbers of graduates and the ebb and flow of history. There were examples of this in China during the Cold War and elsewhere, just as a tiny few of the tens of thousands of our U.S. citizen graduates may have been less than a source of pride. I can draw no conclusion, however, other than that MIT, the United States, and the world have overwhelmingly benefited from the international character of our student body.

The National Context

What is the broader national context?

Over the last twenty-five years, the number of foreign-born scientists and engineers in the United States has grown in all degree levels, in all sectors, and in most fields of study. The largest group of foreign students are those studying in our business schools. Currently, 25 percent of all U.S. doctorate holders, and roughly 45 percent of PhD engineers and computer scientists, were born abroad. One-third of the science and engineering PhD's working in our industries were born elsewhere, with this number exceeding 50 percent in engineering and computer science.

Over the years, the dominant national origins of international students studying science, engineering, and computer science in the United States have shifted, largely propelled by the strength of various national economies, and attenuated by political conflicts. When I was a young faculty member, the largest numbers of international students in U.S. engineering programs came from Iran and Nigeria; today, they come from Asian countries.

When considering the large influx of international students in engineering and science, we must recognize that these demanding studies and professions are not highly valued in our popular or political cultures. It is incumbent on us to strengthen our K–12 science and math education, and for the government and private sector to maintain exciting research and educational environments to attract bright young Americans. I should note that as federal funding for biomedical research has dramatically increased during the last few years, in that field the percentage of doctorates granted to U.S. citizens has begun to increase, albeit slowly.

As we consider the implications for homeland security of our openness to international students, we should be cognizant that other national emergencies have raised similar questions in the past. In the late 1970s, during the Iranian hostage crisis, grave concerns were raised about Iranian students in this country, and strong actions were contemplated, and to some extent taken, against them. In the late 1980s and early 1990s, MIT and other universities were castigated because of our visitors from, and interactions with, Japan. It was feared that the Japanese would milk advanced technology from our university laboratories, commercialize it, and drive our economy into the ground. Indeed, a U.S. senator widely circulated a diagram titled "The Circle of Shame" with MIT depicted at the heart of this presumed nefarious activity.

Three Conclusions
From this background and context, I draw three conclusions:

• First, the openness of U.S. research universities to foreign students and scholars has been overwhelmingly successful in building the excellence of our institutions, enhancing the educational experience of our students, contributing to American industry and academia, advancing nations around the world, and disbursing good will toward and understanding of our system and values.

• Second, nationally, the proportion of foreign students in science and engineering doctoral programs continues to grow. This, however, is largely a reflection of problems in our own secondary educational system, coupled with a popular culture that does not promote or value the dedication and long years of hard work required for success in these fields.

• And third, our openness to international students and scholars has been questioned or reviewed many times throughout our history, including during the most recent decades.

We now find ourselves in perilous times that require that we consider, in partnership with our federal government, whether our openness to foreign students requires modification. Indeed, statutory requirements for such determinations are already in place. We have the harsh reality that a few of those responsible for the bombing of the World Trade Center in 1993, and the mass killings in New York, Washington, and Pennsylvania last year, entered this country on student visas. We also have the concern that future catastrophic terrorism—unlike that committed to date—might require advanced scientific knowledge or materials that could be acquired in university classrooms or laboratories.

Thus two questions are raised: Should we track the whereabouts of foreign students, and should there be restrictions on what they study?

Tracking International Students

Students and visiting scholars must be issued visas by U.S. consular officers around the world after they have been admitted to study at a U.S. university. The consuls have the responsibility for judging the appropriateness of admitting each such student. This is the proper division of labor—universities evaluate academic credentials, and federal officials in the State Department determine admissibility to the United States.

It is broadly agreed that once students arrive in this country universities should maintain and provide to the government fundamental "directory information" including whether each individual is enrolled and what area of study he or she is pursuing. It certainly is legitimate for the government to track non-immigrant students and scholars, and determine whether they are pursuing the purposes for which they were admitted. Despite numerous comments by journalists and politicians to the contrary, the higher education community has supported, and continues to support, such tracking.

The problem has been that this information, which is already collected by the universities, gets buried in a vast amount of paper that cannot be processed or analyzed in a timely manner. A new computer system, SEVIS (Student and Exchange Visitor Information System), is under rapid development to correct this situation. MIT supports the deployment of SEVIS, and so does every major higher education association.

Sensitive Areas of Study

Presidential Decision Directive No. 2, issued by President Bush in October 2001, requires that the federal government, in consultation with the higher education community, determine "sensitive areas of study" that should be off-limits to students from certain nations.[1] Even this is not a new concept. There has existed for some time a State Department system called Mantis that is alerted when a potential student from certain countries applies to study in a field that appears on the Technology Alert List, such as nuclear engineering, lasers, sensors, ceramics, radar, electronic guidance systems, or munitions. The State Department must then generate a specific opinion as to whether the student should be granted a visa.

Nonetheless, I am deeply concerned about where implementation of this directive could lead. The basic framework, developed by the White House in consultation with agencies such as the State Department and the Department of Justice, and with considerable discussion with the higher education community, is fundamentally sound. The core of this framework is the Interagency Panel on Advanced Science and Security (IPASS). The proposed task of IPASS is widely understood to be to determine whether students or scholars applying to enter the United States will engage in research activities that provide access to advanced science or technology of direct relevance to the development, deployment, or delivery of weapons of mass destruction.

This framework, if I have accurately portrayed it, has two important positive features. First, it establishes a high-level review panel, rather than generating a list of specific subjects or courses considered off-limits. Second, it applies to matters associated with weapons of mass destruction, which, as I will explain later in this essay, seems appropriate to me. Third, it places this judgment with the admitting authorities *at the time of visa application*, thus maximizing the openness of our institution to students once they are properly admitted to the United States.

Where could the IPASS framework go wrong and unreasonably disrupt the basic workings of research universities? I would suggest the following potentialities as troubling or inappropriate:

• Moving beyond criteria that are based rather narrowly on weapons of mass destruction;

• Expanding criteria to cover academic courses and classes, rather than very specific research and development activities; and

• Applying new academic restrictions to students after they have begun to study at the institution for which they were properly granted a visa.

Indeed, the MIT Ad Hoc Committee on Access to and Disclosure of Scientific Information, chaired by former U.S. secretary of the air force Sheila E. Widnall, in its report "In the Public Interest," recommended that "No foreign national granted a visa by the U.S. government should be denied access to courses, research or publications generally available on campus."[2]

This committee further stated,

The well-being of our nation will ultimately be damaged if education, science, and technology suffer as a result of any practices that indiscriminately discourage or limit the open exchange of ideas.

We recommend that no classified research should be carried out on campus; that no student, graduate or undergraduate, should be required to have a security clearance to perform thesis research; and that no thesis research should be carried out in [intellectual] areas requiring access to classified materials.

Scientific Materials and Information

Terrorism to date has been decidedly low-tech, although its worst instances have been very sophisticated organizationally. Truck bombs, commandeering of commercial aircraft, and credit card fraud appear to have been the primary tools used by those who have done us great harm. The materials they used have been things such as fertilizer, diesel fuel, and off-the-shelf chemicals. None of this has involved scientific or technical information that is advanced or difficult to obtain. This is an important observation, although it is no guarantee of the future course of events. Indeed, the as-yet undetermined origin of anthrax attacks in the United States gives rise to important concerns.

The nebulous, diffuse nature of terrorism makes a simple prescription for the responsibilities of academic institutions impossible. Nonetheless, let me suggest a basic framework for thinking about it, by parsing the issues among the most commonly discussed mechanisms for terrorist attacks of a technological nature.

This framework reflects the nature of the information and materials required:

• The use of *nuclear weapons and missiles* is a singular matter. The information required to construct a nuclear weapon is acquired over many years. It is generally not the stuff of classroom learning; rather it is largely sophisticated "know-how" developed by experience, testing, and advanced computational simulation. Most nations can only acquire the critical components and materials required for construction of a nuclear weapon by illegal means.

• *Cyberterrorism* is the use of computer and communication technology to disrupt, corrupt, or disable our military or commercial IT systems. Potentially it could directly weaken our national security, or it could bring havoc to our economy. The information required by a cyberterrorist can be presumed to be of varying degrees of sophistication, but generally available. It is largely the stuff of hacking. The materials, in this case, are computers and access to the Internet. Having said this, cybersecurity is an urgent issue in all domains of industry, education, and government. It imposes additional administrative burdens and regulatory costs on all organizations, and it calls for more computer scientists and mathematicians who are U.S. citizens, trained to protect our information infrastructure.

• *Bioterrorism* could involve the propagation of disease and the defeat or disruption of therapies to counter it. The information required is likely to be available in published literature. Some experientially gained "know-how" might be involved, but it could generally be obtained by a wide variety of experiences in laboratories, medical establishments, or pharmaceutical companies. Some specialized equipment or facilities might be required, but they would likely have widespread applicability to legitimate activities. This situation is distinctly unlike the case of nuclear weapons and poses some of the most vexing issues. The needed biological materials may or may not be readily available.

• *Chemical or explosive attacks* are somewhat less commonly discussed, but are, in my view, among the things we should be most worried about. The information required for many forms is readily available, even to the layperson. Some dangerous agents are difficult to obtain, but others can be purchased off the shelf. The terrible destruction of lives by an angry American at the Alfred P. Murrah Building in Oklahoma City and the use of Sarin gas in Tokyo are prime examples.

Having reviewed these categories, I would say that nuclear weaponry seems to be an almost singular case. Critical knowledge and "know-how" should be, and are, highly restricted by the normal security classification processes of the Department of Defense and the Department of Energy. These are not things that students should be required to access in the conduct of university research; they cannot be taught in a normal classroom. It is an area that, in my view, is appropriate for reasoned decision making by IPASS. But we should depend primarily on our well-established classification and security mechanisms.

I do not believe that cyberterrorism, bioterrorism, or the use of chemical explosives pose threats that could in a meaningful way be countered or avoided by restrictions on what is taught in our university classrooms, or on the country of origin of our students. This is basic knowledge, and as in most instances in life, basic knowledge can be used for good or ill. The knowledge of what makes a virus virulent is also the key to medical therapies and disease prevention. This may be an uncomfortable reality, but it is a reality.

The *material* (as distinct from the information) needed to cause terror by chemical or biological means is a different matter. It is a clear responsibility of universities not to be a *source* of such materials for use by those who would do harm. Access to pathogens and dangerous chemicals must be carefully restricted and monitored in the normal course of doing science. Inventories should be minimized. Location, quantities, and security should be maintained effectively and accurately. We are working hard to establish best-practice in this regard at MIT.

It is the further responsibility of universities to educate all of their research and laboratory students about security issues regarding their materials and equipment. This should be integrated with education and training regarding the health, safety, and environmental responsibilities of laboratory practice. Rules as basic as not working alone in chemical and biological laboratories must be reinforced.

Select Agents

The term "select agent" came into the scientific vernacular when, on June 12, 2002, the president signed into law the Public Health Security and Bioterrorism Preparedness and Response Act of 2002 (H.R. 3448, Pub. L. 107–188).

As a first step in this law, all researchers in the life sciences were required to report to their institution and to the government (Department of Health and Human Services) by September 10 their inventory of forty "select agents" that might be used as bioweapons. Other provisions of the law will include similar reporting requirements for potentially lethal agricultural materials and security measures for laboratories that keep such agents. In addition, only those researchers found to have a legitimate need will be allowed access to these materials, which will not be available to students or scholars from countries that are considered to be sponsors of terrorism or to people with histories of mental illness or felony or drug convictions.[3]

By and large, the academic community has treated this as a reasonable approach and, of course, will comply with the law. But even this seemingly straightforward approach is not without a huge potential price to be paid in the advancement of science, and therefore in our health and welfare. The MIT Ad Hoc Committee on Access to and Disclosure of Scientific Information was deeply concerned about the path down which we may be starting, noting that the Secretary of Health and Human Services has the statutory power to expand the list of select agents. The committee expressed the view that we could soon arrive at a level of restriction of access to materials by our students, faculty, or staff on the basis of their citizenship, for example—something that would be incompatible with our principles of openness, and would cause us to withdraw from the corresponding research topics on our campus.

Publication of Scientific Information

The most difficult challenge as we balance prudent measures to maintain our security with the openness that is so essential to America's basic principles, to the excellence of our universities, and to the conduct of science, is associated with publishing information in the life sciences.

Why is this so complicated?

Science is a collective endeavor. Science increasingly is an international endeavor. The weight of these two statements is compounding at lightning speed as the complexity of science increases, and because, like all of society, scientists are tied together through the Internet. Science progresses not just by singular discoveries, but also by the independent verification and interactive discussion of discoveries. Knowledge is honed through ongoing dialogue that takes unexpected twists and turns. It thrives in openness, and suffers in isolation.

Thus, in fields such as microbiology, the very nature of science, when combined with the dual nature of information—that is, its use for good or for ill—presents a challenge in an environment filled with well-justified concern about terrorism.

I worry that the broad advance of biological science is open to compromise. Restrictions that have been or may be imposed by our government as it struggles to carry out its most fundamental mission of protecting its citizens are not the only issue. The politics of subjects such as in-vitro fertilization and stem-cell research have removed them from the sphere of federally funded university and government laboratory research, where the mission is to achieve basic scientific understanding. Former director of the National Institutes of Health Harold E. Varmus, among others, has raised deep concern about distortions in the conduct of these and certain other areas of basic biological research that, as a result of such federal policies, can go forward *only* in industrial labs, where "commercial realities must be considered along with scientific progress, where full disclosure is not the norm, and where oversight is limited."[4]

Three Suggestions

The resolution of matters of open publication when our security is challenged is not easy. A panel of the National Academy of Sciences has been established to provide guidance on this matter. It is chaired by MIT professor Gerald R. Fink, former director of the Whitehead Institute for Biomedical Research. While looking forward to their wisdom, let me offer three suggestions for the resolution of the issues of sensitive areas of study, select agents, and publication of scientific information:

• First, *consultation* by the Federal Government with the academic and scientific communities is essential. This must be continuous and directly effective consultation at both the policy and operational levels. As pointed out with great clarity by John J. Hamre, former U.S. Deputy Secretary of Defense, all too often security professionals do not understand or trust scientists, and scientists may be quite unaware of some real risks associated with their work.[5] This has been a major problem within the nuclear weapons arena since its beginning. It will be even more complex as we worry about basic research in universities in the diffuse, little-understood context of terrorist threats. But there is no viable alternative to substantive consultation and mutual effort.

• Second, *distinct boundaries* must be drawn where it is actually possible and appropriate. It is the ambiguity and uncertainty of what is inappropriate to publish, or in the use by the government of ill-defined terms like "sensitive but unclassified," that creates danger for the scientific enterprise and invites bad decisions. Well before September 2001, difficult issues were arising regarding the application of export controls on the uses of computers and satellites for basic research, and even control of certain unclassified but export-controlled library documents. Productive collaborations with scientists in other countries and the work of noncitizen graduate students and scholars have been prohibited by increasingly broad interpretation of the International Traffic in Arms Regulations (ITAR). Similar problems with export control arose in the 1980s. The problem was settled effectively when President Reagan issued National Security Decision Directive 189 (NSDD 189). Basically NSDD 189 stated that scientific information is either classified or unclassified. It generally exempted fundamental research from security regulations. This distinct boundary was fundamentally clear and effective for many years. Then, over time, its interpretation by the bureaucracy became increasingly broad and its effectiveness was diminished by application of other statutes—an opportunity afforded by the compromise insertion of one open-ended clause when it was drafted. NSDD 189 should be reaffirmed, and its spirit should be applied in other domains. The default in fuzzy areas should be to keep basic research open and unencumbered.

• And third, we should not underestimate the power of *voluntary agreements* within the scientific community. The decisions about publication of detailed results faced by many scientists, especially biologists and biomedical researchers, simply do not lend themselves to decisions by security personnel. In the end, most decisions will be made by the scientists who perform the work being reported, because, given the dynamic evolution of scientific knowledge, they do not lend themselves to simple regulatory rules. We also must be keenly aware that regulations in the United States are limited in their effectiveness in an age when important frontier science is done in many nations around the world. (Indeed, the incident that first brought this issue to the public's attention occurred when an Australian group reportedly learned how to make a virus related to smallpox 100 percent virulent.) It may be that the most effective thing to do is to create a framework or forums from which scientists can gain guidance and advice from their peers as they wrestle with such daunting decisions.

Here too there is precedent of sorts. In the war years preceding the development of the atomic bomb, Allied scientists stopped publishing research associated with uranium physics, although they continued to discuss the topic privately among themselves. And when recombinant DNA first became possible, leading scientists, led by David Baltimore, established a moratorium on their work, pending open discussion among themselves and a wide range of lay people to establish standards. Work and open publication proceeded smoothly thereafter. Neither of these examples provides a direct guidance for the less focused situation we face today, but the point is that the scientists themselves, in consultation with many others as appropriate, found an effective path forward.

In Conclusion

The debate about security and openness is not new. In 1958 Norbert Wiener opined, "To disseminate information about a weapon . . . is to make practically certain that it will be used."[6] As if in rejoinder, Edward Teller said in 1987 that "secrecy is not compatible with science, but it is even less compatible with democratic procedure."[7] These statements by two brilliant scientists with experience in defense work reflect the fact that virtually all science and engineering knowledge, or most other knowledge for that matter, can be used for good or ill.

This certainly does not mean that we can wash our hands of the responsibility to address hard questions about the safety and security of our fellow citizens. But in an age when the "weapon" may be a truckload of explosives, a computer virus, a commandeered aircraft, or finely milled bacterial spores, "dissemination of information" is a nebulous matter. And in an age when the rapid advance of science and technology is essential to sustaining our health, economy, and quality of life, Teller's observation is of crucial importance.

Traditional American values of openness in education and research must prevail. But this will be possible only if we in research universities contribute our talents to maintaining the security of our homeland, and if the federal government and academia maintain a respectful, substantive, and effective dialogue between those who do science and those who are charged with protecting the nation.

Notes

1. "Homeland Security Presidential Directive—2," October 29, 2001, President George W. Bush.

2. "In the Public Interest," Report of the Ad Hoc Faculty Committee on Access to and Disclosure of Scientific Information, Massachusetts Institute of Technology, Sheila E. Widnall, Chair, June 12, 2002, p. 15; subsequent citations at pp. ii and iii.

3. See Diana Jean Schemo, "September 11 Strikes at Labs' Doors," *New York Times*, August 13, 2002, page F1; and David Malakoff, "Tighter Security Reshapes Research," *Science* 297 (September 6, 2002): 1630.

4. Harold E. Varmus, "The Weaknesses of Science for Profit," *New York Times*, December 4, 2001, p. A21.

5. John J. Hamre, "Science and Security at Risk," *Issues in Science and Technology* 18, no. 4 (Summer 2002): 51–57.

6. Norbert Wiener, quoted in Robert Jung, *Brighter than a Thousand Suns* (Harmondsworth: Penguin Books, 1958).

7. Edward Teller, *Better a Shield than a Sword: Perspectives on Defense and Technology* (New York: The Free Press, 1987).

13

Moving On
2002–2004

The moving finger writes; and, having writ, moves on.
—*The Rubaiyat of Omar Khayyam*

This final essay, to some extent, speaks to the state of MIT as I prepare to leave its presidency. It covers essentially the past two years, rather than a single academic year. In it, I reflect somewhat on what I had learned in nearly fourteen years, and cite a few lessons I thought might be of some value as MIT prepares to move on to its next stage. It is of a more personal nature than the essays that preceded it, but it is neither a laundry list of accomplishments nor a guess at the legacy of a presidential tenure. Rather, it reflects some values and characteristics that I have observed, learned about, or built on as I worked with my MIT colleagues during these years.

Among these values and characteristics are excellence, perseverance, boldness, and optimism, which have permeated the actions of MIT as an institution, and legions of individuals within its community. These characteristics have had a great deal to do with the path that MIT has taken from 1990 to 2004. My role during these years has given me many opportunities to understand some of the origins and manifestations of academic excellence. It has also given me a deeper understanding of the values of perseverance, boldness, and optimism, and occasionally to find them within myself. Of course, these characteristics and values are not new; they have dominated critical moments throughout the history of MIT.

In the essay for academic year 1998–1999, I wrote, "Colleges and universities teach by their actions as well as through their curricula." Herein are a few of the actions by which MIT has taught, and some of the foundations on which American higher education has achieved greatness and relevance.

Universities endure. Their work is never complete. To paraphrase Vannevar Bush, they forever pursue the endless frontier. The role of individuals is transient. We make our contributions, do our work, exert our influence, pursue our passions, chase our dreams, teach and learn, succeed and fail, give substance to the present, help shape the future, and then move on.

And as we move on, we should reflect on our times and what we have learned—but only for the purpose of helping ourselves, and others, to travel more wisely into the future. Having had the rare privilege of serving as president of MIT for nearly fourteen years, through the change from the twentieth to the twenty-first century, I am indeed compelled to reflect on what I have learned. It is far too soon for me to claim more than a hint of understanding of the institutional legacy my colleagues and I leave, and that is for others to determine in any event.

Excellence

I have learned about excellence.

Faculty

Most of us go through life adding incrementally to knowledge, polishing a concept here or there, doing an experiment, contributing a few leaves—or, if we are lucky, a twig—to the tree of knowledge. But there are the few who change fundamentally what we know or can do.

Tom Everhart, when he was president of Caltech, once observed to me that, "one truly excellent scientist is more valuable than 1,000 very good scientists." MIT is blessed with a remarkable number of excellent scholars, teachers, and researchers. The joy of serving as president of the Institute is to be in constant contact with such people. And the challenge is to work effectively with colleagues, who in any given conversation or situation, will know infinitely more about the topic at hand than you could ever learn. Of course, academic administrators and leaders enjoy this, but must cope with how to make wise decisions in such an environment.

At an MIT memorial service for the late Claude Shannon, Professor Robert Gallager observed that when one studies the outstanding work of others, for example, Shannon's application of Boolean algebra to describe computing, the natural reaction is "I wish I had thought of that!" But, said Gallager, when he was introduced to Shannon's concept of information channels and the mathematical theory of information, the only possible reaction was "How did he ever think of that? I never could have." That is an elegant illustration of what scholarly excellence is. It is also an overly modest statement about Bob Gallager's own contributions.

MIT history is replete with radical thinkers like Claude Shannon who have truly founded or transformed major fields of scholarship or technology—Noam Chomsky in linguistics, Paul Samuelson in economics, Norbert Wiener in cybernetics, and Tim Berners-Lee with the World Wide Web, to name but a few. I am confident that the current generation of MIT faculty includes many others whose contributions will prove in time to be of fundamental and lasting value. They set the stage for institutional excellence.

How do we maintain such individual excellence as the institution progresses? I believe that the primary mechanism is the much-maligned tenure system. Yes, tenure. When we make the hard decision to award tenure to a colleague, we are setting the standards of the institution for the next thirty or so years, so we do so with great care and a sense of responsibility. It is a hard-edged system within a community that thrives on collegiality. We first give enormous choice and opportunity to new faculty members, but several years after that, the tenure system focuses our minds on a clear, informed evaluation of the quality and impact of each candidate's accomplishments in research, scholarship, teaching, and to a lesser extent, service.

Many in the corporate world criticize tenure as simply job security and sinecure. But they are wrong. In a serious university, tenure is first and foremost a strong form of evaluation and accountability. Only between 30 and 50 percent of those who enter as assistant professors are ultimately tenured.

By the way, the tenure system is still justified, in my opinion, by the protection it provides against political interference in controversial scholarship. Undoubtedly, the system has been abused from time to time, but in first-rate institutions its implementation is one of our most important obligations, and it is a primary means for maintaining long-term excellence.

To paraphrase Winston Churchill's famous characterization of democratic government, the tenure system is the worst possible academic system—except for all the others.

Institutional excellence is more than a simple sum of the contributions of individual scholars. We are an academic community in which interaction and synergy define us to be far more. Good colleagues beget more good colleagues. Excellent students come to MIT to be taught by excellent faculty, and excellent faculty work at MIT in large measure because of our stellar students. Excellent faculty and students can accomplish their goals only when enabled by appropriate resources and skilled and committed staff. If any link in this chain is broken, there is danger of a downward spiral. Balancing all these factors is the prime responsibility of provosts, deans, department heads, and other academic leaders as they allocate resources.

Higher Education in America

Excellence also extends beyond individual scholars and institutions—it extends to systems. A basic question I have been asked innumerable times, especially when traveling abroad, is, Why is America's system of higher education so good? It is, as has been said all too often, the envy of the world.

I think that there are seven primary reasons for the excellence of U.S. higher education relative to that in other countries:

• We have a broad diversity of institutions ranging from small liberal arts colleges to Ivy League schools, to the great land grant universities, and to somewhat more focused institutions like MIT or Caltech. This diversity provides a wealth of environments and opportunities, from which individual students can select a school that best matches their needs and capabilities.

• We offer new assistant professors a wide-open field of freedom to choose what they teach and the topics of research and scholarship they engage. We reject the hierarchical systems of many other nations in which junior faculty are subservient to, and indeed apprenticed to, senior professors. We therefore enjoy a constant flow of new ideas, passions, and approaches that keep us fresh and robust.

• In our research universities we meaningfully weave together teaching and research. This too brings a freshness, intensity, and constant renewal that is a critical component of institutional excellence.

• We welcome to our nation and our institutions students, scholars, and faculty from other countries. It is not possible to overstate the intellectual and cultural richness that immigrants have brought to U.S. campuses. They have joined us to create what we are. Even the constant flow of international visitors to our campuses, and our faculty to theirs, is critically important.

• We have an implicit national science and technology policy that recognizes the support of frontier research in our universities as an important responsibility of the federal government. This policy is intended to provide financial support to researchers, in whatever institution they are located, based on their merit in a competitive marketplace of ideas. It has the additional feature, elegant in its simplicity, that funding for infrastructure is attached to grants and contracts, and therefore flows to the researchers with the most meritorious ideas and track records.

• We have a tradition of individual philanthropy through which our alumni and others who believe in excellent education support our colleges and universities. They enable talented students from families of modest means to attend even the most costly schools. We have tax laws that encourage and enable such support, to an extent that is unique in the world.

• We have a system of free competition for faculty and students. Such inter-institutional competition, though it may be the bane of academic administrators' daily lives, drives excellence.

As has been explained in my reports during the last thirteen years, most of these seven factors are constantly in danger. The political winds shift and change—raising barriers to international flow of students and scholars, corrupting the merit-based, peer-reviewed award of federal research funds through rampant "pork barrel" congressional earmarking of projects and facilities, and raising the specter of price controls on higher education rather than emphasizing financial aid for needy students. Some private foundations and philanthropists blow hot and cold on supporting the academic enterprise, and often suppress creative forces by being overly prescriptive. Governing boards, especially in public institutions, occasionally attempt to interfere inappropriately with the freedom of faculty to choose the subjects of their research and teaching.

All those who believe that it is important for the United States to have the best system of higher education in the world must therefore be constantly vigilant and advocate effectively for sustaining these elements of success.

Perseverance

I have learned about perseverance.

Continuity and Change

Universities are about change. They look backward to learn and preserve the lessons of the past; they are engaged in the affairs of the present; and they look forward to shape and invent the future. MIT, by its nature and founding mission, is strongly focused on the present and future.

In 1991, as our new MIT administration set its foundations, the Academic Council held a retreat. We devoted the first half of our time together to envisioning what we thought the world would be like ten or twenty years in the future, and we devoted the second half to identifying the characteristics MIT should develop in order to map onto our emerging view of the future.

We summarized our thoughts, only partially tongue in cheek, in the acronym NIRRD. This stood for Nimble, International, Robust, Resourceful, and Diverse. (I admit that the second R actually stood for Rich, but we thought it prudent to use gentler language to display our understanding that excellence requires financial resources.) So while we would continue to respect MIT's famous Nerd Pride, the celebration of focused brilliance and technical prowess mixed with irreverence for the more mundane social norms, we would set our larger plans and strategies toward relevance and opportunity for service to a changing world.

All this is to say that both change and continuity are important for universities, but we must get the balance right. Stewarding both continuity and change requires perseverance. Perseverance is crucial because people and externalities will try to change what should be continued, and continue what should be changed. It is all understandable, and usually well intentioned, but individuals and institutions must try to make wise choices and then stick with them. They must also know the difference between thoughtful perseverance and simple stubbornness.

Scientific Accomplishment

In 2001 MIT physics professor Wolfgang Ketterle shared the Nobel Prize for his creation of a Bose condensate, an ultra-cold form of matter dominated by quantum effects. This was a testimony to Professor Ketterle's prodigious scientific knowledge and technical skills. But arrival at this Holy Grail of atomic physics was also a culmination of scientific and collegial perseverance through several decades. The origin of the MIT group formalized as the Center for Cold Atoms is in our second-world-war Radiation Laboratory, and traces through several "generations" of physicists at Harvard and MIT. This group persevered as the field of atomic physics oscillated in and out of scientific popularity, building superb laboratories and cadres of faculty, students, and researchers.

Dan Kleppner is the intellectual and organizational "father" of the current group, and Dave Pritchard led it into a new level of experimental sophistication through his path-breaking development of laser trapping. When a faculty position in the area became available, the group and the physics department waited for several years until they were confident that they had identified the best person to fill it. That person was Wolfgang Ketterle, then a postdoctoral researcher in the group. Of course other leading institutions, including in his native Germany, recognized Ketterle's excellence, so keeping him at MIT would be a challenge. So close-knit and collegial was this research group, that Professor

Pritchard literally gave control of his own laboratory and major research grant to Ketterle. Ketterle stayed at MIT, and eight years later he shared the Nobel Prize with two other researchers, both of whom had been educated in the MIT group.

After returning from the Nobel ceremonies in Stockholm, Ketterle walked into Dave Pritchard's office, said, "I have something for you," and gave his Nobel medal to his mentor and colleague. This postscript to perseverance is also a testimony to the deep sense of humanity that still permeates much of the scientific world.

Cultural and Institutional Change

Lou Gerstner, who during ten years as chairman and CEO of IBM led one of the most remarkable turnarounds in U.S. business history, spoke in 2003 at the MIT Sloan School of Management. In the discussion that followed his talk, a student asked him what he had learned during those ten momentous years. Gerstner replied, "I learned that culture is everything."

He went on to explain that he had once thought that institutional culture was just one of a long list of functions one learns about in business school—finance, marketing, governance, auditing, and so on. He found that management could deal straightforwardly with most of those matters, but changing a company's culture requires an entirely different level of perseverance, and success is never guaranteed in advance. I would add that for the most part, success only comes if the underlying idea behind the change is appropriate.

I think often of three examples of cultural or institutional change at MIT that require perseverance: building a renewed sense of community, achieving diversity, and charting new architectural directions.

In 1996 then-dean for students and undergraduate education Rosalind Williams and I worked together to establish and charge a presidential Task Force on Student Life and Learning. This was a group of distinguished MIT faculty members from a wide variety of disciplines and academic traditions who devoted enormous thought and effort to establishing an improved framework for student life and learning at MIT that would make sense for our times and for the future as best as they could envision it. They engaged large numbers of students, faculty, alumni, and many other stakeholders, and in 1998 they issued a very important report. Their central conclusion was that MIT, traditionally considered to rest on two pillars, research and teaching, should build its future on three pillars—academics, research, and community.

"Community" sounded soft and unfamiliar to MIT ears, including my own. We were more used to rigor, intensity, metrics, and hard work. But as leaders of the faculty, students, alumni, and staff continued to think, they slowly but surely began to understand the wisdom of the task force in promoting this dimension—raising our sights to more truly become a community of scholars with a more holistic view and increased commonality of purpose that gave greater weight to life beyond the classroom and laboratory.

Over a period of about three years, the term "community" slowly became common in hallway conversation and in meetings, despite the fact that any ten MIT people would likely have ten different definitions of the word. The evolving concept of community became a major factor in restructuring our housing system, in orienting our first-year students, in allocating our budgets, in structuring the administration, in designing our buildings, and in how we think about each other. We continue to debate the relative merits and roles of micro-communities and macro-community. But after six years of perseverance, I believe that MIT is well into a journey that will create an even greater, more supportive, and more enjoyable academic community, while making no compromises in its rigor and academic excellence.

Diversity

Diversity, of all the attributes of American universities, is the one that requires the greatest perseverance to establish and maintain. Diversity has a broad connotation in academia—variety in disciplines, missions, pedagogical styles, world views, motivations; and in assembling a student body—variety of specific talents, economic and social backgrounds, geographic origin, educational preparation, life experiences, cultural and religious heritage, demonstrated creativity, personal accomplishments, and so on. But here I want to concentrate on diversity of race and gender, because we are an institution in which science and engineering are central, and women, African-Americans, Latinos, and Native Americans have long been underrepresented in these fields.

I believe deeply that such diversity is important to the quality of education of all students, and that MIT has a particular responsibility to educate a diverse scientific and engineering workforce and leadership for our nation. (We made these points in an amicus brief during the crucial U.S. Supreme Court consideration of affirmative action in student admission at the University of Michigan. Joining us in this brief were Stanford University, IBM, Du Pont, the National Academy of Sciences, the National Academy of Engineering, and the National Action Council on Minorities in Engineering.)

When I began my career as a teaching fellow and then as a young assistant professor at the University of Michigan in the 1960s, it was extraordinary if I had more than one African-American student in my classes every couple of years. In fact, it was extraordinary if I had more than one or two women students in a class. And if I had either, it was a near certainty that they would be one of the best two or three students in the class, because only through unusual drive and commitment would these students have come to study engineering.

In that context, when I consider that in 2004 MIT's undergraduate student body is 42 percent women, 6 percent African-American, 12 percent Hispanic American, 2 percent Native American—as well as remarkably diverse in so many other dimensions as well—it seems to me that a miracle has happened.

But that is just the point. It is not a miracle. It is not a natural occurrence. It is the result of determined, conscientious effort, over more than three decades, often against seemingly insurmountable odds; it is the result of institutional leadership and occasional courage; it is a result of the determination of innumerable families and communities. The goal was as simple as it was profound: to give bright young people from every range of our society the opportunity to succeed.

I also conclude that despite the length of this journey, our nation is a better place than it was three decades ago. The perseverance to get where we are today has been great; the perseverance that will be required to achieve similar diversity in our graduate-student population and in our faculty will be even greater.

Why? Because the efforts to do so place academia at the nexus of a complex of historical, social, political, legal, and philosophical forces that not only militate against success; they continually change. It deals with the congruence, or lack of congruence, between the interests of individuals and the interests of society. And of course our community has a wide range of views on the topic. I would have it no other way. But surveys show that we have an extremely strong consensus on the goal and value of diversity.

We must continue this important quest. In my view, we must persevere for the foreseeable future in employing appropriate forms of affirmative action, and we must continue MIT's historical leadership in outreach and mentoring to inspire and enable young people of color to pursue rigorous education in science, engineering, mathematics, and management. And we must continue to find the strength within ourselves, and within our institutional frameworks, to eradicate the subtle and not so subtle biases that can cause the career experiences of women and men to differ in irrational and unfair ways.

Race still matters in America. And women and men can still experience seemingly identical careers very differently. I look forward to the day when the proverbial playing field is truly level, when we can have a pure meritocracy that is color blind and gender blind. But we are not there yet. Reaching that day will require Perseverance with a capital P.

Campus Renewal

Campuses evolve in momentous bursts. Roughly every twenty-five years, need, opportunity, and economic forces seem to converge to make possible major renewal of campus buildings and infrastructure.

Need is brought about by physical decay, evolving technology, student and faculty expectations, advancing instrumentation, changing forms of artistic expression, new pedagogies, and interinstitutional competition. Opportunity stems from new faculty with new ideas, changing scientific and scholarly directions, the evolving needs of society, dynamic patterns of federal research policy and support, and the innate drive to move to still higher levels of excellence. Economic forces derive from—well, the health of the economy and stock markets.

All of these forces, and many others, converged for MIT in the late 1990s and gave us a historic opportunity to renew our campus through both new construction and the renovation of existing facilities. We took vigorous advantage of that moment, moving forward with a building agenda to match and enable our aspirations in student life and community, and in our future-oriented research and academic agenda. The upshot is that almost 25 percent of today's MIT campus has been constructed since 1990.

One could view this as an enormous cost. Indeed, new construction since 1998 has totaled over $1 billion. But those of us among the faculty, administration, and trustees who planned and executed this campus renewal believe that it has been an essential investment in MIT's future excellence and leadership. The new and renovated buildings serve essential functions for teaching, research, and campus life.

But this renewal has been about more than functionality. It has also been about architectural boldness, livable, inspirational spaces, and our search for a new sense of community. Frankly, as we enter the twenty-first century, our architectural boldness echoes MIT's heroic creation of its Cambridge campus at the beginning of the twentieth, and in the same spirit in which MIT invested in Baker House, Kresge Auditorium, and the Chapel in the 1950s. The "Student Street" in the Ray and Maria Stata Center will indeed take us to a new level in inspirational and congenial spaces for teaching, study, discussion, dining, and mingling. And I defy anyone to cite a facility that has more rapidly and effectively transformed the sense of campus community for students, faculty, and staff than the Al and Barrie Zesiger Sports and Fitness Center.

But just as a strong economy and unprecedented investment returns gave us courage to pursue a new campus vision and gave many extraordinary donors the confidence to help us realize that vision, so too did the subsequent economic downturn create a back-pressure against it. Therein lies another personal lesson about perseverance.

There is a premium to be paid in commissioning some of the greatest architects of one's times—people like Frank Gehry, Steven Holl, Fumihiko Maki, Kevin Roche, and Charles Correa. And major gifts become more elusive when an economy cools. MIT was subjected to these forces. On top of that, soon after several of these projects were started, Boston area construction costs rose at an historically unprecedented rate, driven by the massive "Big Dig" project that saturated the markets across our region and well beyond. For almost two years, in many trades, one could not find even two subcontractors to compete on price. Furthermore, when the economy began to decline, the construction markets did not immediately follow suit, because the "Big Dig" had guaranteed government funding.

Pressures mounted to stop our projects, and to replace bold designs with more utilitarian structures before proceeding. We engaged, as we had a responsibility to do, in debates about what debt levels we could afford, and whether we had sufficient gifts, or could expect them in the future. We had to continually remind ourselves of the important role that federal reimbursement for the costs of research facilities would play as we moved into important new fields of research.

I had seen this before. In the early 1990s MIT prepared to construct the wonderful new South Laboratory Building at the MIT Lincoln Laboratory. It had taken eight years to arrange the proper federal funding and the private financing for this large project. But then the nation went into a deep recession, and Lincoln Laboratory was downsizing substantially as the "Reagan Buildup" in the Department of Defense passed through its peak and moved to a large decline following the end of the cold war. There was an almost unanimous opinion that it would be a mistake both symbolically and functionally to start construction under these circumstances.

But we realized that it would take many years to restart the project, especially in light of the federal complexities, and that the real symbol should be that we believed that the lab had a bright future. So we plowed ahead. As it turned out, it was indeed the start of a renaissance, and the MIT Lincoln Laboratory is very healthy today, and is conducting much of its work in this attractive, state-of-the-art facility.

In the early 2000s MIT again decided that the long view—the new academic agenda, and the quest for inspiration and community—would dominate. The buildings are not ends in themselves; rather they are the structures that will enable our students and faculty to realize their dreams and contribute to society. MIT's evolving campus is the reflection of a bold university that is confident of its future.

In other words, we must persevere.

Boldness

I have learned about boldness.

Boldness does not come naturally to me. Indeed, I have observed that for the most part, academics save their boldness or radicalism for their intellectual endeavors, rather than for their day-to-day lives and behavior, or for the organizations they inhabit. And universities are inherently conservative institutions. They should be, for there is much that is good and important within them that must be conserved.

But there are instants when both institutions and individuals must decide whether or not to strike out in new directions, or to seize a moment. The conclusions they come to at such junctures make all the difference. Boldness, courage—call it what you will—seems not at all to have a mysterious origin. Rather it is the simple application of core values at a critical moment in time.

The values may be institutional, or personal. I would hope that they can be both at once.

MIT has taken many bold, perhaps even courageous, steps at the turn of the century: the decision to publish all of our course materials on line, to be freely available to anyone in the world; the public acknowledgement that the senior women faculty in our School of Science had been marginalized and the determination to change that situation; the dedication to visionary architecture that is marking our evolving campus; the decision to offer health benefits to same-sex partners; the confidence that launched a $1.5 billion fundraising campaign. These decisions were reflections of a spirit of courage and values that has marked MIT from its beginning. To illustrate more fully what I mean by institutional boldness or courage, I will take one case in point. It was literally a "case," involving a lawsuit against MIT by the Department of Justice on the matter of student financial aid.

Student Financial Aid and the Justice Department
My first lesson in boldness at MIT came early.

In May 1991 U.S. attorney general Richard Thornburgh brought a formal complaint against the eight Ivy League universities and MIT, charging that they illegally colluded in the Overlap Group—a set of colleges and universities that held meetings to ensure that financial aid to students applying to more than one of these institutions was awarded only on the basis of financial need. The next week he left the administration to run for the U.S. Senate. This was a bizarre application of the Sherman Antitrust Act. Indeed, it was the first time that a non-profit organization had been sued under this act. That fact undoubtedly added to the zeal of Justice Department attorneys, who sensed a new legal frontier to pursue.

The other eight institutions signed a consent decree—essentially a way of saying that they had done nothing wrong, but wouldn't do it again.

As a neophyte president, I was lobbied kindly but firmly by more experienced fellow presidents I greatly admired not to challenge the Justice Department. The stakes, and potential treble damages, they said, were too high to risk in a court battle.

Then the moment came—I was on the phone in my study talking with Thane Scott, a fine young attorney, and Constantine Simonides, a remarkable MIT administrator and a spiritual force in the Institute. They explained that time had run out. I had to tell them whether to sign a consent decree or go to court.

After a long pause, I said, "We are going to court."

What was this decision all about?

The Justice Department would claim that the institutions were conspiring to set financial-aid levels in a noncompetitive way, but what really was at stake was the future of a view that the role of financial aid is to enable those who would not otherwise be able to attend a fine university to do so.

MIT believed strongly that there was an important principle to be upheld, and so did I. It had been well articulated by my predecessor, Paul Gray, during his term in office.

MIT had long believed, and believes today, that undergraduate financial aid exists to enable bright students who come from families of modest means to attend college. We admit students on the basis of their merit and we distribute financial aid on the basis of their need. For many years prior to 1991, the eight Ivy League schools, MIT, and about forty other institutions had been mutually committed to these principles. Every year we compared data on the financial need of those students who had been admitted to more than one of our institutions. Using a common methodology, we compared the judgments of our financial-aid officers on each of these families' ability to pay a share of the cost of their child's education. We made no common decisions about what tuition to charge or how much aid to provide, but we did make a common assessment of their need.

What happened?

There was a protracted and dramatic legal battle. Economic experts argued, newspapers editorialized in our favor, and eloquent witnesses testified about the virtues of MIT's system of merit-based admission and need-based financial aid. We predicted that if we did not prevail, the nation's financial aid system would spin apart, and more and more financial aid would become "merit-based," that is, be given to very good students who did not actually need it in order to recruit them to campuses.

MIT lost the case in the U.S. Circuit Court in Philadelphia. Within hours, to the utter astonishment of the Justice Department, I held a press conference and announced that we would appeal the ruling. The three-judge appellate court heard our arguments, and ruled on September 17, 1993. There were three legal points in question. The court ruled unanimously in favor of MIT on two points, and split two to one in MIT's favor on the third point. It remanded the case back to the lower court. For all intents and purposes, we had won a strong victory. On this basis, we negotiated a settlement with the Justice Department that defined terms under which limited agreements and after-the-fact data comparisons could be effected by colleges. These ground rules were further expanded and refined in subsequent reauthorizations of the Higher Education Act.

The appeal hearing, normally a very brief and dry affair, had some real drama. The distinguished jurist Leon Higginbotham, who had served as chief justice of that very court until only a few weeks before the hearing, had asked to present the amicus briefs to the court. He later stated publicly that in his career the two legal endeavors he was most proud of were representing Nelson Mandela and testifying on behalf of MIT. Why? Because he deeply believed that the decades of commitment by the Overlap schools to merit-based admission and need-based financial aid had been a fair and powerful tool in advancing talented underrepresented minorities in American society.

Nonetheless, the Ivies remained under the consent decree for a decade, use of merit aid grew across the country, and federal grants were increasingly replaced by loans. All these factors have combined to cause a massive shift of financial support away from the poorest students and families to those with somewhat higher incomes. Despite the very real pressures on middle-class families during the last dozen years, I consider that the world of financial aid is less noble and fair than it once was.

In 2001 a group of twenty-eight leading universities and colleges, including Cornell, Stanford, Yale, and MIT, signed a public document committing themselves to merit-based admission and to a common methodology for measuring need. This is an attempt to nudge the system back in the general direction of its pre-1991 configuration. It is helpful, but the merit-aid approach is strong in many other universities. Many colleges and universities now bargain with parents, matching offers of other schools and trying to maximize the number of top students they can attract with a given financial aid budget. This is known as enrollment management. An entire cottage industry of advisors has grown up to assist families in the wheeling and dealing.

Despite this imperfect ending, MIT is still regarded with respect for having stood on principle. We resisted unwarranted government intrusion into the business of private universities. Our stance strengthened our institution. And I earned my MIT spurs.

Optimism

I have learned the value of optimism.

Indeed, it is hard to live and work within the environment of discovery and accomplishment on the campus, and to observe the impact of our graduates on the world, without being optimistic about the future. But optimism is challenged from time to time.

Every fall for fourteen years I have had the opportunity to speak to our first-year students at convocation during their first week on campus. This is the first time that they are together in one place. The air is electric with excitement, enthusiasm, and apprehension. It brings to me a wonderful sense of renewal, and an opportunity to say some things that I think are important about the adventure on which they are embarking—whether or not they care or remember a word of it!

A few years ago, notably before such shattering events as the attacks on September 11, 2001, the bursting of the dot.com bubble, or U.S. engagement in war, one of the freshmen wrote an editorial in the campus newspaper. He took me to task for being so optimistic in my convocation message. That puzzled and troubled me.

Here was an absolutely stellar group of young men and women about to begin their studies at one of the world's greatest universities. They had a common bond of dedication to, and superb capabilities in, science, mathematics, and engineering. They were in the right place at the right time. The field of opportunity before them was unparalleled. It was arguably the most exciting period in human history for science—the human genome was being sequenced, life science was reinvigorating engineering, the information-technology revolution was playing itself out, instruments of unprecedented accuracy and resolution were giving us new insights into the human brain and the nature of the universe, it was a golden age of mathematics, new interactions among social science, engineering, and management were beginning to blossom, and the power of computers to analyze and simulate complex phenomena was about to enter a whole new level.

Furthermore, the world ahead would need bright workers and leaders grounded in these disciplines in order to cleanse our environment, provide us energy, improve human health and security, and enable other nations to climb the ladder of well-being. The young people who would follow them would need to be educated. It was the dawn of the knowledge age, and they had come to learn from, and contribute to, one of the world's great knowledge resources.

How could MIT freshmen not be optimistic?

The reason, of course, is that they knew about poverty, disease, war, and human failings. One can always find reasons to be pessimistic, but it is no way to launch a college experience or a life of learning.

When I was young, I sat in our comfortable home in front of a black-and-white television and watched an interview with Dr. Tom Dooley, an American medical doctor serving people in Asia in the midst of unfathomable poverty and dire living conditions. Dr. Dooley held up in front of the camera a tiny, ill, starving child with a distended belly. Now, in the 1950s, such sights were never seen on television, or in magazines. It was shocking, and I recoiled emotionally. But then he calmly said, in essence, "When you look at this child you see something horrifying, but I look at this child and know that I have the knowledge and skill to make him well."

I have never forgotten that simple statement. It symbolizes for me an important part of what a great university, especially one with the focus of MIT, can do. Through its own work, and especially through the lives and works of its graduates, a university can strive to make the world well. On our campus we can, through the arts, humanities, and fundamental science, advance the human condition at the most sophisticated level. And beyond our campus, we and our graduates have unbounded opportunities to improve life for the many. The knowledge we generate, the things we come to understand, and the devices we build, can improve health, economies, security, and the quality of life.

In the end, I believe that knowledge and skill trump ignorance, and that optimism trumps pessimism. If we believe that and act accordingly, our personal happiness will benefit, and our talents will be well used.

MIT, too, must continue to be optimistic in its vision of why we are here and what we can do. For then our students will be inspired to take on the great challenges of the world, with excellence, perseverance, and boldness.

Index